CW00536816

Behind
enemy lines

Manchester University Press

Cultural History of Modern War

Series editors   Peter Gatrell, Max Jones, Penny Summerfield and Bertrand Taithe

Already published

Jeffrey S. Reznick   *Healing the nation: soldiers and the culture of caregiving in Britain during the Great War*

Penny Summerfield and Corinna Peniston-Bird   *Contesting home defence: men, women and the Home Guard in the Second World War*

Colette Wilson   *Paris and the Commune, 1871–78: the politics of forgetting*

Centre for the
Cultural History
of War

Behind enemy lines

Gender, passing and the
Special Operations Executive
in the Second World War

JULIETTE PATTINSON

Manchester University Press
Manchester and New York
distributed exclusively in the USA by Palgrave

Published by Manchester University Press
Oxford Road, Manchester M13 9NR, UK
and Room 400, 175 Fifth Avenue, New York, NY 10010, USA
www.manchesteruniversitypress.co.uk

Distributed exclusively in the USA by Palgrave
175 Fifth Avenue, New York,
NY 10010, USA

Distributed exclusively in Canada by UBC Press
University of British Columbia, 2029 West Mall,
Vancouver, BC, Canada V6T 1Z2

British Library Cataloguing-in-Publication Data
A catalogue record for this book is available from the British Library

Library of Congress Cataloging-in-Publication Data applied for

ISBN 978 0 7190 7569 8 *hardback*

First published 2007

16 15 14 13 12 11 10 09 08 07   10 9 8 7 6 5 4 3 2 1

Typeset in Minion
by Koinonia, Manchester
Printed in Great Britain
by Antony Rowe Ltd, Chippenham, Wiltshire

For Graeme

Contents

List of figures

List of tables

Acknowledgements

This book stems from my interest in gender and war which was fostered by Professor Penny Summerfield during my undergraduate and postgraduate degrees at Lancaster University between 1994 and 2003. It was her suggestion that I research the SOE (Special Operations Executive) for my doctorate. I am deeply indebted to both her and my other supervisor Professor Maureen McNeil for their support and encouragement.

The veterans who shared their wartime memories with me deserve a special mention, in particular those who feature prominently in the book: Yvonne Burney, (née Baseden), Francis Cammaerts, Gaston Collins (né Cohen), Claire Everett (pseudonym), Sydney Hudson, Roger Landes, Bob Maloubier, Bob Sheppard, Lise Villameur (née de Baissac), Nancy Wake and Cyril Watney, several of whom have since died. Conducting the oral history interviews was certainly very pleasurable and I was touched both by their hospitality and their willingness to reflect upon wartime experiences, some of which were painful. Without their contribution, this book would not have been possible.

The research on which this book is based would have been so much harder to undertake without the financial assistance I received from the Economic and Social Research Council (R00429934346), as well as the two small grants from the Iredell and Sheppard funds from Lancaster University's History Department.

On a more personal note, my heartfelt thanks go to my colleagues at the University of Strathclyde and especially to both my partner Graeme and my parents Val and Steve for their many different kinds of help and support and for living for so long with my research – they now know almost as much about the SOE as me!

Abbreviations

ANZAC	Australian and New Zealand Army Corps
ARP	Air Raid Precaution
ATS	Auxiliary Territorial Service
BEF	British Expeditionary Force
BFI	British Film Institute, London
F Section	French Section of SOE, independent of de Gaulle
FANY	First Aid Nursing Yeomanry
IWM SA	Imperial War Museum Sound Archive, London
NCO	Non-commissioned Officer
RAF	Royal Air Force
RF Section	Gaullist section of SOE, operated in France
SOE	Special Operations Executive
STO	Service du Travail Obligatoire
WAAF	Women's Auxiliary Air Force
WRNS	Women's Royal Naval Service
WT	Wireless Telegraphy

1

Reconstructing the Special Operations Executive

'If I had accommodated one man, the word would have spread around. They would have been coming over from the next mountain! [laughs] I would have had a very sore arse! [raucous laughter] The pine needles! And when would I have done the work which I had done and would those men have had respect for me? They wouldn't have. They wouldn't have.'[1] Sitting at the bar in the Special Forces Club near Harrods in the summer of 1999, Nancy Wake, the most highly decorated woman of the Second World War, was recalling a conversation she had had with the producer of an Australian mini-series about her wartime experiences resisting the Nazi occupation of France. Aware that Wake had spent several months living and working with seven thousand maquisards on the hillsides of the Auvergne, the producer, who was keen to inject more romance, had said: 'You must have had a love affair in the mountains?' Wake recognised that despite being accepted by the men any overt reminders of her femininity would result in her losing their regard and admiration. Being a woman in this very masculine environment had its complications and over several gin and tonics Wake told me about this period of her life including the time when some of her male colleagues observed her urinating and another occasion when they photographed her changing from her khaki uniform into her pink satin nightdress. She dismissed these incidents, reasoning: 'But could you blame them? Out there? I didn't get cross about it, but I didn't want it. But I figured that if I had been with a bunch of women that hadn't seen a man, maybe I would have done the same!'[2] Despite having climbed over the Pyrenees, been trained in silent killing techniques, parachuted into Nazi-occupied France, risked her life by undertaking sabotage missions and cycled over 500 km in 72 hours through enemy territory without any identity documentation in the hope that she would be mistaken for a young housewife out shopping, she asserted: 'What you've got to remember is that I was just a normal young woman.'[3]

Behind enemy lines is about the extraordinary experiences of ordinary men and women like Wake who were recruited and trained by a British organisation and infiltrated into France to encourage sabotage and subversion during the Second World War. The book draws upon personal testimonies, in particular oral history and autobiography, as well as official records and film to examine how these law-abiding civilians were transformed into paramilitary secret agents. It is concerned with the ways in which the SOE veterans reconstruct their wartime experiences of recruitment, training, clandestine work and for some their captivity, focusing specifically upon the significance of gender and their attempts to pass as French civilians.

This chapter introduces the organisation, discusses the publicity that the SOE has generated both in print and on screen, situates the book within the broader debates around British women's wartime contributions and the emerging literature on masculinity and outlines the book's conceptual framework by explaining the theories of 'passing' and 'performance'.

What was the SOE?

In 1938, a clandestine organisation called Section D was created, so called because of the 'destruction' caused by sabotage and subversion undertaken in the Balkans. In the summer of 1939, MI R (Military Intelligence, Research) concluded that guerrilla warfare could assist in diverting enemy troops if used in conjunction with the regular armed forces. Following the Nazi 'blitzkrieg' of the Low Countries, the withdrawal of the BEF (British Expeditionary Force) from Dunkirk and the capitulation of France, the new War Cabinet under Winston Churchill agreed to afford a higher priority to acts of sabotage and subversion. On 27 May 1940, they agreed to a restructuring of the bodies concerned with subversive activities, which led to the establishment of the Special Operations Executive on 1 July. A War Cabinet memorandum dated 19 July 1940 noted: 'A new organisation shall be established to coordinate all action, by way of subversion and sabotage, against the enemy overseas. This organisation will be known as the Special Operations Executive.'[4] The new strategy was fuelled by Churchill's memories of quasi-guerrilla fighting on the north-west frontier and in South Africa, as well as by the success of T. E. Lawrence who had demonstrated the possibilities of irregular warfare. Sabotage and subversion were thus given increased prominence in Churchill's war strategy: 'We regard this form of activity as of the very highest importance. A special organisation will be required and plans to put these operations into effect should be prepared, and all the necessary preparations and training should be proceeded with as a matter of urgency.'[5]

The SOE was organised according to territories, with each country having its own section and staff. France was unique in that it was comprised of not one but four sections: F (which was independent of de Gaulle and is the focus of this book), RF (the Gaullist section), EU/P (Poles in France) and D/F (escape lines and clandestine communications). F Section built up a network of independent *réseaux* or circuits throughout France, incorporating an organiser who was responsible for building up the resistance group, an arms instructor or saboteur whose job it was to train new recruits and plan and conduct sabotage missions, a wireless operator who regularly contacted the base stations to arrange the dropping of supplies and an *agent de liaison* or courier who undertook a wide variety of tasks, such as conveying weapons, passing messages from one resister to another and locating dropping grounds. Each circuit was given a name, usually that of an occupation, such as SALESMAN or HEADMASTER, and they were to be independent of neighbouring groups. In total, 480 British agents were sent to France by F Section. Despite heavy losses and German penetration, F Section agents played an important role increasing the pace of resistance against the Nazi regime by recruiting, training and arming resisters, by establishing communication networks, by arranging parachute drops and, especially in the run-up to D-Day, by conducting sabotage operations which delayed German troops getting to the Normandy beaches.

Post-war representations of the SOE

These clandestine activities of SOE operatives were being made public even before the Second World War had ended. Newspaper articles told of the exploits of the two female agents, Sonya Butt and Paddy O'Sullivan, who had been publicly named. The *Sunday Express* for example, ran an article on 11 March 1945 entitled 'WAAF girls parachuted into France'.[6] Such articles provided positive accounts of women's capabilities and efforts in helping to win the war, which mirrored the image presented in newsreels including *Jane Brown changes her job*[7] and *Nightshift*,[8] films such as *The Gentle Sex*[9] and *Millions Like Us*,[10] propaganda posters such as 'Serve in the WAAF with the men who fly',[11] as well as adverts such as one for Weetabix which depicts a female barrage balloonist and the by-line 'On a man's job and equal to it'.[12] As well as encouraging women to enlist (or buy their product), these different forms of media emphasised that despite undertaking previously male roles in industry and in the services, and being clothed in uniforms and overalls which had a distinct gender tag, women had retained their femininity. Hence, newsreels showed factory women clamouring to get in front of the mirror to put on their make-up, films demonstrated that female war workers were still attractive to men by incorporating a love interest and both posters and adverts used illustrations of young, attractive women. It was especially important to reassure the public that the women who had engaged in clandestine warfare, undoubtedly the most masculine of roles given their proximity to combat, were feminine. The *Sunday Express* article, for example, asserted: 'The interesting thing about these girls is that they are not hearty and horsey young women with masculine chins. They are pretty young girls who would look demure and sweet in crinoline.'[13] This article appeared before the horrors of concentration camps were widely known and there is certainly a rather naive, condescending tone given that these women had risked torture, deportation and execution.

After the war when the public knew about the camps, articles on the fate of the missing female agents who had failed to return from Germany began to appear, prompted by Violette Szabo's father, Charles Bushell, who was publicly demanding to know what had happened to his daughter.[14] The post-war trials of concentration camp staff brought further coverage of the female agents of this clandestine organisation. The *Daily Telegraph and Morning Post*, for example, ran an article on 30 May 1946 with the headline 'British women burned alive: German camp staff charged'.[15] The tone of these articles was quite different and instead of the frivolous preoccupation with their appearances, journalists reported on the proceedings of the trials and information gleaned on the women's missions and deaths. Horror at the use of young women to fight the Nazis pervaded these articles. One journalist wrote: 'What more appalling and unlikely, until our own time, has befallen women than to be dropped by parachute behind enemy lines, to be betrayed, arrested, tortured, put to death?'[16]

The awarding of prestigious medals to female agents, including the George Cross[17] to Odette Sansom in August 1946 for her actions during captivity, and posthumously to Violette Szabo in December 1946 and Noor Inayat Khan in April 1949, generated more newspaper articles. The editor of the *Daily Herald* commissioned a nine-part series entitled 'Commando Girls' which told the stories of individual women.[18] Publicity also accompanied the unveiling of a plaque in 1948 at St. Paul's Church in Knightsbridge, the wartime headquarters of the First Aid Nursing Yeomanry (FANY). The tablet was inscribed with the names of fifty-two

FANYs who had been killed during the war, thirteen of whom had been F Section agents. The FANY was a voluntary civilian women's organisation established in 1907 to bridge the divide between the front line and medical stations. FANYs had been employed by the SOE as secretaries, coders and wireless operators at the base stations in Britain, North Africa, Italy and the Far East and the female agents had all been seconded to the FANYs in order to ensure that those who did not belong to one of the auxiliary services had officer status. The unveiling of the plaque was featured in the press, along with a list of the names of the thirteen female agents and photographs of Odette Sansom and Yvonne Baseden, both of whom survived Ravensbrück concentration camp.[19] The identities of the ninety-three male agents who were killed remained unknown.

The pattern of biography publication also illustrates the preoccupation with the experiences of female agents. Six of the thirty-nine women sent to France by F Section have been subjects of published biographies (three of whom have been written about by more than one author)[20] and five books have been published which provide chapter-biographies of several female operatives.[21] In contrast, of the four hundred and forty-one men who were infiltrated into France, only two have had full-length biographies written about them[22] and just two books provide chapter-biographies of male agents.[23] On the other hand, male veterans have been more likely than their female colleagues to write their autobiographies. Three have each written more than one book about their experiences with the SOE[24] and a further nine have written a single volume.[25] In contrast, only three women have published their memoirs.[26] That most written SOE testimonies are male-authored reflects a more widespread pattern in published autobiographies; whereas men represent themselves, women are more likely to be represented by others. One agent, who failed to find a publisher for her autobiography, was told that the manuscript lacked drama and was advised to 'pad it out' by injecting more excitement into the descriptions of resistance in France and life in Germany as a prisoner.[27] Those who were successful in locating a publisher generally adhered to the conventions of the spy and thriller genre; these were gripping tales of derring-do and close shaves. Hence, the agents themselves were involved in shaping the public's image of the clandestine operative.

Two F Section agents were also involved in constructing the filmic representation of SOE operatives' recruitment, training and operational work. *School for Danger*,[28] a feature-length public information film produced by the RAF Film Unit, featured Harry Rée and Jacqueline Nearne. It had been shot in 1944 in the liberated villages of the south of France, but it did not have its premiere until 7 February 1947. It received mixed reviews.[29] The decision to use ex-agents, rather than actors, was thought to be an error by the *Evening Standard*'s film critic: 'I know it is a cherished theory of documentary film-makers that it is unethical to use real actors when reconstructing reality; but personally I find the hunted looks and quavery dialogue of a group of self-conscious amateurs most embarrassing.'[30] A reviewer from the *Daily Graphic* also commented on the use of real actors, noting: 'Clearly they found the camera more frightening than the Nazis.'[31] This would appear to have been the case: in an article for the *Evening Standard*, Nearne is quoted as saying that *School for Danger* 'depicts the job hundreds of us did during the war, and we would do it again if we had to, but I do not think I would make another picture. Filming was more nerve-racking than parachuting.'[32] Certainly, the film was a rather dull, awkwardly-acted portrayal of SOE agents' work behind enemy lines in France, lacking in both plot and drama, which contrasts with later heroic representations in *Odette*[33] and *Carve Her Name with Pride*.[34]

Indeed, the biographies about Odette Sansom and Violette Szabo, with their mix of adventure, suspense and romance, quickly attracted the attention of film directors. The film of Jerrald Tickell's 1949 biography about Sansom had its world premiere at the Gaumont Palace in Lewisham on 17 April 1950. *Odette* starred Anna Neagle in the title role, and had Maurice Buckmaster, the head of F Section, appearing as himself and Peter Churchill, Sansom's organiser, making a cameo appearance as a local resister. The film depicted Sansom's recruitment, training and work, as well as her arrest, torture and incarceration in a German concentration camp. The film was well received and came fourth in the list of box office hits of 1950,[35] perhaps boosted by the public's knowledge that 'Odette' had married her organiser, played by Trevor Howard, which had made the headlines in 1947.[36] However, at least one critic was less than impressed: 'She grows steadily uglier all through the film ... she never wears a pretty frock. Woollen stockings make her legs look slightly bowed. Her hair, under an ugly scarf, seems to be tied up with old pieces of string. She looks like a kick-about old cushion, with a face.'[37] The adaptation of R.J. Minney's 1956 biography *Carve Her Name with Pride* had its world premiere at Leicester Square Theatre on 20 February 1958. The appearance of Virginia McKenna, who starred as Violette Szabo, was also the focus of one review: she 'is no curvaceous glamour girl, but her integrity and exceptional acting ability more than atone for her modest vital statistics.'[38]

While Ian Fleming wrote about the fictional adventures of James Bond, it was, then, with the real life female agents that a particular fascination developed, fuelled by these films, biographies, awards and newspaper articles. M. R. D. Foot, author of the official history of F Section, noted the over-representation of female agents in popular culture, and stated in interview: 'Odette Sansom was in her day as famous as Princess Diana was'[39] and Gervase Cowell, the ex-Adviser to the Foreign Office, noted:

> The story of a woman agent facing danger and bringing home the goods or being tortured makes the media drool. Odette, who was the first one to do this, was seized on and there, I suppose, you could say there's a hint of exploitation if you like. It was realised that it would make very good propaganda to parade this pretty woman who'd been in love with the man she met, you know when she touched ground they sort of ran in slow motion [laughs] and so she was given a sort of promotional tour.[40]

By virtue of their gender (and the concomitant disruption of social mores precipitated by the recruitment of women), female agents have generated much interest in both popular literature and film. The organisation, however, has not always been portrayed in a positive light. Public knowledge of the deaths of several women prompted Elizabeth Nicholas to write a damning critique of the London headquarters of F Section for sending naive twenty-somethings to an occupied country where they were called upon to undertake highly risky operations having been inadequately prepared to outwit highly-trained, experienced German counter-espionage officers.[41] This view was echoed by Jean Overton Fuller, the author of four books[42] about the organisation which raised awkward questions about double agents and German penetration: 'What qualifications other than idealism and bravery had young girls like Denise and Madeleine to pick their way in that complex underworld into which they were dropped?'[43] Fuller's and Nicholas' criticisms of F Section prompted Dame Irene Ward M.P. to propose a motion in the House of Commons in December 1958 which demanded an investigation into the effectiveness of the organisation. Ward, who was writing a history of the FANYs which included a chapter on the SOE women,[44] wanted to know why the files on agents who had died had not been made available to historians as she believed this prevented their achievements being made known to the public. The underlying assumption was that the government was attempting to conceal errors which cost the lives of seven women in particular. The media turned these questions into an uproar. *Time* magazine printed a picture of Diana Rowden with the caption, 'Burned alive as a decoy?' and noted that the 'thought that the seven girl agents, and a hundred others, might simply have been decoys handed over to certain death in order to mask other intelligence activities was an unpalatable one for many Britons.'[45] That several male agents may also have been sacrificed was not considered newsworthy.

In order to address Dame Irene's charges and the growing indignation about the deaths of agents incurred in the wake of Nicholas' and Fuller's books, Prime Minister Harold Macmillan ordered the Foreign Office to commission a history of the SOE in one country. This resulted in the publication in 1966 of M. R. D. Foot's *SOE in France*[46] which defended F Section's actions against the charges from Fuller, Nicholas and Ward. Their comments were clearly uppermost in his thoughts as he wrote his introduction: 'In recent years SOE has suffered from too little publicity of the right sort and from too much of the wrong; these pages are meant to restore the balance.'[47]

The fascination with the female agent shows no sign of ebbing as evidenced by the popularity of television dramas of the seventies and eighties, such as *Secret Army*,[48] *Wish Me Luck*[49] and, especially, *'Allo 'Allo!*[50] which began as a spoof of *Secret Army* and ran for nine series spanning a decade. Each of these programmes focused upon women undertaking resistance: in *Secret Army*, Jan Francis led a Belgian escape line with the assistance of two other women, *Wish Me Luck* dramatised the exploits of female wireless operators and couriers in France, and in most episodes of *'Allo 'Allo!*, René, the rather spineless café owner, reluctantly got drawn in to assist Michelle ('I shall say this only once') and her band of gun-toting female resisters. Not only were these programmes popular in their time but they continue to remain so: repeats are broadcast on both terrestrial and satellite channels, fans can purchase the DVDs and there are internet websites dedicated to each series. Media producers have recognised the ongoing interest in the female agents and have capitalised upon this: there have been three documentaries about individual women,[51] a three-hour Australian mini-series which fictionalised the wartime experiences of one agent,[52] and two documentaries which used excerpts of interviews with several female agents.[53] One of these, *Behind Enemy Lines: The Real Charlotte Grays*, coincided with the release of the film in 2002.[54]

Even the commemoration of the SOE has been feminised, leaving little space for an articulation of male experiences. We have already seen that the first memorial was to the SOE-FANYs. Plaques and memorials at Dachau, Natzweiler and Ravensbrück concentration camps also testify to the sacrifice made by female agents who died for their country. However, there are a few memorials which do not gender the dead, remembering all who died, such as the F Section monument at Valençay in Indre,

France, and plaques at Westminster Abbey and Tempsford aerodrome in Bedfordshire.

Female agents also feature more prominently in museum exhibitions. The Imperial War Museum's permanent display, 'Secret War', includes Yvonne Cormeau's wireless set, along with her dress and suitcase, replete with bullet-hole and blood. On display in the 'Victoria Cross and George Cross' gallery are two dolls made by Odette Sansom while she was imprisoned at Fresnes in Paris and the gun belonging to Violette Szabo. A museum opened in 2000 in a house where Szabo stayed between her two missions in Wormelow, Herefordshire; a wall mural can be seen in Stockwell where she attended the local school and a wall plaque has been erected outside the house where her family lived in Burnley Road, Stockwell.

These biographies, films, documentaries and museum displays which predominantly focus upon female agents have resulted in the public being much more familiar with female operatives than with their male counterparts. Violette Szabo and Odette Sansom are household names, whereas few have heard of male veterans such as Francis Cammaerts and Roger Landes who played important roles in the SOE. Hence, much of the literature contrasts with other historical fields in which an emphasis is placed on male figures and their activities. Perhaps one explanation for why the female SOE agents have struck such a chord in popular literature and film is that wars are generally fought to safeguard women and children and thus the women who were executed died in a war which was fought to protect them. War has generally been seen as organised round a clear gender divide with a combatant male fighting to protect the non-combatant female. Women's attributed 'innate' attachment to the domestic sphere strengthened by their reproductive capacity and the cultural myth that women are inherently peace-loving has precluded their undertaking a more active role in wartime. Women tend to be viewed as 'victims' in war and not as active agents. And although there is a cultural inability to acknowledge women as combatants (given the presumed affront to notions of femininity that any kind of combat would represent), there is a voyeuristic fascination with the women who do undertake a wartime role. The execution of middle-aged British nurse Edith Cavell in 1915 generated a wealth of propaganda images and memorials testifying that 'patriotism is not enough', while Mata Hari remains a potent cultural icon epitomising the alluring and dangerous femme fatale. Boudicca, Joan of Arc, Flora Sandes and Maria Botchkareva's Russian Battalion of Death also retain enduring appeal precisely because they transgressed conventional codes of behaviour and notions of women's 'appropriate' role in war by not simply waiting patiently for the return of their husbands and sons, keeping the home fires burning. This interest in war women is heightened when it becomes common knowledge that young women, trained in unarmed combat and silent killing techniques, were infiltrated behind enemy lines to wage war against the might of the Nazi war machine which swept through the Low Countries and France at lightning pace and which proved ruthless in its activities in the East and against resisters. In this case, there is no longer a separation of the battle and home fronts or of the roles of male combatants and female civilians. In a total war, anything goes and it is this which is of infinite interest to the public.

Behind enemy lines moves beyond the dominant representations of the female agent found in print and on screen. She was not the naive idealist who, out of her depth fighting the Nazis, was ruthlessly sacrificed by a morally corrupt organisation, as Elizabeth Nicholas and Jean Overton Fuller would have us believe. But equally, she bears little resemblance to the heroic filmic portrayals of Sansom and Szabo. In the chapters that follow, we shall see that rather than being idealistic, they were highly motivated, often driven by the desire for revenge and hatred for the Germans, were alert to the dangers they faced, were determined to proceed with their missions despite the obstacles that were put in their way and accomplished their work with varying degrees of success. Similarly, filmic representations of the heroic female agent are shown to be one-dimensional. The book scratches away the patina to reveal issues, such as fear, boredom and post-war psychological problems, which have not been the subject of scrutiny. Instead of providing descriptive biographies of the female agents, *Behind enemy lines* traces the significance of gender during the recruitment and training procedures, considers the ways in which gender impacted upon both the implementation of their clandestine role and their experiences during captivity, analyses whether the war changed conventional gender norms and, crucially, it reinserts male agents back into the SOE and does so, in part, by examining the gendering of their experiences also. By analysing the impact that participating in clandestine warfare has upon notions of masculinity and femininity, it is hoped that the book will extend the debate about wartime gender relations.

Gender and war

The study of gender and war is advancing apace. There is a great deal of interest today in women's involvement in military enterprises. Labour shortages, deskilling and the demand for equal rights have coincided to widen women's participation in the armed forces. This controversial development in the composition of the services has challenged the common assumption that war is essentially the concern of men fighting to protect women and children and has stimulated interest in the history of women and the military. Historical interest has focused on situations in which women were involved in combat. Studies have been undertaken of women's involvement in the wars of the twentieth century. In the British context, interest has concentrated particularly on the Second World War. In contrast to the First World War, in which trench warfare was a predominately male affair, the demands of total war made the Second World War gender inclusive. It witnessed an unprecedented level of female mobilisation: by 1943, about 7.5 million British women were employed in full-time and part-time paid and voluntary work including 90 per cent of single women aged between eighteen and forty and 80 per cent of married women.[55] Following the passing of the National Service (No. 2) Act of December 1941,[56] which made single women aged between twenty and thirty liable to conscription, women entered industries from which they had previously been excluded and many joined the auxiliary services which brought them closer to the front line and to traditionally masculine military roles than they had been previously: women served on anti-aircraft batteries in the ATS (Auxiliary Territorial Service), managed barrage balloons in the WAAF (Women's Auxiliary Air Force) and worked as plotters in the WRNS (Women's Royal Naval Service).

Research on British servicewomen in the Second World War focuses on the issue of the extent to which gender equality characterised women's involvement in military forces. In considering the conceptualisation of gender relations in wartime, historians such as Penny Summerfield,[57] Gerard DeGroot,[58] Tessa Stone[59] and Julia Rosenzweig[60] contend that despite making incursions into the military services, which were a bastion of masculinity, this did not entail much disruption of traditional gender roles. Women remained marginalised as equality stopped at the point at which combat began: servicewomen could not pull the trigger on anti-aircraft guns and could not accompany regiments into battle, were precluded from flying planes in combat situations and were not permitted to serve on ships. Moreover, a large number of the 470,000 women in the auxiliary services were concentrated in traditional women's work: cooking, cleaning and administration. Thus, although the war compelled a relaxation of gender norms, it did not result in their abolition. Furthermore, this was largely temporary. The substitution of women for men in a range of civilian and military jobs did not lead to long-lasting changes to women's status. While Arthur Marwick,[61] Alva Myrdal and Viola Klein[62] have claimed that the twentieth-century wars were periods of great social upheaval which liberated women from rigid, gender-defined roles, research during the last twenty years has unsettled this established evaluation. Gail Braybon,[63] Penny Summerfield[64] and Harold Smith[65] argue that women made gains on an individual basis but they each dispute the claim that the wars permanently destabilised established gender relations. With reference to the Second World War, the post-war reversals of wartime gains, the persistence of women's subordinate position within the sexually-segregated labour market, women's resumption of traditional gender roles and the baby boom all suggest that conventional gender norms were maintained, or even strengthened, rather than undermined.

However, this book examines the one British organisation which did deploy women in a combat situation and by so doing potentially destabilised conventional gender norms. An analysis of the recruitment practices, the training schedule, female agents' experiences while both undertaking their clandestine work and during captivity, as well as an examination of their post-war lives will enable conclusions to be drawn on the extent to which this potential was realised. *Behind enemy lines* thus extends the historiographical debate on the transformative effects of the Second World War on women, which to date has focused on women in industry and the auxiliary services, by investigating the experiences of women who belonged to a paramilitary organisation.

While women's official exclusion from combat has resulted in studies using a gender perspective to analyse women's roles on the home front, the taken-for-granted status of fighting as a male activity has meant that studies on war rarely mention masculinity in any explicit way. And yet war is clearly a fruitful site for analysing notions of masculinity. 'Hegemonic masculinity', a key term in gender studies which was first used by Bob Connell[66] to refer to the form of maleness that is culturally extolled and is hierarchically positioned above other, marginalised and subordinated, masculinities, is highly appropriate in this context. Some historians have turned their attentions to the gendered experiences of men in wartime, perhaps stimulated by the burgeoning historiography of women and war. Edited collections by Stefan Dudink, Karen Hagermann and Josh Tosh[67] and also by Paul Higate[68] ensure that the field of gender and war is not solely the study of women and femininity.

The First World War in particular has generated considerable research with cultural historians examining masculinity as both practice and representation. Notable studies include those undertaken by Paul Fussell,[69] Graham Dawson,[70] Alistair Thomson,[71] George Mosse[72] and Mike Paris.[73] Focus has centred particularly on the gulf between romanticised notions of the glorious, chivalric and heroic nature of conflict in which boys become men and war is a game, akin to the sports field, as promulgated in juvenile adventure fiction studied by Paris, and the distinctly less glamorous reality of combat with its lengthy casualty lists, physical injuries and shell shock, as noted by George Mosse and Alison Light.[74] They both assert that the 1920s and 1930s saw a change in ideals of manliness: the hard, plucky and lion-hearted nature of Edwardian masculinity was replaced by a softer, nervy and feminised maleness which was more domestic, pacifistic and anti-heroic. This seeming feminisation of British men in the inter-war period was in direct contrast with the apparent hyper-masculinisation of German manhood.[75]

Because the Second World War was more gender inclusive, less has been written on masculinity in this period. Work undertaken by Sonya Rose indicates that constructions of British hegemonic masculinity, the soldier hero, continued to be differentiated from the Nazi's ultra masculine image, as well as from emasculated British men, such as conscientious objectors.[76] Rose terms this downplaying of bravado 'temperate masculinity' and this is most clearly personified by the unflappable RAF pilot in the newsreel *All in a fighter's day's work*.[77] If the man in uniform was the soldier hero, what space did that leave for the civilian male? Work undertaken by Penny Summerfield and Corinna Peniston-Bird on the Home Guard suggest that this was a site in which constructions of masculinity were rather uncertain.[78] Men who were precluded from undertaking military service as they were either too old, too young or considered medically unfit, as well as those who were in reserved occupations, were eager to reclaim masculine pride by joining the Home Guard. In this way, they were able to play a role in defending the nation from attack and thus fulfilled their part of the wartime gender contract. Yet because they were a voluntary, civilian force which was never tested, was ill-equipped and often worked alongside the ATS on anti-aircraft batteries, their masculinity was somewhat undermined. Representations of the unit, including the much loved BBC television series *Dad's Army*,[79] have added to this ambiguity.

Surprisingly, there is also some uncertainty within the representations of male agents' manliness. *Behind enemy lines* examines constructions of masculinity in personal testimonies, official documents and in film in order to examine how these men, who were members of an elite organisation, composed their masculine selves. While some accounts depict a soldier hero, others portray a more tempered masculinity; for example, films have shown male agents as physically less capable than women ('Tony Fraser' in *Carve Her Name with Pride*), anxious and dependent on a woman's inventiveness ('Peter Churchill' in *Odette*) and, within the narrative genres of oral history and autobiography, some male veterans have provided stoic accounts in which they recall enduring anxiety, boredom, loneliness and frustration. Tracing the significance of masculinity in male veterans' testimonies was not easy as men generally do not reflect on gender relations and do not perceive their lives as gendered. Correspondence with three male veterans emphasised this: one wrote 'gender did not exist. It took the present generation to invent it'. Another noted in his letter that 'gender has simply nothing to do with it' and a third wrote that 'the question of gender did not arise as the organisations were all male.'[80] Gender is often regarded as something which women alone 'possess' and thus gender dynamics are more likely to emerge overtly or be highlighted in the testimonies of women than in those constructed by men. Yet gender dynamics are always a relevant and constituent element of social life and were significant in every aspect of male SOE agents' experiences, as we shall see.

Thus, *Behind enemy lines* extends the literature on war and gender in two key ways: firstly, the book reconsiders the debate, outlined above, on the Second World War's impact on conventional gender roles by analysing the one British organisation which offered women the opportunity to engage in combat; and secondly, by analysing the testimonies of male agents, which include references to self-imposed sexual abstinence for example, it goes beyond the dominant representation of clandestine masculinity offered by James Bond. In order to uncover new meanings of what it meant to be an agent behind enemy lines, the analysis of key experiences in veterans' accounts is underpinned by two cultural theories, passing and gender performance.

The phenomenon of passing

In their testimonies, veterans often refer to the necessity of concealing their British paramilitary identities and describe immersing themselves in the culture of the country into which they had infiltrated by employing the term 'passing'. They are using it in its general, literal sense: to be mis/taken for. The Oxford English Dictionary defines passing as 'to be accepted as equivalent to; to be taken for, received, or held in repute as. Often with the implication of being something else.' Benjamin Cowburn for example, wrote in his autobiography: 'I was to pass for an average Frenchman, while secretly organising the sabotage of selected targets'[81] and Peter Churchill noted that fellow SOE agents Isidore Newman and Edward Zeff 'were English but spoke faultless, rapid French and their appearance was such as to make them pass unnoticed in any French crowd, train or restaurant.'[82] Others did not specifically use the word 'passing' in their testimonies, but invoked terms such as 'covering', 'concealing', 'acting' and 'playing' which all imply that new identities were assumed.

The term 'passing' has its origins in literary criticism[83] (key texts include *Uncle Tom's Cabin* and *Running a Thousand Miles for Freedom*[84]) and has been primarily associated with black slaves passing as white in order to escape servitude. Enabled by 'white' physical features, black passing subjects cross a racial border in their assumption of a new identity which attributes status and apparent opportunities. The concept has been discursively applied to other aspects of a subject's identity, such as gender (the performances of drag queens and kings[85]), class (dissimulating a working-class identity in the hope of accessing the status attributed to the middle classes[86]), religion (Jews assuming the accoutrements of Christianity to pass as Aryans during the Second World War[87]) and sexuality (gay men and lesbian women passing as heterosexual by utilising the institution of marriage.[88]) Passing, then, is the term used to refer to the process whereby individuals of one race, gender, class, religion or sexuality attempt to appropriate the characteristics of the 'Other' and desire not to be recognised as different. It is generally assumed that prior to passing the subject has a fixed identity and thus the act of passing is often regarded as transgressive. Passing subjects show the visible to be an unreliable signifier of authenticity – you do not necessarily 'get' what you 'see'. Passing can never be a solitary exercise since it requires both the individual to perform and relies on an audience to authenticate their passing.

The concept is applied throughout the book to explain the assumption of alternative identities by SOE agents who had to conceal their British paramilitary status. There were a number of identity borders, including occupation, nationality, religion, gender, class and sexuality, that agents crossed in their attempts to distance themselves from their clandestine identity and which enabled them to carry out their undercover work. Intersections of gender and nationality in identity formation are specifically scrutinised.

Performing gender

As notions of 'masculinity' and 'femininity' underpin this book, it is useful to reflect upon them. Although they are concepts which are frequently invoked and may seem fairly easy to recognise, it is exceedingly hard to identify what masculinity and femininity actually 'are'. For the purposes of this book, I shall invoke the now familiar definition which characterises them as sets of social and cultural meanings and significations which are traditionally regarded as antithetical. Femininity, for example, is understood in such a way as to both distinguish it from and to enhance masculinity. Thus, mastery, competence, aggression, action, logic, competition and confidence are traditionally associated with masculinity. Characteristics that have been conventionally ascribed to women, and can thus be seen as feminine, include compassion, tenderness, weakness, helplessness, emotion and passivity. These antithetical significations indicate why war has been perceived as a masculine activity. Furthermore, perhaps the ultimate conceptualisation of masculinity and femininity rests on the gendered connotations of combat and non-combat.

A crucial concept in discussions about gender is 'performativity' which was first used by Judith Butler in her groundbreaking book *Gender Trouble*[89] in which she argued that gender is a public and performative act; an ongoing, often unconscious repetition of gestures, which are neither natural nor optional. Gender identities, according to Butler, do not pre-exist practices of femininity and masculinity but emerge from performances that conceal their constitutiveness. Gender is, then, a series of acts, rather than an attribute: a 'doing' rather than a 'being'. The act of 'doing gender' has become so routine, so thoroughly unexceptional and mundane, that it is taken for granted, like stopping for a red traffic light. Butler also introduced the notion of 'performance' which, in contrast to 'performativity', is a one-off event which is intentionally undertaken. Her invocation of drag illustrates that there is an acknowledgement that the representation is merely an act and that the 'authentic' self can be located behind or underneath the representation.[90] Not only does drag suggest that femininity can be mimicked by men and masculinity by women, it reveals that women also imitate femininity and men masculinity and that it requires work to accomplish (appropriate) femininity and masculinity. Hence, gender is a performance which masks the mechanisms of its own status as performance and erases the means by which it is produced. The display so seamlessly imitates 'reality' that it goes undetected as performance and is read as authentic and original.

Butler's concept of 'performance' is useful to this analysis as a striking feature of SOE agents' testimonies was the emphasis placed on acting. Referring to her duping of German soldiers, Nancy Wake noted: 'I was a bit of an actress and I adored that you see. In truth, I enjoyed that.'[91] Acting often entailed transforming appearance and many agents assumed disguises and different personalities to carry out their missions and to evade capture. Thus, SOE agents experimented with different presentations of selves involving specific forms of masculinity and femininity. Acting entailed assuming specific roles appropriate for the context and agents adopted a variety of different personalities and lifestyles, as we shall see. Comparing her strategies to those of her female colleagues, Yvonne Baseden noted: 'They played it quite differently.'[92] Her use of the word 'play' explicitly connotes a deliberately undertaken performance. The term 'performance' is used throughout this book to inform discussions of the individual and one-off enactments which constituted the passing strategies of male and female combatants.

The above discussion of passing and gender performance indicates the approach taken to the auto/biographical sources, archival documents and film that were collected, as well as to the oral history interviews. In addition to consulting the transcripts of interviews conducted by media companies for various television documentaries[93] and listening to the tapes held at the Imperial War Museum Sound Archive, I conducted sixty-six interviews with veterans. Twenty of these have been used in the preparation of this book. [See Appendix for brief biographical details.] Oral history, once perceived as a maverick offshoot of the traditional discipline of history, has, since its growth in the mid-1970s, become an accepted sub-discipline. It developed alongside feminism, women's history and socialist history in Britain and North America and the development of feminist theory has contributed to its growth. The focus on subjectivity and the recovery of 'hidden voices' to create new histories within both oral history and feminism illustrate their compatibility. This book, an interdisciplinary study informed by socio-cultural history and feminism, is located primarily within this field.

Nevertheless, oral history, with its reliance upon personal memory, has been criticised for being unreliable and inaccurate. A. J. P. Taylor, for example, claimed: 'Memoirs of years ago are useless except for atmosphere ... old men drooling about their youth.'[94] Interviewees can forget, lie, embellish, conceal information, become confused and simply get things wrong. The temporal gap between the experience and the reconstruction of the experience in the oral history interview is often cited as resulting in a lack of precision as memories can become 'culturally contaminated' during the intervening years. Memory, interpretation of experience and the forms of narration can all change in the telling. Denise Riley, a feminist commentator, recognises the problems inherent in using personal testimony and claims that in conferring authenticity upon subjects' memories, oral historians are 'assuming a clear space out of which voices can speak'.[95] The oral history interviews which I conducted took place over fifty-five years after the Second World War so such criticisms appear particularly valid. However, if we recognise that oral history interviews are not reproducing the experience as it happened but rather constructing a representation of it, the fragility of memory seems less significant. Criticisms of oral history based on the perceived unreliability of memory suggest that interviews are only about eliciting facts. Understanding why someone represents the past in particular ways may be as important as the details of the narrative recounted (the so called 'facts'). Personal memory elicits material of great richness and complexity because it enables interviewees to reflect upon the past in the present. What emerges are not unmediated accounts of a remembered past. As will be discussed in chapter four, interpretations offered by interviewees are bound to have been influenced by cultural attitudes developed during the intervening years.

Undertaking my own oral history interviews with veterans enabled me to ask specific questions about their passing performances and the relevance of gender to their experiences. These concepts complement each other in that they emphasise the non-originality of routine practices and offer a framework for the analysis of the dynamics and demands of disguise indicating that these meant far more than simply 'looking the part': they were about acting out a way of life and performing an identity. Thus, this book uses the notions of passing and gender performance in order to examine SOE agents' manipulation of national and gender identities. It considers the necessity of concealing a British paramilitary identity and examines the significance of gender in all aspects of agents' experiences within the SOE. An analysis of the ways in which the recruitment practice operated will serve as a suitable starting point for this examination.

Notes

1 Personal interview with Nancy Wake.
2 Personal interview with Nancy Wake.
3 Personal interview with Nancy Wake.

4 National Archives, CAB 121/305.
5 National Archives, CAB 66/7.
6 S/Ldr W. Simpson, 'WAAF girls parachuted into France', *Sunday Express* (11 March 1945).
7 *Jane Brown changes her job* (1942) Dir. Harold Cooper.
8 *Nightshift* (1942) Dir. Paul Roth.
9 *The Gentle Sex* (1943) Dir. Leslie Howard.
10 *Millions Like Us* (1943) Dirs. Sidney Gilliat and Frank Launder.
11 'Serve in the WAAF with the men who fly' (1941), artist Jonathon Foss.
12 'On a man's job and equal to it', Weetabix, *Picture Post*, 6 June 1942.
13 Simpson, 'WAAF girls parachuted into France'.
14 For example, 'Girl who was dropped over France missing', *News of the World* (17 March 1946); 'The story behind a tragic picture: women agents' death mystery solved: last hours in concentration camp after parachute leap', newspaper unknown (31 March 1946); 'Story of the woman who knew how to die: Nazi firing squad was moved', *News Chronicle* (30 March 1946); 'First British woman GC: fought gun battle alone with the Gestapo', *Daily Graphic (and Daily Sketch)* (18 December 1946). See also 'British women burned alive: German camp staff charged' [on Andrée Borrel, Vera Leigh, Diana Rowden and Sonia Olshanesky who were killed by lethal injection at Natzweiler on 6 July 1944] *Daily Telegraph and Morning Post* (30 May 1946.)
15 'British women burned alive', *Daily Telegraph and Morning Post* (30 May 1946).
16 M. Lane, 'The story of four British secret service women: parachutists did not return'. Newspaper unknown and undated. Clipping held at FANY HQ.
17 The George Cross, created in 1940 by King George VI, is the highest Commonweath decoration given to civilians. It is awarded for 'acts of the greatest heroism or of the most conspicuous courage in circumstances of extreme danger' which are not in the face of the enemy.
18 J. Gleeson, 'Commando Girls: beginning today: a story that will thrill you and make you proud', *Daily Herald* (24 April 1950) [on Peggy Knight]; 'Commando Girls: Part II: Peggy blows up a German convoy', *Daily Herald* (25 April 1950) [also on Peggy Knight]; 'Caught by the Gestapo: today's instalment of Commando girls', *Daily Herald* (26 April 1950) [on Yvonne Baseden]; 'Torture – despair then rescue', *Daily Herald* (27 April 1950) [also on Yvonne Baseden]; 'Commando Girls: her bluff saved three men from death', *Daily Herald* (1 May 1950) [on Christine Granville]; 'Commando Girls: the radio "widow"', *Daily Herald* (2 May 1950) [on Lise de Baissac]; 'Commando Girls: the mother who died and the sisters', *Daily Herald* (3 May 1950) [on Violette Szabo and Jacqueline and Eileen Nearne]; title unknown, *Daily Herald* (5 May 1950) [on Pearl Witherington]; 'Commando Girls: she led 3,500 guerrillas', *Daily Herald*, 6 May 1950 [also on Pearl Witherington]. See also James Gleeson's article 'The secret heroines' in the *Sunday Graphic* (22 June 1952).

19 Franklin, 'Britain pays tribute to her war heroines'.
20 J. Tickell, *Odette: The Story of a British Agent* (London: Chapman and Hall, 1949); J. Overton Fuller, *Madeleine* (London: Gollancz, 1951); R.J. Minney, *Carve Her Name with Pride: The Story of Violette Szabo* (London: George Newnes, 1956); R. Braddon, *Nancy Wake: The Story of a Very Brave Woman* (London: The Book Club, 1956); M. Masson, *Christine: A Search for Christine Granville* (London: Hamish Hamilton, 1975); S. King, *Jacqueline: Pioneer Heroine of the Resistance* (London: Arms and Armour Press, 1989); P. Fitzsimons, *Nancy Wake: The Inspiring Story of One of the War's Greatest Heroines* (London: Harper Collins Entertainment, 2002); S. Ottoway, *Violette Szabo: The Life That I Have: The Heroic Tale of a Female Spy in Nazi-Occupied France* (Barnsley: Leo Cooper, 2002); S. Basu, *Spy Princess: The Life of Noor Inayat Khan* (Stroud: Sutton, 2006). SOE agent Bob Maloubier told me in the summer of 2002 that he had just finished writing a biography of Violette Szabo. This has yet to be published.
21 J. Gleeson, *They Feared No Evil: The Stories of the Gallant and Courageous Women Agents of Britain's Secret Armies, 1939–45* (London: Hale, 1976); L. Jones, *A Quiet Courage: Women Agents in the French Resistance* (London: Corgi Books, 1990); B. Escott, *Mission Improbable: A Salute to the RAF Women of SOE in Wartime France* (Sparkford: Patrick Stephens Limited, 1991); R. Kramer, *Flames in the Field: The Story of Four SOE Agents in Occupied France* (London: Penguin Books, 1995); M. Binney, *The Women who Lived for Danger: The Women Agents of SOE in the Second World War* (London: Hodder and Stoughton, 2002).
22 E. Le Chêne, *Watch for Me by Moonlight: A British Agent with the French Resistance* (London: Eyre Methuen, 1973) about Robert Burdett (né Boiteux), a colleague of Pierre, the author's husband who was also an F Section agent; D. Nicolson, *Aristide: Warlord of the Resistance* (London: Leo Cooper, 1994) about Roger Landes.
23 E. H. Cookridge, *They Came From the Sky: The Stories of Lieutenant Colonel Francis Cammaerts, DSO, Légion of Honour, Major Roger Landes, MC and Bar, Légion of Honour, and Captain Harry Rée, DSO, OBE* (London: Heinemann, 1965); M. Binney, *Secret War Heroes: Men of the Special Operations Executive* (London: Hodder and Stoughton, 2005).
24 C. Burney, *The Dungeon Democracy* (London: William Heinemann Ltd, 1945); C. Burney, *Solitary Confinement* (London: Clerke and Cockeran, 1952); G. Millar, *Maquis* (London: William Heinemann Ltd, 1945); G. Millar, *Horned Pigeon* (London: William Heinemann Ltd, 1946); P. Churchill, *Of Their Own Choice* (London: Hodder and Stoughton, 1952); P. Churchill, *Duel of Wits* (London: Hodder and Stoughton, 1953); P. Churchill, *The Spirit in the Cage* (London: Hodder and Stoughton, 1954).
25 G. Langelaan, *Knights of Floating Silk* (London: Hutchinson, 1959); B. Cowburn, 1960, *No Cloak, No Dagger* (London: Jarrolds, 1960); P. de Vomécourt, *Who Lived to See the Day* (London: Hutchinson, 1961); D.

Rake, *Rake's Progress* (London: Leslie Frewin, 1968); R. Heslop, *Xavier: The Famous British Agent's Dramatic Account of His Work in the French Resistance* (London: Rupert Hart-Davis, 1970); J. Poirier, *The Giraffe Has a Long Neck* (London: Leo Cooper, 1995); G. Zembsch-Schreve, *Pierre Lalande: Special Agent. The Wartime Memoirs of Guido Zembsch-Schreve* (London: Leo Cooper, 1996); B. Sheppard, *Missions Secrètes et Déportation* (Paris: Heinandal, 1999); S. Hudson, *Undercover Operator: An SOE Agent's Experiences in France and the Far East* (Barnsley: Leo Cooper, 2003).

26 A.-M. Walters, *Moondrop to Gascony* (London: Macmillan, 1947); D. Rochester, *Full Moon to France* (London: Robert Hale Limited, 1978); N. Wake, *The Autobiography of the Woman the Gestapo Called The White Mouse* (Melbourne: Macmillan, 1985).

27 Personal interview with Yvonne Baseden. Sadly, the manuscript was lost en route to Africa and she did not attempt to write down her experiences again, apart from a three-part series which appeared in the *Sunday Express*. 'The tremendous things that happened to a quiet little English secretary: secret mission', *Sunday Express* (9 March 1952); 'The tremendous things that happened to Yvonne Baseden: an English secretary meets the Gestapo', *Sunday Express* (16 March 1952); 'An English Secretary in the torture cells of the Gestapo', *Sunday Express* (23 March 1952).

28 *School for Danger/Now It Can be Told* (1944) Dir. Teddy Baird, starring H. Rée and J. Nearne (RAF Film Unit/Ministry of Information).

29 *To-day's Cinema* (7 February 1947); *The Times* (7 February 1947); *Sunday Express* (7 February 1947); *Kinematograph Weekly* (13 February 1947); *The New Statesman and Nation* (15 February 1947); *Showmen's Trade Review* (22 February 1947); *Punch or the London Charivari* (5 March 1947).

30 P. Kirwan, *Evening Standard* (6 February 1947).

31 *Daily Graphic* (undated). Held at the British Film Institute.

32 'He and She, 'chutists, start new jobs', *Evening Standard* (undated). Held at the British Film Institute.

33 *Odette* (1950) Dir. Herbert Wilcox, starring Anna Neagle, Trevor Howard and Peter Ustinov.

34 *Carve Her Name with Pride* (1958) Dir. Lewis Gilbert, Prod. Daniel Angel, starring Virginia McKenna.

35 'British films take honours: five among six winners at Great Britain's box offices during year', *Motion Picture Herald* (6 January 1950). The American film *Annie Get Your Gun* topped the list.

36 'Odette G.C. [George Cross] wed today' (newspaper unknown and undated); 'Couple who fooled Gestapo marry' (newspaper unknown and undated). Clipping held at FANY HQ.

37 *Daily Express* (7 June 1950).

38 J. Billings, *Kinematograph Weekly,* n.26367 Vol. 25, No 291 (1 April 1958).

39 Personal interview with M. R. D. Foot.

40 Personal interview with Gervase Cowell.

41 E. Nicholas, *Death Be Not Proud* (London: Cresset Press, 1958).
42 J. Overton Fuller, *Madeleine: The Story of Noor Inayat Khan, George Cross, M.B.E., Croix de Guerre with Gold Star* (London: Victor Gollancz, 1952); J. Overton Fuller, *The Starr Affair* (London: Gollancz, 1954); J. Overton Fuller, *Double Webs: Light on the Secret Agents' War in* France (London: Putnam, 1958).
43 J. Overton Fuller, *Double Agent? Light on the Secret Agents' War in France* (London: Pan Books, 1961), p. 183. Denise and Madeleine were the codenames of Andrée Borrel and Noor Inayat Khan.
44 I. Ward, *F.A.N.Y. Invicta* (London: Hutchinson, 1955).
45 'Painful Memories', *Time* (15 December, 1958).
46 M. R. D. Foot, *SOE in France, An Account of the Work of the British Special Operations Executive in France 1940–1944* (London: HMSO, 1966).
47 Foot, *SOE in France*, p. xvii.
48 *Secret Army* (1977–9), BBC2, starring Jan Francis, Angela Richards and Juliet Hammond-Hill.
49 *Wish Me Luck* (1987), ITV, starring Kate Buffery, Suzanna Hamilton and Jane Asher.
50 *'Allo 'Allo!* (1982–1992), BBC1, starring Gordon Kaye, Vicki Michelle and Kirsten Cooke.
51 *For Valour: 'Pearl Witherington'* (BBC1, 1995); *The Story of Nancy Wake: Codename The White Mouse* (White Mouse Productions, 1997); *Homeground: 'Secret Agent: The True Story of Violette Szabo'* (Channel 4, 2002).
52 *Nancy Wake: The Story of the White Mouse* (1987).
53 *Conflict* (History Channel, 2000) and *Behind Enemy Lines: The Real Charlotte Grays* (Channel 4, 2002). Both male and female agents appeared in *Timewatch: Secret Memories* (BBC2, 1997); *Churchill's Secret Army* (Channel 4, 2000) and *Secret Agent* (BBC2, 2000).
54 *Charlotte Gray* (2002) Dir. Gillian Armstrong, Prods. Sarah Curtis and Douglas Rae, starring Cate Blanchett.
55 J. Hooks, *British Policies and Methods of Employing Women in Wartime* (Washington: US Government, 1944).
56 National Archives, National Service (No. 2) Act, 1941.
57 P. Summerfield, *Reconstructing Women's Wartime Lives: Discourses and Subjectivity in Oral Histories of the Second World War* (Manchester: Manchester University Press, 1998).
58 G. DeGroot, '"Whose Finger on the Trigger?": Mixed Anti-Aircraft Batteries and the Female Combat Taboo', *War in History*, 4:4 (1997).
59 T. Stone, 'Creating a (Gendered?) Military Identity: The Women's Auxiliary Air Force in Great Britain in the Second World War', *Women's History Review*, 8:4 (1999).
60 J. Rosenzweig, 'The Construction of Policy for Women in the British Armed Forces: 1938–1948' (M.Litt dissertation, University of Oxford, 1993).
61 A. Marwick, *The Deluge: British Society and the First World War* (London:

Macmillan, 1965); A. Marwick, *Britain in the Century of Total War: War, Peace and Social Change, 1900-67* (Fakenham: Cox and Wyman Ltd, 1968).

62 A. Myrdal and V. Klein, *Women's Two Roles: Home and Work* (London: Routledge, 1956).

63 G. Braybon, *Women Workers in the First World War: The British Experience* (London: Croom Helm, 1981); G. Braybon and P. Summerfield, *Out of the Cage: Women's Experiences in Two World Wars* (London: Pandora, 1987).

64 P. Summerfield, *Women Workers in the Second World War: Production and Patriarchy in Conflict* (London: Croom Helm, 1984).

65 H. Smith, *War and Social Change: British Society in the Second World War* (Manchester: Manchester University Press, 1986).

66 B. Connell, *Masculinities* (Cambridge: Polity Press, 1995).

67 S. Dudink, K. Hagermann and J. Tosh (eds), *Masculinities in Politics and War: Gendering Modern History* (Manchester: Manchester University Press, 2004).

68 P. Higate (ed.), *Military Masculinities: Identity and the State* (London: Praeger, 2003).

69 P. Fussell, *The Great War and Modern Memory* (Oxford: Oxford University Press, 1975).

70 G. Dawson, *Soldier Heroes: British Adventure, Empire and the Imagining of Masculinities* (London: Routledge, 1994).

71 A. Thomson, *Anzac Memories: Living with the Legend* (Oxford: Oxford University Press, 1994).

72 G. Mosse, *The Image Of Man: The Creation of Modern Masculinity* (Oxford: Oxford University Press, 1996).

73 M. Paris, *Over the Top: The Great War and Juvenile Literature in Britain* (Westport: Praeger, 2004).

74 Mosse, *The Image Of Man*; A. Light, *Forever England: Femininity, Literature and Conservatism Between the Wars* (London: Routledge, 1991).

75 Mosse, *The Image Of Man*.

76 S. Rose, *Which People's War? National Identity and Citizenship in Britain, 1939-1945* (Oxford: Oxford University Press, 2003).

77 *All in a fighter's day's work*, 7 October 1940, Gaumont British.

78 P. Summerfield and C. Peniston-Bird, 'The Home Guard in Britain in the Second World War: Uncertain Masculinities?' in Higate, *Military Masculinities*.

79 *Dad's Army*, BBC 1, 1968-1977.

80 Correspondence with SOE veterans (combatants in Greece and the Middle East), 28 March 2000, 14 October 1999 and 3 November 1999.

81 B. Cowburn, *No Cloak, No Dagger* (London: Jarrolds, 1960), p. 42.

82 P. Churchill, *Duel of Wits* (London: Hodder and Stoughton, 1953), p. 16.

83 See for example, E. Ginsberg (ed.), *Passing and the Fictions of Identity* (Durham: Duke University Press, 1996), pp. 2-3.

84 H. Beecher Stowe, *Uncle Tom's Cabin or Negro Life in the Slave States of*

America (London: C. H. Clarke, 1852); W. Craft, *Running a Thousand Miles for Freedom: The Escape of William and Ellen Craft from Slavery* (London: William Tweedie, 1860).

85 E. Newton, *Mother Camp: Female Impersonators in America* (Chicago: Chicago University Press, 1979); R. Baker, *Drag: A History of Female Impersonation in the Performing Arts* (London: Cassell, 1994).

86 B. Skeggs, *Formations of Class and Gender: Becoming Respectable* (London: Sage, 1997).

87 L. Weitzman, 'Living on the Aryan Side in Poland: Gender, Passing and the Nature of Resistance', in D. Ofer and L. Weitzman (eds), *Women in the Holocaust* (New Haven: Yale University Press, 1998).

88 A. Rich, 'Compulsory Heterosexuality and the Lesbian Continuum', *Signs*, 5:4 (1980).

89 J. Butler, *Gender Trouble: Feminism and the Subversion of Identity* (New York: Routledge, 1990).

90 J. Butler, *Bodies That Matter: On The Discursive Limits of Sex* (London: Routledge, 1993).

91 Personal interview with Nancy Wake.

92 Personal interview with Yvonne Baseden.

93 *Churchill's Secret Army* (Channel 4, 2000); *Secret Agent* (BBC2, 2000); *Behind Enemy Lines: The Real Charlotte Grays* (Channel 4, 2002).

94 B. Harrison, 'Oral History and Recent Political History', *Oral History*, 1:3 (1972) p. 46.

95 D. Riley, *Am I That Name?: Feminism and the Category of 'Women' in History* (London: Macmillan, 1988), p. 10.

2

'To pass as a native':
recruiting for operations in France

This chapter considers the initial interview as an opportunity for the recruiter to assess the potential 'passing' skills possessed by the candidate that will enable them to conceal their British paramilitary identities and be taken for French civilians. Many interviewees endowed their initial encounter with a particular significance, since the recruitment interview is regarded as their first experience of the SOE. The first recruiting officer for F Section was Lewis Gielgud, brother of the actor John Gielgud. He was replaced in 1942 by Selwyn Jepson who had written several novels and considered himself a good judge of character. Jepson, who was willing to disregard the cultural taboo on women's involvement in combat, recognised that women might also be useful in clandestine work and began interviewing suitable female candidates. In an interview for the Imperial War Museum's Sound Archive, Jepson remarked:

> I was responsible for recruiting women for the work, in the face of a good deal of opposition from the powers that be, who said that women, under the Geneva Convention, were not allowed to take combatant duties which they regarded resistance work in France as being … It took me some time to find a proper answer to that and then I found it. I discovered that the anti-aircraft units always had ATS Officers on their strength and that when it came to firing an anti-aircraft gun the person who pulled the lanyard that released the trigger was a woman … There was a good deal of opposition from various quarters until it went up to Churchill.[1]

Vera Atkins, F Section's Intelligence Officer remembered 'the heated discussions which took place when the idea was first put forward'.[2] Resistance to Jepson's initiative is evidence of the potency of a cultural prohibition concerning women's involvement in combat situations. Women's exclusion from fighting, which has been seen as amounting to a 'combat taboo', has resulted in women undertaking mainly auxiliary roles in wartime. Despite Jepson's avowal that the prohibition on women's use of arms is codified in the Geneva Conventions, it had no legal foundations. Rather, this was a deeply entrenched notion that women should not use arms. The taboo is found in most cultures, but is easily abandoned or modified if there is a need for women as fighters. In fact, the National Service (No. 2) Act, which extended the previous acts of 1939 to 1941 to include women, stated: 'No woman who is called up for service under the principal Act shall be required actually to use any lethal weapon or to take part in the actual use of any lethal weapon *unless* she has signified in writing her willingness to use lethal weapons or, as the case may be, to take part in the use thereof.'[3]

The SOE did require women and consequently modified, if not ever entirely abandoned, the combat taboo by allowing women to be recruited and trained (although Jepson's recollection of the solution to the question of women bearing arms is erroneous.) He recognised that there might be several advantages to employing women to undertake clandestine work. He believed women had a 'greater capacity for cool and lonely courage than men' and that this would be of use in undercover work. He also thought that women would be able to 'mov[e] about in France without being noticed'.[4] During the two years that Jepson was the recruiting officer for F Section, he enlisted over fifty female candidates many of whom successfully passed the training. That thirty-nine women were infiltrated into France by F Section and a further eleven by RF Section, three by the Dutch branch and two by the Belgian office suggests that women's involvement in this paramilitary organisation offered a challenge to traditional gender roles.

When the recruiting officer became aware (either through an SOE contact or the name being passed on from another organisation) of a female or male candidate who might be suitable, a letter was sent inviting them for interview. The meetings were held in a dilapidated bedroom converted into an office in the Hotel Victoria in Northumberland Avenue, London. Yvonne Baseden recalled 'walking into a nondescript building, in a nondescript office. I couldn't think why on earth I was here'.[5] Extensive research on candidates was undertaken prior to each interview and the recruiting officer possessed a dossier chronicling the personal histories of interviewees as Roger Landes recollected: 'Gielgud had a file with all the things about me. When I'd been born, trained, that I could speak

French fluently and that I was a wireless operator.'[6] Interviews enabled the recruiting officer to learn more about the candidates and to ascertain their feelings about the German occupation of France. Selwyn Jepson recalled: 'It would be a sort of conversation on various subjects leading up to the background of a potential recruit, what they did in civilian life, what their families were like … It was always a general conversation in which it would be possible to get to know quite a lot about the person concerned.'[7]

Interviews lasted about twenty minutes and were conducted in French, enabling the interviewer to test the linguistic proficiency of candidates. The recruiting officer would ask questions inquiring how they had come to speak French and about the parts of France with which they were familiar. Jepson recollected: 'I simply went on with the fiction, or rather with the cover, that they might have in having languages and a knowledge of France and so forth, they might be of value in the war effort.'[8] If, as M. R. D. Foot, the author of the official history, noted, 'the French proved so inadequate that there was no hope of passing, in France, as French, he would politely close the meeting.'[9] However, if the recruiting officer considered that they could pass as French, the subject of returning to France was broached. This could be raised at the first meeting or during subsequent interviews. To most interviewees, this was quite an unexpected turn and the revelation was likely to have been particularly surprising for female candidates considering the taboo on women participating in combat. Moreover, most believed they were there for other purposes: Odette Sansom, for example, had sent in some photographs of France that she thought might be of some use to the war effort, Violette Szabo had thought she was collecting her widow's pension and a number of female candidates believed they were being interviewed for interpreters' jobs. Roger Landes recollected the speed with which Gielgud raised the issue of returning to France: 'He explained that if I wanted to go back to France, I could. "If you're caught by the Gestapo, there's a good chance you would be tortured and shot." He told me that straight away. He then gave me five minutes to make up my mind.'[10] Yvonne Baseden, who was interviewed by Jepson, also remembered the subject of France being introduced:

> He said, 'Would you be interested to do something more in relation to France?' Of course I was thrilled and I said, 'Yes, of course'. He said, 'It's not going to be very easy and you'd have to leave the WAAF for a little time and you'd have to have special training.' And I said, 'I don't mind.' And he said, 'Well, of course, the thing is there are different ways of getting you over there if you are found suitable. It might imply parachute or landing.' I said, 'Well

that all sounds quite exciting' [giggles], particularly at that age. So I said, 'Ok'
… And that's how it all started. 1 June 43.[11]

Baseden's account recreates the excitement surrounding the official interview. Her use of the words 'thrilled' and 'exciting', coupled with her giggling
as she recalled the event, point to her enthusiasm about something for
which she was unprepared, but which she greeted with relish. Baseden
and Landes were recruited, but this raises the questions of why were they
considered suitable and who were the other candidates?

The recruits

The successful candidates recruited to F Section came from a variety of
backgrounds. Some had been active in the local Resistance and used the
established routes to cross the Pyrenees. However, most recruits were not
living in France at the time of the occupation and had no experience of
resisting.

Selwyn Jepson noted that there was a marked social homogeneity
among the recruits: 'It would all be middle-class, perhaps slightly upper
middle-class because of the education which would have brought them
into contact with France and French … Working-class … wouldn't
have the qualifications in terms of knowledge and language. They just
wouldn't have it.'[12] In spite of his assertion, candidates came from a variety
of backgrounds and were by no means all upper middle-class: Andrée
Borrel, for example, had worked in a bakery and Violette Szabo, whose
father was a lorry driver, worked at Woolworths before joining the ATS.
There were schoolteachers, journalists, secretaries, entertainers, racing
drivers, artists, industrialists, authors and hairdressers. Many of the
women were recruited from the WAAF and a number of the young male
recruits had finished their schooling at the outbreak of war and joined
either the British or French army.

A number of potential recruits were suggested by those already employed
by the organisation, which would suggest that the 'old boy network' was
in operation. Foot told me, 'It had to be in the beginning dependent on
the old boy network. How else could you recruit? If you'd been to public
school with somebody, you knew whether he was any good … Women
could come in equally as people would have sisters, cousins etc, who they
would know and invite them to join it.'[13] Yvonne Baseden, for example,
became friends with Pearl Witherington in the WAAF: 'Unbeknownst
to me, she had been asked "if you see or hear of anybody who could do
this sort of work, give us the names." And I gather she recommended my

name. So that's how I got involved with the Special Forces.'[14] Similarly, Claude de Baissac recommended his sister, Lise, Jacqueline Nearne was proposed by Maurice Southgate and Francis Cammaerts was suggested by Harry Rée.

Many of the recruits were Anglo-French, but there were also candidates who came originally from Mauritius, Switzerland, Australia, Poland, Canada, Russia and India. They came from a variety of religious backgrounds as well: there were Jews, Roman Catholics, Buddhists, Quakers and a Muslim Sufi. The recruits were of varied age, ranging from early twenties to middle age. Some recruits were married with children, others were newly-weds, some were widows, a few had been divorced, some were homosexual and many heterosexual men and women were single. Hence, recruits came from a wide variety of backgrounds and were differentiated by gender, nationality, class, occupation, religion, age, marital status and sexuality.

What they all had in common however, was that they were interviewed by a recruiting officer who required that they possessed a number of qualities which would enable them to pass and undertake their clandestine work. Gervase Cowell, the SOE adviser to the Foreign Office (1988–96), noted: 'Well, the first qualification was that they had to be able to pass as a native of the place they were in, so they had to be French or speak native French and they had, obviously, to look French and as if they would be able to have all the other necessary qualities for it.'[15] My interview with Cowell was conducted before I recognised the significance of passing in the testimonies of F Section agents and, hence, his explicit reference to passing was unprompted by me. The main priority in recruitment, according to Cowell, was to recruit people who could be assimilated into the culture of the country that they were infiltrating and who could 'pass as a native'. He isolated three qualifications which the recruiting officer was likely to look for in potential recruits: French nationality or alternatively an ability to speak French 'like a native', a typically 'French appearance' and various other 'necessary qualities'. Examining each of these factors in turn, it becomes apparent that not all of these criteria were rigidly adhered to in the selection of agents.

Nationality and upbringing

Cowell's first point, that the agents should be French, was more of a preference than a realisable criterion as this was complicated by the fact that de Gaulle's RF Section employed only men (and eventually women) who were French nationals. This meant that F Section could not recruit candidates who were one hundred per cent French. In the following statement, Maurice Buckmaster, the head of F Section, recalled the effect this had on recruitment practices:

> We were not allowed to recruit people with French passports, with French nationality. They had to go to de Gaulle, which meant that we had to find people of non-French nationality whose French was that of a French person. That, strangely enough, was not the most difficult part of the task. Looking at it in advance so to speak, I thought we'd never find English people whose French is good enough to let them pass as French people … People who'd either been brought up in France, been at a French university, had lived half of their life or possibly even all their lives virtually in France but who were English and who had escaped, got out of France before the Occupation.[16]

The recruitment practices of F Section were structured around legal definitions of French citizenship. However, the organisation did not adhere rigidly to the rule imposed upon them. Some recruits such as Bob Maloubier did in fact have full French legal status. F Section was able to circumvent the legal restrictions on recruiting native French men and women in a variety of ways. Some of the agents recruited were French citizens who had acquired British nationality through marriage to a British subject. For example, Odette Sansom (née Brailly) was the daughter of French parents. However, through her marriage to Englishman Roy Sansom, she acquired British nationality and was thus able to be recruited by F Section. According to the 1914 British Nationality and Status of Aliens Act, which revised the 1870 Naturalisation Act: 'The wife of a British subject shall be deemed to be a British subject, and the wife of an alien shall be deemed to be an alien.'[17] Upon marriage, therefore, women automatically took their husbands' nationality. Thus, Frenchwoman Odette Brailly became British subject Odette Sansom. It was not until 1 January 1949, following the passing of the British Nationality Act (1948), that British women were able to retain their nationality upon marriage to a foreigner.[18]

A number of the agents, including Yvonne Baseden and Bob Sheppard, had British fathers who married French women following the First World War. Children of these Anglo-French unions assumed the nationality of their fathers and were issued with British passports, which precluded them from serving in RF Section. These British legal subjects of Anglo-French origin, with their mixed parentage and French upbringing, were considered ideal recruits. Having lived in France for a number of years and attended French schools, they had acquired knowledge of French customs.

Their schooling played a vital role in their socialisation as French citizens: in the same way that British schools taught a distinctly British heritage of Shakespeare and the British Empire and socialised pupils into being Britons, French schools instilled an equivalent French cultural tradition. The transmission of the dominant ideology by the schooling system and the exposure to French cultural values and norms were essential in shaping French national identity. The significance of education systems as vehicles for the transmission of national heritage and the inculcation of patriotic consciousness has been noted by Benedict Anderson. He has contended that through this medium 'imagined communities' are constructed which bind citizens into a collective national identity.[19] Hence, nationalist education socialises pupils into a common culture, forges a sense of collective identity and evokes a shared history which secures allegiance and mobilises subjects in times of crises.

It was not only Anglo-French men and women who had been raised as children in France who were suitable candidates for recruitment. British nationals who spent significant periods of their childhood in France were also likely to have developed an understanding of French habits. For example, from the age of three, Claire Everett lived with her mother on the Riviera. Her upbringing and French education equipped her with knowledge that would, years later, help her to pass as a French civilian: in particular, a familiarity with French customs and an understanding of the nuances of social interaction. In other words, she had developed a French 'habitus'.

Pierre Bourdieu's concept is useful to this discussion of attributes and qualities as habitus refers to the partly unconscious 'taking in' of culturally determined bodily dispositions, such as manners, language and accent, as a result of lengthy immersion in a specific culture. In his examination of the social practices of individuals in their everyday lives, he noted that actions cannot simply be regarded as matters either of conscious individual will or as mechanical reactions determined by wider structures. His concept of habitus bridges the gap between these two explanations of practice and enables an understanding of identities premised upon familial legacy and socialisation. According to Bourdieu, the family is a key habitus-generating institution which slowly inculcates its members from early childhood with an appropriate habitus. Young children, attentive to the gestures and postures of the adults around them, observe their facial expressions, ways of using cutlery, modes of walking and styles of talking. This process of imitation soon becomes second nature and 'instinctive', rather than a strategic intention. Habitus is inculcated less by explicit instruction than

by social experience and socialisation in early life. The 'matrix of perceptions, appreciations and actions'[20] which are acquired in the family are
then developed by schooling and interaction with others. Thus, individuals like Claire Everett, who had been raised in France, were ideal recruits.
Their ability to speak colloquial, 'native' French, which Cowell believed
was essential if the candidate was not a French national, was also indicative
of the acquisition of a French habitus.

Accent and language

Language, as a system of rules which determines meaning, pronunciation
of words and sentence structure, is not simply a medium of communication. It also carries cultural meaning and signifies national identity. Each
national culture has a language which is central to its identity. Exploring
the relationship between nationalism and social communication, Karl
Wolfgang Deutsch noted that 'processes of communication are the basis
of the coherence of societies, cultures and even of the personalities of
individuals'.[21] Language conveys a sense of history and tradition and, as
Bourdieu argued, is 'the most important part of the cultural heritage'.[22]
Given that SOE candidates' ability to speak French was often linked to a
specific cultural heritage, the relationship between linguistic ability and
cultural background is significant.

Because of the centrality of language to everyday communication, it
was essential that the agents spoke fluent French and were, in addition,
cognisant of acceptable grammatical usage. Most of the recruits were
not French subjects and thus it was important that candidates of other
nationalities could speak French fluently to enable them to pass successfully. In his written account of F Section, Maurice Buckmaster noted:
'Language was, naturally, the first and vital hurdle ... We could not afford
to jeopardize valuable agents through the inability of a colleague to speak
the French of a Frenchman. It was necessary to exclude from the start all
those candidates who failed to convince our examiners that they could
be taken for Frenchmen by a Frenchman.'[23] He reiterated the importance
of linguistic ability in an interview for the Imperial War Museum: 'The
main requirement was absolutely perfect French, I mean the French of a
Frenchman and not that of someone who has learnt French. The natural
Frenchman.'[24] The organisation wanted candidates whose first language
was French. Given that this was rarely possible, they required individuals
whose French was so fluent that they blurred the distinction between the
French of a French national and that of a fluent foreigner.

'To pass as a native': recruiting for France

As we have seen with reference to Yvonne Baseden and Claire Everett, for many candidates, their ability to speak fluent French was a result of their cultural heritage: they had lived for lengthy periods in France, had experienced a French education and had interacted over long periods of time with French people. In other words, their immersion in French culture as children had equipped them with a French linguistic habitus. This enabled the future agents to acquire a linguistic habitus which Bourdieu noted is the cultural propensity to not only speak in a grammatically correct manner but also the instinctive capacity to say socially acceptable words appropriate to the situation.[25] F Section agent, Tony Brooks, for example, recalled: 'I think in French. I mean if I catch my finger in a door, I don't say "damn", I say "merde". Even now ... It comes naturally. I think in French. I dream in French.'[26] This illustrates the 'taken-for-grantedness' of habitus: dispositions become so ingrained that they operate below the level of consciousness. Furthermore, Brooks' instinctive reaction also suggests that habitus is durable and once acquired not readily displaced.

However, not all of the agents that F Section recruited were raised in France as children. Some had moved to France as adults and had learned to speak French as a second or foreign language. Their French habitus was acquired through a long period of residence in France and marriage to a French national. For example, Nancy Wake arrived in Paris in 1934 unable to speak the language. As an Australian, Wake did not possess any French cultural inheritance but, following her move to Paris to work as a journalist and her later marriage to a Frenchman, she slowly acquired a French habitus. This involved the studied imitation of the Parisian style of Frenchwomen: 'I had to work at it ... I started copying the way the French women presented themselves.'[27] Her biographer, Peter Fitzsimons, noted:

One as effervescent as Nancy simply could not live cheek by jowl by towel [sic] with the French without picking up some of their ways, and it was only a short time before, like them, she started having little more than a tiny strong coffee for breakfast, before she started buying ingredients for her meals immediately before cooking them, wearing scarves in a certain way around her neck in the classic European fashion, smoking way too many Gitanes until they burnt the back of her throat, and drinking cognac that had already been warmed up in the palm of her hand to produce more of the delicious vapour that was one of the key pleasures of drinking it. She learnt early, that on seeing any of her expanding coterie of French friends for the first time in the day, she did not simply nod and smile by way of greeting – as she had back in Australia – but instead kissed them on both cheeks. Every day! If they had become particularly close friends, then four or even six kisses was the go.[28]

Thus, when Wake moved to France, a different cultural 'field', she incorporated into her habitus appropriate values and dispositions. As well as undertaking specific French customs, she began to speak French without an accent and learned typically French slang and swearwords. When she was parachuted into Montluçon on the 29 February 1944, she had lived in France for a decade: 'I had lived in the country so long I could think like them and feel instinctively how they would react to certain situations. In a nutshell, I was French, except by birth.'[29]

Bourdieu sees habitus as transmitted exclusively through the family and the education system. In the case of many F Section recruits, these were crucial habitus-generating institutions, demonstrated with reference to the upbringing of Yvonne Baseden and Claire Everett. However, the example of Wake illustrates that habitus could be acquired in other ways, for example, through employment, residence and marriage and that agents who had not been brought up in France as children could work (and succeed) at acquiring a French habitus. Her references to instinctively 'feeling' French, to thinking as the French do and to reacting in a typically French manner were indicators of a French habitus.

Wake's immersion in French culture also furnished her with knowledge of the grammar and nuances of the French language: 'I have all the expressions of Provence because my French husband used to teach me what to say. He used to say, "Nanny, now if that [silence] say [silence]". He taught me those things so I could speak to them [French nationals].'[30] Wake's ability to intersperse conversation with colloquialisms signified a high level of communicative competence and suggested French nationality. Her command of the French language, knowledge of French vocabulary, syntax, pronunciation and intonation and the absence of an accent would have been clearly demonstrated in the initial interview, held in French.

Another indication of candidates' possession of a French habitus was the use of slang. Robert Boiteux, an Anglo-French agent, recalled: 'I speak French like a Frenchman; I know the slang ... [I] spoke fluent French.'[31] His statement resonates with Buckmaster's assertion that F Section wanted men who could speak 'the French of a Frenchman'. Boiteux parachuted into France and worked alongside Bob Sheppard who presented his linguistic ability in similar terms: 'I spoke French like a Frenchman. I could speak French and I knew France entirely. I not only spoke French, but I lived in France, went to school in France.'[32]

Recruits who had lived in France as children were likely to speak fluent French, even if their parents were British. Claire Everett, for example, asserted: 'At that time, I was more at home speaking French than I was speaking English.'[33] Immersion in French culture had an impact on her acquisition of a French habitus. Agents such as Gaston Cohen, who did not live in France, learned to speak perfect French because they spoke it on a daily basis: 'My father was very pro-French and my mother didn't even attempt to learn English and I went to a French Protestant school in London so I always spoke French.'[34] Although Cohen only visited France during summer holidays, he spoke the language fluently as this was his 'mother tongue'. Thus, individuals who spoke French continuously, as Cohen did, could acquire an appropriate French habitus which made them suitable recruits for F Section.

However, not all recruits possessed French linguistic fluency. Like Cohen, Englishman Harry Rée only lived in France during the holidays: 'I'd never had a long spell in France.'[35] In contrast to Cohen who spoke French every day and regarded French as his first language, Rée was unable to speak fluent French: 'My French was far from colloquial. Very much schoolteacher French ... My French wasn't good enough to wander round Clermont; there were too many Gestapo about.'[36] In another interview, Rée noted: 'I had an ordinary Englishman's French accent ... My French wasn't very good.'[37]

Before the war, Rée had been a teacher and, by referring to his linguistic ability as the standard of 'schoolteacher French', he draws a distinction between his grasp of French as used in his lessons and the fluency expected of nationals. Although he possessed an extensive vocabulary, Rée spoke French with an English accent.[38] This is noticeable in the film *School for Danger* in which he starred. He suspected that the Germans stationed in Clermont-Ferrand would be able to detect his English inflection. Accents could be accounted for using ingenious cover stories which implied that the person had French colonial origins, had been educated in Switzerland or employed in Belgium, for example, but an English accent was difficult to justify. However, despite the inadequacy of his spoken French, Rée was recruited. This suggests that he possessed other qualifications and qualities which compensated for his language deficiencies. Indeed, Selwyn Jepson named him as a 'particular agent that I remember and admired ... really a first-class agent ... I can remember when I interviewed him, thinking immediately, here's a good one. And I hardly had to explain to him at all what the work was. He knew instinctively what I was after. Very, very good indeed.'[39]

Rée's lack of a French habitus was likely to be a handicap when he attempted to pass as French. Before moving on to establish his own circuit, he spent a few days with the STATIONER network and had to be accompanied by its courier, Jacqueline Nearne, whenever he ventured into Clermont-Ferrand. Unlike Rée, Nearne could convincingly speak 'native French', having been educated in France from a young age.

Rée was not the only male agent of British origin who pronounced French in an English way. Francis Cammaerts was informed by Alec Rabinovitch, a fellow SOE agent, that he spoke French with a distinctive English accent[40] and Ben Cowburn recalled: 'Before the war, I did speak French with an English accent. In preparation for my trip I had practised pronouncing the r's from the throat as the French generally do and my friends had said that I sounded just like a Frenchman from the eastern provinces.'[41] Cowburn worked hard trying to improve his French accent. Nevertheless, when he was in the field, three French nationals asked Cowburn whether he was English, which suggests that his efforts were not wholly successful.

Rée, Cammaerts and Cowburn were just some of the male agents who did not speak fluent French and who retained a discernible English accent. These were not exceptions. Jepson remembered that there were recruits 'who couldn't pass very well for long or very safely because of limitations of education ... who had all the qualifications except their French had an English accent.'[42] Jepson's view that an agent's failure to pass was related to unsatisfactory or incomplete education reinforces the suggestion that schooling was a key institution for the transmission of habitus. His recollection of his recruitment of candidates who could only pass temporarily because of language problems undermines the emphasis placed on linguistic skills as a necessary prerequisite to recruitment.

Interestingly, Jepson refers to a gender dimension by asserting that 'it was always the men' who spoke French with an English accent, which, unfortunately, the Imperial War Museum interviewer did not probe further. Yet there is evidence to suggest that some of the female agents also had difficulties: Yvonne Baseden noted that the 'technical side of my French was practically non-existent'[43] and instructor, A/Lt Shley wrote on 7 September 1943 in Violette Szabo's personal file: 'I seriously wonder whether this student is suitable for our purpose ... she speaks French with an English accent.'[44] Nevertheless, it would appear that many more men than women spoke imperfect French, but, given the greater number of men recruited and infiltrated into France, that is hardly surprising. Jepson's comment about gendered linguistic inabilities may be linked to the roles female agents undertook. Women were not sent in as organisers of Resistance networks. Twenty-eight women were infiltrated into France by F Section as couriers and eleven as wireless operators. Couriering in particular required fluent French as it entailed mobility and searches were a daily occurrence. Consequently, the women who were recruited had to be fluent French speakers. Furthermore, as local women could be recruited in the field for this work, there was less need for female recruits to undergo the SOE training in England. Hence, F Section could select the most fluent women available. Although many more men were recruited, they were in short supply because of the urgent need for organisers, saboteurs and wireless operators. As a result, some were recruited because they possessed skills other than linguistic competence. Perhaps Jepson's expectation of female recruits' linguistic abilities was higher for this reason. Female agents had to possess various attributes but of paramount importance was their linguistic skill, which, because of gendered role allocation, was vital, while male agents could be recruited who lacked French language skills. This suggests that gender was a significant factor in the recruitment procedure.

As there was a limited supply of French-speaking Britons who could pass as French in France, it was soon recognised that in order to meet the growing demand for suitable agents, the SOE would have to recruit from within the Commonwealth more widely. F Section recruited siblings Claude and Lise de Baissac from the French-speaking British colony of Mauritius, as well as enlisted several French-speaking Canadian nationals. Although many possessed fluent French, some had a Canadian accent and did not have an intimate knowledge of France and French culture, having never visited the country. Edward Yeo-Thomas, an RF Section agent who was incarcerated at Buchenwald concentration camp with Canadian F Section agents, Frank Pickersgill and John Macalister, queried: 'Why on earth were they sent out on such a dangerous job when their French was so faulty that they could never hope to pass themselves as Frenchmen?'[45] An answer is that, although most French nationals would be able to detect those who were foreigners, Germans would not. Cyril Watney recollected: 'German soldiers couldn't tell the difference because they had difficulty in speaking French themselves.'[46] Moreover, this was a period of significant geographical mobility and displacement and the south of France especially was inhabited by many refugees from north-west Europe. Perhaps appearance, which was also identified by Cowell as a crucial factor in the recruitment of candidates, was a more significant criterion than the ability to speak fluent French as agents' lack of fluency could only be detected when they engaged in conversation with percep-tive, French-speaking German soldiers.

Appearance and looks

The recruiting officer was likely to note whether candidates' appearance would facilitate their passing. Maurice Buckmaster, who asserted that candidates had to be able to pass as Frenchmen, noted that 'this applied to appearance as well as to speech'.[47] A number of agents suggested that dark hair, olive skin and medium height were indicators of a French nationality. British legal subjects of Anglo-French origin generally conformed to the stereotype of the 'French' national since they often inherited culturally-relevant characteristics from their French parents. Yvonne Baseden, who was dark-haired, olive-skinned and petite, noted: 'I looked very French anyway, in those days particularly.'[48] Anglo-French agent Robert Boiteux noted 'in France, I was [a] Frenchman. I was small, dark.'[49] Boiteux passed as a Frenchman because his appearance visually aligned him with stereotypical 'French looks'. This would suggest that certain features were indicators of 'French appearance'. The visual signs of their French nationality alone would not have recommended them to the recruiting officer, but in conjunction with their ability to speak 'native French', Baseden and Boiteux were considered suitable.

However, there were also candidates who were recruited who did not possess these features. Boiteux parachuted into France with Anglo-French recruit Bob Sheppard who was blond, 1m 90 tall and according to Boiteux, 'looked like a British Officer'.[50] Sheppard also recognised this: 'The appearance was difficult because I looked too much like a young Englishman. I had beautiful blond wavy hair.'[51] The skin colour of Noor Inayat Khan may have made her visually distinctive in a predominantly white culture and Francis Cammaerts was unlike most Frenchmen at 1m 95. Their appearance may have inhibited their passing as 'French natives' since they did not possess stereotypical 'French looks'. However, Cammaerts did not think that his height was a problem: 'Rabinovitch [an SOE colleague] … thought I looked much too English … Height, like accent, was enormously affected by the swarm of refugees you know, the people from naturally "tall" countries like Scandinavia. But they didn't stand out. People didn't go round roasting someone because they were six inches taller than other people.'[52] In his debriefing interview, Cammaerts commented upon his appearance and asserted that his height had its advantages: 'For train controls, informant discovered that his appearance … stood him in good stead, as he was tall and blond, and was very often passed over by the Germans who would immediately pick up a small, dark and probably Jewish-looking man in the compartment.'[53] Implicit in

Cammaerts' comment is the view that it was dangerous to be potentially physically identifiable as Jewish. Paradoxically, the description provided corresponds with that of the stereotypical French national.

In addition to recruiting candidates whose appearance was considered typically British, a number of men and women were recruited by F Section that, according to Yvonne Baseden, 'were so obviously Jewish'.[54] She felt that the SOE was endangering the lives of Jews who visually conformed to stereotypically Jewish appearance by sending them to France which was occupied by an anti-Semitic force. In a situation in which French Jews were forced to wear the Star of David and were subjected to deportation, SOE agents who were Jewish ran great risks.

This notion that Jewishness was physically identifiable has been contested, since it invokes stereotypes (rigid, fixed, oversimplified and sometimes pejorative evaluative descriptions) of the distinguishing physical characteristics of Jewish men and women. Sander L. Gilman asserted: 'The statement that someone "looks Jewish" … reflects the visual stereotype which culture created for the 'other' out of an arbitrary complex of features'.[55] He noted that this visual stereotype is only very tenuously rooted in reality. Moreover, the statement 'looks Jewish' solidifies traits as fixed and immutable. Testimonies of Holocaust survivors indicate that there were many Jews who had blond hair and blue eyes and who were able to pass as 'Aryans'.[56]

If passing involves the assembling and construction of visual signs which are designed to invoke very specific readings of the body, then those individuals who were visibly distinctive through their height, their skin colour or their features could fail to pass as French nationals. However, this stereotypical classification is a rather unconvincing method of categorising individuals, suggesting a fixing of difference in so called national characteristics. The notion that appearance can be regarded as a key signifier of national identity needs to be interrogated and the adequacy of an account which places over-riding emphasis upon visible signifiers called into question. French nationals did not all look alike and to speak collectively of a 'French appearance' suggested a greater degree of uniformity than was the case. Visual signs clearly are not infallible markers of nationality: most obviously, agents who possessed a stereotypically 'French appearance', but who were *not* French, could successfully pass as 'French natives'. But confidence in appearance as a signifier of nationality was rather simplistically expressed by the SOE recruiting officer who, in practice, employed some individuals who did not conform to these stereotypes. Like the criterion of speaking fluent and unaccented

French, the principle of recruiting individuals with 'French looks' was not rigidly adhered to and a number of interviewees with a markedly 'English appearance' were enlisted. Promising recruits who possessed other qualifications were not rejected because of their appearance at the recruitment stage. Passing did not operate exclusively on visual signs and depended on other factors and candidates who possessed other valuable skills, but who lacked a visual alignment with stereotypical 'French looks', could, therefore, still be selected.

Other necessary qualities

In addition to criteria relating to nationality, linguistic ability and appearance, prospective agents had to demonstrate that they possessed various other desirable qualities. An applicant's personality was an important factor in recruitment: Maurice Buckmaster noted that character was second only to language. Unlike language skills, which could be tested in the initial interview and were perhaps the simplest quality to assess, personality was much more difficult to appraise. Buckmaster noted that they wanted 'a rugged honesty and singleness of purpose', 'people who would obey instructions, blindly but intelligently; people who could be inspired with confidence and passionate belief; people who would carry on, however hopeless perseverance seemed to be.'[57] Candidates needed to be able to work both autonomously and as part of a group as it was imperative that agents could forge a good working relationship with local resisters upon whom they would rely for further contacts and accommodation.

According to both Buckmaster and Jepson, candidates' motives for joining the SOE were also assessed. Buckmaster noted:

> We used to try to impute motives to our candidates. Did they come to us, we asked ourselves, out of boredom with their own jobs, or from motives of pecuniary gain (quite misplaced so far as our service was concerned, for we paid the pay of the rank plus a trifling extra for 'talent')?[58] Or did they seek escape from a nagging wife or a financial embarrassment? Or were they impelled by sheer love of adventure and glamour? Or did they just drift into it? Or – and these were the interesting cases – did they come to us because they felt that only in this or similar work could they achieve their maximum contribution to the war effort? It was sometimes difficult to tell, but it was only this last class that interested us.[59]

For Jepson, loyalty to Britain was a prerequisite:

So they had ... a British father and a French mother. And they were very good because they had, in the case of the women whose first loyalty would be to the father in the normal psychological picture of a family, a British father and a French upbringing and a French mother was ideal because the loyalty to the father meant loyalty to Britain. And ... a question of loyalty was always at the bottom of it all ... Loyalty to France was useful because it meant that they were against the Germans who were occupying their country. But on the whole it was loyalty to Britain that I was looking for. It's the safest loyalty because ... France being a divided nation as it was then, and tends always to be in times of trouble, it wasn't safe to rely on loyalty to France.[60]

Before raising the possibility of returning to France, the recruiting officer quizzed potential candidates about their feelings concerning the German occupation of France and Vichy collaboration in an attempt to ascertain whether they would be suitable and to inquire if they were driven by patriotism.

Previous conflicts with Germany were often mentioned as motivating factors. French national Bob Maloubier recognised the historical precedents for fighting for his country: 'We hated the Germans. My grandfather fought in the 1870 [Franco-Prussian] war, my father the 1914 war, I was meant to fight in the Second World War.'[61] Maloubier indicated that it was his destiny to fight for the French against Germany, as had his forefathers in previous wars.

The First World War was particularly significant in agents' accounts of their motives for enlisting. Pearl Witherington recollected her rage at the German occupation: 'There's this question of being so mad with the Germans ... I didn't like the Germans. I never did. I'm a baby of the 14–18 war ... There was the question of trying to do something useful for the war. But it was also, the biggest part of it was, I think, this fury that I had against the Germans cos I really was mad with them.'[62] Women were as susceptible to patriotic rhetoric as men were and Witherington was able to channel her indignation by working against the Germans.

Like Witherington, many of the agents were children of veterans of the First World War which had a profound impact upon them. A number of them acknowledged that the timing of their childhood meant they were exposed to anti-German sentiments. Odette Sansom was two and a half when her father was killed and she reflected upon the impact this had on her: 'I was brought up with the image of my father who had been a very brave man. Every Sunday morning after church, I would be taken with my brother to his grave. My grandfather used to say "in twenty or twenty-five years' time, there is going to be another war. It will be your duty, both of you, to do as well as your father did." I listened to that for years ... the seed was there.'[63] Couching her narrative in terms of a 'seed', Sansom implies that her childhood circumstances instilled in her a kernel which was nurtured and subsequently flourished when the opportunity arose to fulfil her grandfather's prediction. Hearing stories of German cruelties as a child and growing up fatherless undoubtedly made her less tolerant of a second German invasion and she felt that it was her duty to continue the battle on her father's behalf.

Familial relationships were significant motivating factors for involvement in other ways. Noor Inayat Khan allegedly wanted to distance herself from her overbearing mother and saw involvement in the SOE as an escape (although a 2006 biography has not given this impression).[64] One interviewee suggested that Lilian Rolfe joined the organisation in order to forget her marriage which had to be annulled after a month following the reappearance of her husband's wife, who had been presumed dead. There were other familial relationships, such as the death of a husband in the war, which motivated several women to accept Jepson's invitation to join the organisation. With the death of a husband, the traditional male role of fighting to protect wife and children was vacated and wives could step into the vacuum. Yvonne Cormeau was prompted to join in order to assume the place of her husband who had been killed in the Blitz: 'I think this was something my husband would have liked to do and, as he was no longer there to do it, I thought it was time for me to do it.'[65] Similarly, according to an article in the *Daily Graphic*, Violette Szabo said, in response to an officer who begged her to withdraw, 'It is my job. My husband has been killed. I am going to get my own back somehow.'[66]

There were other familial ties which motivated individuals besides marital bonds. Maternal responsibility was a factor which motivated some women to join F Section. Odette Sansom was prompted into involvement through her desire to liberate her home country for her three daughters: 'I used to say, well, I've got children and they come first. It's easy enough to go on thinking that way. But I was tormented ... Am I going to be satisfied to accept this like that, that other people are going to suffer, get killed, die because of this war and trying to get freedom for my own children. Let's face it. So am I supposed to accept all this sacrifice that other people are making without lifting a finger in any way?'[67] Sansom felt torn between her immediate maternal responsibilities and her patriotic duty. Coupled with this was her allegiance to the memory of her father, his reputation as a war casualty and her grandfather's expectation of the forthcoming war and her participation in it. Being confronted with the knowledge that her survival chances were very low if arrested and that she risked her children being orphaned, it was a difficult decision for Sansom to make. Furthermore, motherhood and combat are often viewed as mutually exclusive, since one is seen as conferring life and the other as taking it. Sansom was not the only mother to be recruited: Violette Szabo and Yvonne Cormeau also had young children. Motherhood was, then, not a barrier to women's involvement and did not automatically preclude them. Rather, it could provide a major impetus for their involvement.

It appears that some motives for joining the SOE were gender-specific. There is an assumption that in most cases men were solely inspired by patriotism. Although British propaganda posters continually alluded to a paternal protection motif, not one of the male agents that the Imperial War Museum, the media companies or I interviewed referred to fatherhood as a motivating factor. Perhaps this is aligned with stereotypes of masculinity: in making overt other motivations, such as paternal duty, the male combatant risks losing the right to perform that particular mode of patriotic masculinity. In contrast, a number of the female agents made reference to both patriotism and family in their accounts of why they enlisted. This could be partly because women have a discourse available to them which enables them to articulate a compulsion to fight for their children. It may be problematic for women to suggest that they were motivated by patriotic fervour alone, since this implies a transgression of gender boundaries, whereas it is more acceptable for women to make overt their claims to familial responsibility. Joanna Bourke has argued that one explanation for why women killed, which was propounded by the female armed services during the Second World War, centred on the maternal instinct.[68] According to this thinking, although women lacked 'the killer instinct' which compels men to fight, many had a protective quality which enabled them to kill to safeguard their young. Rather than preventing women from killing, the maternal instinct was considered to transform them into formidable killers. Bourke cites W. N. Maxwell, an amateur psychologist, who, writing in the immediate aftermath of the First World War, noted that many women would have been prepared to fight 'under the sway of the maternal instinct, with its protective impulse and its tender emotion, which had been roused by the sight of the wounded or the stories of outrage.'[69] Consequently, Bourke argued that traditional notions of femininity were not undermined by women's involvement in combatant work precisely because of the assumption that the urge to kill is oriented to motherly love. The potential tumult that women's involvement in combatant situations entailed was thus both mediated and enflamed by their maternal duties: mothers could be motivated to fight, which was considered noble and just, but their involvement was simultaneously regarded as controversial given the risk of orphaning children.

Whereas motherly love was a crucial motivation for several of the female agents, it has been alleged that one woman enlisted because she could not have children. Shortly before joining the SOE, Diana Rowden had undergone a hysterectomy. An interviewee claimed that Rowden reasoned that her life was expendable as she was no longer a 'real woman'. My informant maintained that, as Rowden could no longer perform the feminine reproductive function, she felt that she could undertake the traditionally male role of combatant. Such a perception ignores the fact that fathers were not hampered by familial considerations. Whereas a father could jeopardise his life and risk making his child fatherless, mothers had to contend with much stronger cultural disapproval. In contrast to Yvonne Cormeau and Violette Szabo who had to take into consideration their daughters and the impact their possible death would have on their already fatherless children, Rowden was spared this decision. Rather than identifying as a man, as my informant implies, Diana Rowden may have identified herself as a (female) non-parent, her lack of dependants enabling her inclusion in the organisation. This atypical example illustrates that motives were often gender-specific.

Familial connections could even motivate recruits who had registered as conscientious objectors. Francis Cammaerts, who resigned from his teaching post in May 1940, began working as a farm labourer on a pacifist community in Lincolnshire. The death of his brother, a pilot in the RAF, prompted him to join the SOE, as he concluded that the fight against National Socialism was a 'just war'. Harry Rée was motivated by the Nazis' anti-Semitic policies to abandon his pacifism: 'I was fairly far to the Left at the time and I realised that this was much more than a capitalist war and I think the concentration camp business and the anti-Jewish business convinced me that I, with the rest of the country, should do everything possible to defeat the whole Nazi thing because of its racial policies. My father was part-Jewish, but you couldn't live in Manchester in the twenties without having a lot of Jewish friends.'[70] The way the Germans were fighting the war motivated a number of recruits, including Gaston Cohen: 'Well I hated them cos being in the anti-aircraft, I saw a lot of the Battle of Britain, and the way they went about it all was really cruel in my opinion. Targets weren't the object. They were destroying villages and towns.'[71] However, feelings about France, specifically, were not necessarily strong. For example, Cohen recollected his indifference to the occupation of France: 'I was in the army. When France was invaded I was so busy preparing for the invasion of the UK, especially being in Southampton, so it didn't strike me in any way. I was very young. Didn't ring a bell really except I knew I had a brother who was in France.'[72] Cohen was not the only agent who remembered feelings of apathy. When I asked Bob Sheppard how he felt when France was occupied, he noted: 'It's hard to say. At my age at the time [eighteen], we didn't care really. We said, "It's a period we must go through." But then father and mother being arrested, I was alone. I decided then to join England and to enter the British army.'[73] It was the sudden arrest of his parents that compelled Sheppard to reassess his feelings about the occupation and which aroused his patriotic fervour. This indifference seemed to contradict the literature on the trauma of occupation and metaphors of rape that have been used to symbolise the Nazi invasion and occupation of France.

Some recruits were mobilised by apprehensions about enduring a dull and unadventurous war in Britain and were eager to utilise their language skills. Lise de Baissac recollected: 'I went to England [from Paris] to help with the war effort and I thought that I was more useful doing that sort of thing [working with the SOE], and more interesting also than working in an office in London.'[74] Sonya Butt was 'thoroughly bored doing admin and wanted to move on to something else ... I felt that I wasn't contributing to anything in the WAAF and I thought at least I would be doing something ... I liked the excitement of it.'[75] A report by Lieutenant Holland on 19 April 1943 claimed that Noor Inayat Khan 'felt that she had come to a dead end as a WAAF, and was longing to do something more active in the prosecution of the war, something which would make more call on her capabilities and perhaps demand more sacrifice.'[76] Female recruits appear to have been especially keen to escape from the mundane work generally assigned to women in wartime.

There were a number of reasons why individuals joined the SOE, many of which were gender-specific: the death of a spouse, the desire to protect children and the need to escape dull routine work were factors mentioned only by female recruits; only male candidates appear to have been motivated by the recognition that, although they had pacifist leanings, this was a 'just war'; while the hatred of Germans and Nazi policies, patriotism and family legacy have all been identified in both male and female agents' testimonies.

In order to undertake clandestine work, candidates needed to be obedient, intelligent, principled, persistent, resolute, highly motivated and to be able to work both independently and as a team. These qualities were not in themselves reasons to recruit candidates as they needed to show an aptitude in the skills outlined by Cowell before being recruited. The potential recruit might well possess the right 'qualifications' (nationality, a French education, residence, linguistic competence), but still lack the qualities (patriotism, adaptability, single-mindedness) which were also required. Nevertheless, the recruiting officer may well have turned a blind eye to potential recruits' lack of qualifications because the qualities recruits possessed were suitable. Moreover, the approach to D-Day, coupled with the arrest of increasing numbers of agents, meant that more individuals had to be recruited, trained and infiltrated. In the later phases of the Second World War, it is likely that the perceived need for infiltrations may have resulted in candidates being recruited who previously would have been rejected.

Conclusion

Maurice Buckmaster, the head of F Section, asserted: 'The recruiting of course was a very specialised job. We didn't just take any old person that came along. We recruited them and sieved them with very great care before we allowed them to get anywhere.'[77] Given that SOE recruitment was a very thorough process, it is easy to assume that only suitable candidates who fulfilled the requirements of fluency, apposite appearance and appropriate motivation were accepted. However, in contrast to Cowell's and Buckmaster's assertions that there was a systematic approach to recruitment, it would appear that the recruitment process was rather haphazard. Foot noted: 'Entry was so largely a matter of accident that there was nothing which deserved the name of a recruiting system; though there was system enough to prevent people from inviting themselves to join, and simply walking in.'[78] By its very nature the SOE was an innovative organisation and it did not adhere to a rigid recruitment regime. Nevertheless, as we have seen, there were elements of a recruitment policy, definite procedures were in operation and enlistment processes were not unsystematic. The recruiting officer worked alone and with evident flexibility, but he operated within a set of criteria concerning a recruit's qualities that was generated by the F Section staff and to whom the recruiter was ultimately accountable.

That a number of recruits were employed who did not meet F Section recruitment criteria can perhaps be explained by shortages of personnel, compensating qualities and the nature of the specific role. Firstly, the textbook 'perfect agent' may have possessed all the necessary attributes, but it was unlikely that F Section could have found many such individuals. Mounting pressures (the shortage of agents in the field, the increasing German penetration of networks and the escalating number of arrests) compelled the organisation to relax its stringent rules and select candidates who met only some of the requirements outlined by Cowell. Secondly, a post-war report from the Security Section commenting on the relationship between linguistic capabilities and success noted: 'The evidence on this is not conclusive … complete fluency is the ideal, but lack of it can be overcome by a high-class agent.'[79] The idea that a good recruit's other skills could compensate for linguistic inability may explain why agents were recruited who did not display the appropriate attributes. In order to exercise Winston Churchill's exhortation to 'Set Europe Ablaze', F Section had to relax its strict criteria in the belief that an agent who spoke French with an English accent or who 'looked British' but was highly intelligent, appropriately motivated and could work both independently and as a team member would overcome these impediments. Thirdly, an agent who had a flawed accent or who 'looked British' could be sent into the field as a wireless operator since operators often led very solitary existences, meeting only the networks' couriers. Rural areas were less subject to cursory checks and so agents who lacked certain French qualities could conceal themselves amongst civilians who were equipped with these traits. Individuals who possessed an especially useful skill, despite not meeting other standard requirements, could, therefore, still be enlisted. Hence, there was sometimes a disjuncture between the characteristics that were considered prerequisites to recruitment and the attributes that recruits actually possessed. Nevertheless, individuals whose life experience had bestowed upon them appropriate types of French habitus had an advantage and were the favoured recruits.

Notes

1 IWM SA, 9331 Jepson.
2 Vera Atkins quoted in script written by James Gleeson for BBC Radio series *Now it can be told*, broadcast 4 April 1950. Script held at FANY HQ.
3 National Archives, National Service (No. 2) Act. Emphasis added.
4 IWM SA, 9331 Jepson.
5 Personal interview with Yvonne Baseden.
6 Personal interview with Roger Landes.
7 IWM SA, 9331 Jepson.
8 IWM SA, 9331 Jepson.

9 M. R. D. Foot, *SOE: An Outline History of the Special Operations Executive 1940–46* (London: BBC, 1984), p. 71.

10 Personal interview with Roger Landes.

11 Personal interview with Yvonne Baseden.

12 IWM SA, 9331 Jepson.

13 Personal interview with M. R. D. Foot.

14 Personal interview with Yvonne Baseden.

15 Personal interview with Gervase Cowell.

16 IWM SA, 9452 Buckmaster.

17 National Archives, LO 3/604. See M. Page Baldwin, 'Subject to empire: married women and the British Nationality and Status of Aliens Act', in *Journal of British Studies*, 40:4 (2001).

18 National Archives, CO 537/1210.

19 B. Anderson, *Imagined Communities: Reflections on the Origin and Spread of Nationalism* (London: Verso, 1983).

20 P. Bourdieu, *Outline of a Theory of Practice* (Cambridge: Cambridge University Press, 1977), p. 83.

21 K. Deutsch, *Nationalism and Social Communication: An Inquiry into the Foundations of Nationality* (Cambridge, MA: The M.I.T Press, 1966), p. 87.

22 P. Bourdieu, 'The school as a conservative force: Scholastic and cultural inequalities', in R. Dale et al., *Schooling and Capitalism: A Sociological Reader* (London: Routledge and Kegan Paul, 1976), p. 114.

23 M. Buckmaster, *Specially Employed* (London: Batchworth Press, 1952), pp. 26–7.

24 IWM SA, 9452 Buckmaster.

25 P. Bourdieu, *Sociology in Question* (London: Sage, 1992), p. 79.

26 IWM SA, 16568 Brooks.

27 Fitzsimons, *Nancy Wake*, p. 49.

28 Fitzsimons, *Nancy Wake*, p. 51.

29 Wake, *The Autobiography of the Woman the Gestapo Called The White Mouse*, p. viii.

30 Personal interview with Nancy Wake.

31 IWM SA, 9851 Boiteux-Burdett. Boiteux changed his name to Burdett when he moved to Australia.

32 Personal interview with Bob Sheppard.

33 Personal interview with Claire Everett (pseudonym).

34 Personal interview with Gaston Cohen.

35 IWM SA, 8688 Rée.

36 IWM SA, 8720 Rée.

37 IWM SA, 8688 Rée.

38 See also Rée's personal file, National Archives, HS 9/1240/3.

39 IWM SA, 9331 Jepson.

40 Personal interview with Francis Cammaerts. See also Cammaerts' debriefing report, January 1945. Arnaud 'declared that he looked much too English and

had a pronounced accent when speaking French.' National Archives, HS 9/258/5.

41 Cowburn, *No Cloak, No Dagger*, pp. 67–8.
42 IWM SA, 9331 Jepson.
43 Personal interview with Yvonne Baseden.
44 National Archives, HS 9/1435.
45 R. Maclaren, *Canadians Behind Enemy Lines, 1939–1945* (Vancouver: University of British Colombia Press, 1981), p. 50.
46 Personal interview with Cyril Watney.
47 Buckmaster, *Specially Employed*, p. 27.
48 Personal interview with Yvonne Baseden.
49 IWM SA, 9851 Boiteux-Burdett.
50 IWM SA, 9851 Boiteux-Burdett.
51 Personal interview with Bob Sheppard.
52 Personal interview with Francis Cammaerts.
53 National Archives, HS 6/568.
54 Personal interview with Yvonne Baseden.
55 S. Gilman, *Seeing the Insane: A Cultural History of Madness and Art in the Western World* (Wiley: New York, 1982), p. xi.
56 E. Hahn Beer and S. Dworkin, *The Nazi Officer's Wife: How One Jewish Woman Survived the Holocaust* (New York: Little, Brown and Company, 2000); H. Moszkiewiez, *Inside the Gestapo: A Young Woman's Secret War* (London: Warner Books, 1998); R. Altbeker Cyprys, *A Jump for Life: A Survivor's Journey from Nazi-Occupied Poland*, ed. E. Potter (London: Constable, 1997).
57 Buckmaster, *Specially Employed*, p. 28.
58 The agents' personal files refer to their pay. For example, a memo in Andrée Borrel's file dated 28 September 1942 stated: 'While she is in the field her bank account will be credited with £300 per annum.' On 1 May 1943, this was increased to £350. National Archives, HS 9/183.
     Lise de Baissac, who parachuted into France with Borrel, was also paid £300 according to a memo dated 25 September 1942. This increased to £350 on 1 May 1943, £375 on 10 April 1944 and to £450 on 1 July 1944. National Archives, HS 9/77/1.
59 Buckmaster, *Specially Employed*, pp. 28–9.
60 IWM SA, 9331 Jepson.
61 Personal interview with Bob Maloubier.
62 IWM SA, 10447 Cornioley.
63 IWM SA, 9478 Hallowes.
64 Basu, *Spy Princess*. In email correspondence, Basu confirmed that she disagreed with this view of Inayat Khan's motivation to join the SOE: 'This is far from the truth. Noor was very close to her mother. When she was in Edinburgh, she used to take her fellow WAAF colleagues once a week to her mother's house, where the Begum would serve them tea and cakes.' Email, 12

October 2006.
65 IWM SA, 7369 Cormeau.
66 'First British woman GC', *Daily Graphic*.
67 IWM SA, 9478 Hallowes.
68 J. Bourke, *An Intimate History of Killing: Face-to-Face Killing in Twentieth-Century Warfare* (London: Granta Publications, 1999), p. 321.
69 Maxwell cited in Bourke, *An Intimate History of Killing*, p. 322.
70 IWM SA, 8720 Rée.
71 Personal interview with Gaston Cohen.
72 Personal interview with Gaston Cohen.
73 Personal interview with Bob Sheppard.
74 Personal interview with Lise de Baissac.
75 Butt, *Behind Enemy Lines* (Channel 4).
76 National Archives, HS 9/ 836/5.
77 IWM SA, 9452 Buckmaster.
78 Foot, *SOE in France*, p. 40.
79 Foot, *SOE in France*, p. 52.

3

'Taught how to play a part': training agents for undercover work

The previous chapter examined the recruitment process, considering the relevant skills and qualities that the recruiting officer looked for in the candidates which he deemed necessary for undertaking clandestine work in France. There was clearly a relation between the possession of a French habitus and success in the interview. Whether a recruit possessed such a habitus was dependent on a number of factors, such as parental nationality, childhood residence and schooling, emphasising that forms of habitus, though best learned unconsciously, could be nurtured and culturally reproduced. The recruiting officer had to test the prospective agent's potential ability to pass by assessing the extent to which various cultural attributes were displayed. This assessment continued during the training. We have also seen that gender was significant throughout the entire recruitment process: some of these attributes were regarded as gender-specific and motivations for joining the organisation were often gendered. Gender relations became even more significant during the training. While the discussion has centred so far on the selection of those thought capable of passing, the focus of this chapter is on the process of testing, preparing and equipping recruits to pass as ordinary French civilians. It is concerned with the ways in which the SOE training can be regarded as a second level of vetting, following the recruits' 'conditional acceptance' by the recruiting officer at the initial interview which had assessed passing skills.

As we shall see, the prospective agents were sent to a succession of secluded country estates located throughout England and Scotland that the SOE had commandeered and used as training schools. The instruction might be considered to be a form of commando training as much emphasis was placed upon improving the recruits' fitness, demonstrating sabotage techniques and teaching them how to use various weapons. In addition, trainees were scrutinised by NCOs (Non-commissioned Officers) of the Security Section to see whether they could pass as ordinary, law-abiding civilians and were given instruction on how to effect passing.

Early female recruits did not attend the same courses as men. Instead, they were sent to Beaulieu in Hampshire on a course only for women that was of a much shorter duration. This was because it was still regarded as highly contentious to recruit and train women for such unconventional work. The first course for female trainees, or 'students' as they were known, brought together in mid-1942, was an experiment to see whether women could complete the SOE training. With the success of some of the women on this first course, including recruit Andrée Borrel, and also of Lise de Baissac on the second course, whose report noted: 'she was very much ahead of her fellow students and, had she been with others as mentally mature as herself, she would have shown herself even more capable',[1] the SOE staff became convinced that women could undertake the established courses and be trained alongside men. Consequently, women who were recruited later in the war trained with men throughout and followed the full programme of courses discussed below.

Preliminary training

The first training school that all except the early female recruits attended was held at Wanborough Manor, near Guildford. The preliminary course lasted three weeks and about a dozen students attended each session. There were two aspects which this school focused upon: students' behaviour, which was closely monitored in order to assess their potential ability to pass as French, and basic army instruction in physical exercise, Morse and the use of weapons to enable instructors to allocate specific roles to students. Both elements of the course at Wanborough were highly gendered.

Students were lectured on the importance of being unobtrusive in their conduct. They were told that drinking excessively could jeopardise their attempts to retain a low profile. Having been thus informed, students were then persuaded to visit the bar, which was open all day. Harry Despaigne remarked 'they tried to get you drunk'.[2] This was to see, according to Derrick Duesbury, a member of the Security Section, 'whether they make themselves conspicuous when they had had one or two or whether they kept in the background'.[3] This was an important exercise in self-control and taught recruits to employ restraint. It is commonly believed that not only does alcohol release inhibitions, but it also lifts the veneer of learnt behaviour. Thus, in endeavouring to get the students inebriated, the instructors could test whether they had internalised what had been taught. The drinking practices of both men and women were monitored. However, women may well have been more harshly judged for consuming alcohol. Instructors' reports in Jack Agazarian's personal file noted that 'when tipsy he becomes aggressive'[4] and 'I have asked No.1 how he feels as regards drink. He reassures me that he feels quite safe in this respect and that he knows where and when to stop'.[5] In contrast, Nancy Wake was promptly sacked for her drinking. She remembered that Selwyn Jepson reprimanded her, saying 'we don't like our girls to drink'.[6] Jepson's comment gives an interesting insight into the social mores of this period, in which alcohol consumption was seen, by some, as unladylike. However, Wake was reinstated by Maurice Buckmaster, F Section's head, who overruled Jepson and she began the training. Gervase Cowell, the ex-SOE Adviser to the Foreign Office, who had seen all the personal files, including those of people still living (only the files of the deceased are open to the public to be viewed at the National Archives), recalled that in Wake's file there is a report of an incident in which 'she was on a charge for being drunk and disorderly in the village outside the training camp'.[7] In her defence, one officer, which may have been Buckmaster, had written: 'It sometimes happens, I think, that this woman's high spirits are mistaken for drunkenness' and underneath, another, perhaps Jepson, had written, 'I rather think that it is her drunkenness that is mistaken for high spirits'.[8]

Because of entrenched thinking about different male and female behaviour, men were sometimes tested in ways that women were not. Although there was no distinction according to gender in the surveillance of students' alcohol consumption, only inebriated male students were encouraged by FANYs stationed at Wanborough to reveal personal details about themselves. The use of young women to extract information suggests that the male students were assumed to be heterosexual. It appears that women were not subjected to this test. This is perhaps because it was thought that unlike men, who were considered liable to succumb to women's advances, female agents were less likely to be duped by *agent provocateurs* into revealing information. The testing of men only illustrates assumptions about the workings of both gender and heterosexuality.

Not all elements of students' preparation for passing were gendered. In addition to monitoring students' consumption of alcohol, security

officers also observed students' eating habits to establish the extent of
their knowledge of French habits and to see whether they had any English
mannerisms that might betray their identity. Derrick Duesbury recalled
that NCOs in the Security Section 'watch[ed] how they used knives and
forks. Whether they lift them like this [mimes French manner] if they are
going to France.'[9] This was because, as Despaigne observed, 'the knife and
fork are handled in different ways in France than they are in England. The
French more or less follow the American idea: they cut their meat first
and then change over.'[10]

Cyril Watney remembered that table manners and the handling of
cutlery were also culturally differentiated:

> If I'm drinking soup here in England, I'd put my soup spoon there and I'd
> drink the soup like that. But no, not in France. In France, you pick up the
> whole thing and knock it back. Now the thing is that when you're getting
> towards the end of your soup, you get the bottle of red wine and you fill up
> your bowl … And then you can pick up the bowl and you drink it like that.
> Now there's a gimmick! There are lots of different things that you've got to
> know. Lots of little strange things. That's one of them.[11]

Watney's discussion of *chabrol*, a custom in rural south-west France
involving pouring wine into the soup tureen and drinking from it,
suggests that ignorance of subtle differences between British and French
regional cultural customs could endanger agents' freedom. Leaving a
few remnants on the plate and aligning cutlery in the typical English
manner, rather than wiping the remaining gravy with a piece of bread
in the French style, could expose a British national identity. It was thus
important for students' eating habits to be monitored and although most
students had experience of French table manners, lectures on French
cuisine and wines were given. Table manners themselves were not taught
and Yvonne Cormeau recorded in her debriefing report that this was an
oversight: 'She thinks that agents should be carefully instructed in the
manners of the country to which they are sent. For instance, she found
herself the only person at the table drinking soup from the side of her
spoon.'[12] Occasionally, however, trips to French restaurants, such as the
Coquille in Soho, gave recruits an opportunity to practise French table
manners. Watney's statement also makes explicit the relationship between
passing and familiarity: in order to pass successfully, British agents had
to perform cultural practices which for ordinary French people would
have been habitual. These bodily dispositions, which are inculcated as a
result of lengthy immersion in a specific culture, can be regarded as forms
of 'habitus'. Bourdieu's concept suggests that crucial aspects of identity

are formed through familial legacy and socialisation.[13] Familiarity with French table manners could be one element in a French habitus which developed as a consequence of lengthy immersion in the culture. Bob Sheppard, for example, claimed that his adoption of French habits was 'a question of contact and education'.[14] However, in their use of French table manners, students were expected to manifest previous experience of acculturation and the training did little to nurture appropriate habits.

A third important test for checking possession of passing skills was listening to students while they slept to ascertain whether they spoke in English or French and to test their reactions upon waking. Security officers undertook such observation because, as Gaston Cohen asserted: 'The reaction is that you go back to the mother language'.[15] For those who were part-French or had lived in France, this caused little problem, as Sonya Butt recalled: 'They'd come into our room at night and wake us up, touch us on the shoulder and see how we reacted ... I'd lived in France all my life so it wasn't difficult for me at all. But for some of the others it was.'[16] Butt regards her childhood in France, during which she spoke French continually and attended French schools, as a cultural preparation and she believes that she was far more adept at assimilation than others. All of the veterans I interviewed asserted that speaking, dreaming and thinking in the French language came naturally to them. The ability to speak French becomes internalised as 'second nature', which renders it 'natural'. Indeed, when I asked Claire Everett about her ability to dream and think in French, her answer indicates that she regarded it as a non-cognitive element of habitus: 'It was natural, it just came naturally to me. I don't think it was any skill. It was just the years I had lived there and as a child I played with French children all the time.'[17] This confirms Bourdieu's argument that habitus is acquired through social immersion and 'because it is embodied, appears as innate'.[18] He uses the example of athletes to illustrate that habitus is 'a feel for the game', an inclination and a practical sense that enables individuals to react in specific situations in a manner which is not premeditated. Habitus is typically 'instinctive' rather than cognitive as performances are produced as a matter of routine without the actors necessarily being conscious of what they are doing.

Thus, instructors observed students' drinking, sleeping and consumption habits not in order to teach them to perform them better, but in order to test whether the students would be able to pass as ordinary French civilians once in the field. While some elements of this observation, such as inspection of female students' drinking practices and of male students' behaviour, were gender-differentiated, others were less so.

The second feature of the training at Wanborough was that it gave the students a taster of what was to follow at subsequent schools. By seeing in which aspects of the course students excelled, instructors were able to allocate appropriate roles. Francis Cammaerts noted: 'It basically started all the things that we were going to do later. You did a little bit of explosive, a little bit of small arms, a little bit of radio, Morse and physical fitness.'[19]

The physical exercise was especially strenuous. From the time that women were training alongside men, they were expected to undertake the same physical exercises. Forty-year-old Vera Leigh was the only woman on her course and reports from her instructors in January 1943 stated: 'She doesn't shun any part of the syllabus and goes in for everything with enthusiasm' and she 'certainly works hard to keep abreast of the others'.[20] Many of the recruits thoroughly enjoyed the arduous exercise and recall in their interviews how active they had been as children, to the extent that some constructed themselves as *garçons manqués*. Sonya Butt recalled: 'I was always a tomboy and a daredevil. I'd been brought up with my brother and had always played with his pals'[21] Lise de Baissac recollected that 'when I was a child I was a *garçon manqué*. I had two brothers and no sisters. So I was really more at ease with jumping and running than playing with dolls.'[22] However, not all the female agents enjoyed rigorous exercise. Denise Bloch's personal file contains a report from an instructor, dated 29 February 1944: 'This student was not very fit on arrival and was rather heavy and found the PT and ground training very tiring and also very stiffening.'[23] Pearl Witherington recalled: 'PT at half past seven in the morning and they expected me to run and I refused and they said, "What are you going to do if the Germans get you?" and I said, "I'll deal with that when it comes [laughs] but you're not getting me running at 7.30 in the morning." No, thank you. [laughs] I couldn't stand it.'[24] Witherington was not the only woman to opt out of PT. Nancy Wake also recalled evading physical exercise on the pretence of having a cold, cheating on cross-country courses and taking short cuts whenever she could.[25] Witherington's refusal to do exercise and Wake's shirking suggests that women were able to subvert the supposedly mandatory requirements of training. Although men may have done the same, it was unlikely that instructors would have excused their evasion. One exception was Denis Rake: 'I was far too old to start doing PT, and I told the very charming ex-Coldstream Guards Officer, Major Roger de Wesselow, who was commandant of the school, that I flatly refused to risk rupturing myself swinging about on those things they call, I think, the parallel bars.'[26] Wake's and Witherington's success in evading PT might suggest that staff at the training schools,

1 Virginia McKenna, as Violette Szabo, failing to overthrow her instructor during the training. Film still from *Carve Her Name with Pride*, 1958.

who were more used to instructing male army recruits, did not know how to supervise women (or, in the case of Denis Rake, flamboyant homosexuals). Evidence supporting this interpretation comes from Odette Sansom's instructor who is quoted as having said, 'I have never before had to teach such things to ladies' and Leslie Fernandez, an instructor who taught students in close combat techniques, who claimed: 'These girls weren't commando material. They didn't have the physique.'[27] Moreover, the training scenes in the film *Carve Her Name with Pride* (1958) intimate that instructors were perplexed by the participation of women and suggest that female students were treated differently, having to endure instructors' patronising attitudes. Analysis of the training scenes in the film, which is based on the experiences of real-life agent Violette Szabo, provides an interesting opportunity to examine the filmic representation of the treatment of female students by SOE instructors. Although its accuracy is questionable as the film is based on a biography of a woman who was killed during the war and thus she was not involved in the production of either, *Carve Her Name with Pride* can be regarded as an appropriate source to examine the paramilitary training as an SOE instructor and another female agent acted as technical advisers on the film.

In one scene, an NCO instructor is seen teaching Violette Szabo defence tactics. Having effortlessly tossed her to the ground with little resistance, he says: 'Look miss, you're going to fight the Germans! You're going to help us win the war! Right?' When she sheepishly assents, he pats her thigh and in a condescending voice says: 'That's a very clever girl'.[28] While the 'us' in his statement could denote Great Britain, it could also refer to men, indicating that Szabo, labelled by him as a 'girl' and a 'miss', irrespective of the fact that she was married and had a daughter, is merely an auxiliary, 'helping' the 'real' combatants. After a second failed attempt to overthrow him, he exclaims: 'It's very simple. A child could do it',[29] thus positioning her as both incompetent and childlike (see Figure 1). Having humiliated and belittled her in front of the other students, he then turns to a fellow male instructor and bemoans that 'this is the best of the bunch! I can't stand this, I'm going off sick'.[30] This lament suggests that he felt that his skills as an instructor were being wasted upon women. The combat instructor struggles to supervise the female students, punishes them for showing initiative during an exercise and begrudgingly praises them when they have been successful: 'It gives me pain, great pain to say it. I'm proud to have you in my section'.[31] He despairs at their lack of military discipline when they prepare to leave his office without being dismissed: 'Blimey, women!' he exclaims. Having given consent to their departure, he then turns to the camera and reflects, 'Well, I suppose Winston knows what he's doing'.[32] Throughout the training scenes, the instructors are represented as sceptical about the inclusion of women. This representation of instruction suggests that, despite assertions that the training was the same for women as it was for men, there was gender differentiation in the practices and attitudes of instructors. The NCO instructor is not only conscious of gender differentiation, which pervaded and shaped the training, but he was in fact constructing these differences with his treatment of Szabo.

The film director's decision to portray the instructor in such a poor light is perhaps symptomatic of the film's timing. *Carve Her Name with Pride* was itself the product of the gender relations of its era. The post-war period was characterised by a conservative backlash which saw many women returning to the home after wartime employment. By showing the instructor's initial bewilderment and resistance to women's inclusion, which is slowly overcome by Szabo's steady progress, the film can address any assumptions the audience was expected to have regarding female combatants: a point we shall return to later. In this particular case, it is clear that another factor is that one of the two technical advisers on the film was Leslie Fernandez who, as we have seen, had very definite ideas about the capabilities of female students and this might have influenced the construction of both Szabo and the combat instructor.

The representation of the NCO instructor in *Carve Her Name with Pride* who was acutely conscious of gender differences was by no means exceptional, as the personal files make evident. Yolande Beekman's file is replete with highly gendered comments: L/Cpl Gordon wrote: 'A nice girl, darned the men's socks, would make an excellent wife for an unimaginative man, but not much more than that.' Lieut. Holland noted: 'She is feminine enough', while Lieut. Wilson stated that she was a 'maternal type.'[33] Françine Agazarian was reported as 'temperamental', 'might blow the gaff in a fit of jealousy', 'might be indiscreet in a fit of pique', 'sometimes exhibited temperament and caprice. Moody; jealous, unattractive to men'[34] and Yvonne Fontaine's file noted: 'She is egocentric, spoilt, stubborn, impatient, conceited and anxious to draw attention to herself … hair worn loose in rather unbecoming disarray, liable to frequent alteration no doubt … very large goggly eyes.' It was also noted that she 'likes a great deal of attention from those whom she is pleased to call "les boys!"'[35] Similarly, Anne-Marie Walters 'will not hesitate always to make use of her physical attractiveness in gaining influence over men.'[36]

Despite evidence of some women avoiding physical exercise and others being criticised in highly gendered ways in their training reports, historian James Gleeson claimed that 'the instructors had little regard for the sex of their pupils – no exceptions and no allowances were made.'[37] Interestingly, when gender differences were not explicitly acknowledged and women were required to accomplish the same feats as their male colleagues, they might perhaps be considered to be in a worse position than when these distinctions were recognised and special considerations for women made. For example, Claire Everett was knocked unconscious when she attempted to climb up a tree and down a perpendicular rope, an arrangement acknowledged as the toughest obstacle which was designed to test students' physical strength and balance. Everett recalled that: 'I was just hanging there. I didn't realise that you have to use your ankles … The instructor was standing down there marking and I looked down at him and he didn't do anything, his face didn't change. He let me drop and I fell thirty feet on to my back and woke up in hospital. After that, the rope training was banned for women but you know, we should have been told. We didn't have any instruction.'[38] Everett was annoyed that the instructor had watched while she struggled and allowed her to fall. She might have been spared this accident if there had been a recognition of differences in the kind of physical training and background that male and female students had experienced prior to their SOE training. Thus, in being treated the same as her male colleagues and not being granted special allowances, Everett was paradoxically in a less desirable position than if gender differences had been recognised either through lifting the requirement or by giving her adequate instruction in how to complete the task successfully. Women were thus trapped in a double bind: if gender disparity was acknowledged then women were often discriminated against, and if differences in prior training at school and in the army were not acknowledged, and women were compelled to undertake physical exercises designed for men, they were likely to fail.

Role allocation

Trainees' schooling in Morse, weapons and explosives gave the instructors an indication of the roles for which each student would be suitable. Yvonne Baseden recalled that 'they graded you according to what you were best at.'[39] Women were often considered suitable for wireless operating. Those who excelled in the initial Morse training were offered the opportunity to train as WT (Wireless Telegraphy) operators. Although wireless operating required technical skills, which are conventionally regarded as masculine qualities ('girls as a rule are not mechanically minded' noted one official report[40]) women were considered to be suitable for WT work because the small, agile fingers and light bones, which women were thought to possess, supposedly aided motor coordination skills. Women were also considered particularly suitable for couriering because they could conceal their clandestine activities behind a façade of domesticity, were not regarded with the same suspicion as men and were seldom searched by male German soldiers on guard at checkpoints, as we shall see.

However, not all roles were considered suitable for female students: indeed, some positions were closed to them. One job they were not trained for was that of organiser. It was thought that, given the traditionally Catholic and conservative attitudes prevalent in France in this period, it was unlikely that local French men would accept the leadership of young women. Yvonne Cormeau felt this was wrong: 'SOE never gave women jobs higher than wireless operator. They thought no French person would obey instructions from a woman, but I found that I had no problems at all in that respect.'[41] However, many Frenchmen were hostile to women playing any role in wartime. Moreover, there was in existence an acute gendered division of labour that isolated women in the home. Women, who played a subordinate role in the public sphere, were associated with the domestic arena with responsibilities for childcare and housework. Francis Cammaerts noted: 'There was a traditional social pattern in rural or semi-rural France, in which the male does one thing and the female does another.'[42] Women's exclusion from the public realm was exemplified by their lack of political rights: French women were not enfranchised until October 1944. As women did not possess the right to vote, it was unlikely that they would be invested with political power and granted positions of leadership.

Women were also thought to be unsuitable for training as saboteurs. This was probably because these positions entailed teaching roles and working with local Frenchmen. It was assumed that few men would accept instruction in weapons training from a young woman. Pearl Witherington was aware of this when she offered training to a group of resisters: 'I said, "Look, I can come and give you instructions on the explosives and arms but if you don't want a woman [silence]." This was Auvergne country and I thought, well, perhaps they won't enjoy having a woman there at all. So I said, "If you don't want me to do it, if they don't want a woman, just tell me and I'll send you somebody else." ... The Auvergne was very closed, it's hilly country, they're not open-minded.'[43] Hence, the 'combat taboo' remained largely intact. A number of female veterans record in their testimonies their pleasure at not being allowed to become saboteurs. Yvonne Cormeau indicates her relief in two separate interviews held at the Imperial War Museum, claiming in one interview, 'Luckily, men only as saboteurs' and 'Well, that I was quite glad of' in the second.[44] Unfortunately, neither interviewer asked her why she appreciated this exclusion. However, one can speculate that she might not have had skills in this area or, perhaps more likely, she wanted to avoid killing. Women's biological ability to bear children was seen to be at odds with terminating life as Pearl Witherington claimed: 'I don't think it's a woman's job, you know. We're made to give life, not take it away. I don't think I could have stood up and coldly shot somebody.'[45] The notion that women's biology rendered them inappropriate for some aspects of warfare was central to the 'combat taboo'. Yet Witherington's SOE work was paradoxically closely linked to combat, which illustrates the strength of gender differences at the time. At the heart of her account is a contradiction in that, while she is evoking gender distinctions central to discourses of that period, she had undermined them by participating in combatant work. Conventional gender norms were thus simultaneously disturbed and defended.

The association of women with giving, not taking, life might explain why Cormeau, who was a mother, was relieved that only men were allotted the role of saboteur. Witherington, however, does not speak for all of the women recruited. When I asked Yvonne Baseden if she would have been prepared to shoot someone in the field, she replied abruptly and decisively: 'Oh yes. Yes, absolutely. I don't know whether I would be prepared to knife them because we were trained to do that as well. Oh yes, certainly I would. It was part of the training and a job to be done.'[46] This suggests that women underwent the same training in armed combat as men and were taught aggressive manoeuvres as well as defensive tactics which indicate that the combat taboo was not enforced. Nancy Wake was even more uncompromising: 'All I wanted to do was to kill Germans.'[47] Wake dispels the myth that women, due to their life-giving capacities, are innately pacifist. Whereas some female students wanted to have no role in the killing of German soldiers, as it seemed to go against the dominant discourse of femininity, others were quite prepared or even desired to do this. Nevertheless, the association of women with reproduction and birth might be one explanation as to why women were not specifically trained for the role of saboteur. Furthermore, the combat taboo may have been in operation in subtle ways: although women were not excluded from basic weapons training, they were prohibited from undergoing extensive training in preparation for the role of saboteur.

Men's and women's work was thus clearly differentiated in terms of tasks and status as a gendered division of labour was established with women being trained as couriers, men as organisers and saboteurs, and both as wireless operators. This is an interesting site of gender construction wherein there is explicit decision-making about the appropriateness of men and women undertaking specific roles. Despite the social and cultural upheavals produced by the war, which enabled women to play a part in clandestine warfare, gender roles and norms remained resilient. Although a small number of women were recruited as agents, they were assigned highly gender-specific positions during their training at Wanborough. This was because various skills, such as communication, leadership and physical strength, were regarded as gender-specific.

Two different types of accounts of the training can be detected: seemingly straightforward narratives recalling equality and apparently ambiguous and contradictory narratives recollecting both equality and discrimination. Some female veterans assert that they only ever experienced equality and claim that they were both unaware of, and later unconcerned by, the gendered division of labour. Yvonne Baseden asserted that 'it didn't occur to me' that the SOE did not train any women as organisers and, when I asked Claire Everett if she recalled feeling aggrieved, she exclaimed: 'Good lord, no. No, no. Well I think Pearl proved it. She had to do it. If faced with it, you take on those responsibilities. You do it. She had to cope and she did.'[48] Everett uses the example of Witherington, who was sent in as a courier but later took on a leadership role following the arrest of her organiser, Maurice Southgate, to assert that, although women were not sent into the field as organisers and saboteurs, in certain circumstances they did assume these masculine roles. Interestingly, although Everett uses Witherington as an example of women taking positions of responsibility, Everett herself also assumed a masculine role when the group's weapons trainer was shot in a Maquis encounter with German soldiers. This is a clear example of self-deprecation, a common theme which was prevalent within many veterans' accounts. Having herself proven that women could undertake these masculine roles, Everett nevertheless was not annoyed that women were excluded from these positions. One explanation for why gender differentiation is denied in these testimonies might be that their emphasis on the positive dimensions of the training makes it difficult for them to conceptualise and make reference to any dissatisfaction or inequality.

In other accounts, gender dynamics were highlighted in more complex ways. Despite her satisfaction that women were not assigned the role of saboteur, Yvonne Cormeau was displeased that only men could be organisers: 'I was rather annoyed to discover men only were used as group leaders. There was real discrimination there.'[49] Cormeau also asserted: 'We must remember that there were no women who were put in charge. All the bosses were men.'[50] Not only was Cormeau conscious of gendered role allocation, she was also eager to have it documented that there were some roles from which women were deliberately excluded. This is particularly remarkable given that her interviewers were asking her general questions concerning the training, rather than questions about gender relations. Despite affirmations of equality, assertions of gender differentiation often pervaded such accounts and some were conscious of being discriminated against and recall that there was a very explicit division of labour with men and women being allotted different roles.

Paramilitary training

Wanborough functioned as 'an elimination school'[51] and students who did not seem adequately assimilated into French culture were returned to their units or sent to 'the Cooler' in Inverlair, Inverness-shire, not knowing the reasons for their elimination.[52] Those individuals who successfully passed this first hurdle graduated to the next course, a much tougher paramilitary commando course that lasted between three and five weeks. It was held in one of the 'Group A' Special Training Schools in Arisaig, a rugged area on the western coast of Inverness-shire. The remoteness lent itself to the type of schooling undertaken there. Students were trained in survival skills, such as fieldcraft, map reading and compass work, as well as being taught by poachers how to live off the land.

Unlike the instruction at Wanborough, which was testing recruits' passing skills, the training at Arisaig focused on honing them physically in order to prepare them for the rigours of living clandestinely in occupied territories. This was important given that many agents would have to undertake demanding physical feats, such as climbing over the Pyrenees in order to return to Britain. Gaston Cohen remembered that there were 'forced marches, 40 miles in the Highlands, in the mist with a minimum of food. Boat training in the loch, very cold, had to swim in the blasted loch.'[53] He found it very tough but managed to successfully undertake the training and derived considerable confidence from it.

In spite of the extreme physical toughness of the training at Arisaig, men and women were trained together and were sent in small mixed groups on hikes. One male recruit on Claire Everett's course had his own trick of ensuring his group worked hard. She recalled: 'He made me lead all the time. I'd be the first of the group of five when we were going on a mission, or doing whatever … His theory was if I did it, they'd have to, even if they found it tough. They'd have to keep up with a girl.'[54] He was playing upon, and implementing, gender differences. He was exploiting men's desire not to be perceived as failing in masculinity by deliberately

putting a woman in front. Moreover, he was playing on their expectation that women were unsuited to either demanding physical exercise or
leadership. Therefore, in successfully completing the job, Everett not only
experienced satisfaction in her own competence but she also provided an
incentive for the others. She felt the pressure of being the only woman in
her group: 'It was harder on me', but, nevertheless, was eager to assert that
she enjoyed it tremendously.

As Everett's testimony suggests, she was not given any special treatment, but instead had to work very hard as she was frequently made
to lead in the exercises. Aonghais Fyffe, a Security Liaison Officer and
head of the lodge at Inverlair, also suggests that women were not given
any concessions: 'There was no distinction between the sexes and all
suffered the same rigours of physical training in the early hours of wintry
mornings, the same mud, muck, soakings in peat bogs on fieldcraft
and the same sore muscles and aching joints from the Arisaig form of
unarmed combat. After all, when they were crawling flat to the ground
over the peaty marshes of Loch nan Uamh, they were all just "bods in
battledress".[55] Fyffe asserted that he did not differentiate between male
and female students and, moreover, that women were not exempted
from any aspect of it. Similarly, Eric Sheppard, who was an instructor in
communications at the school that the wireless operators progressed to
after leaving Arisaig, informed me that every morning before his lessons
began they would have PT:

> We had a proper gym instructor and we all had to join in with that and it was
> PT, gymnastics, jumping over things, acrobatics over this blooming horse,
> to keep fit, you know, generally speaking. The usual thing. And then there
> was always a cross-country run – about three miles that everyone used to do.
> And the women were doing exactly the same as the men – they had to, this
> was the point. So there was no difference in that respect at all. If they were
> going running, they had to do the same running. I mean we had rugby and
> football and all that, but they didn't join in that obviously, but the climbing
> and all that. The girls were equal in respect to what the men were doing but
> obviously from a physical point of view it was a different matter.[56]

Rather than gender being irrelevant, as Fyffe and Sheppard suggest,
I suspect that it was a structuring absence. For example, there was no
relaxing of the rules concerning what women had to accomplish and thus
they were expected to embark upon hikes with their male colleagues.
Ordinary women, whether they had been recruited as civilians or
from the services, however, were unlikely to be able to keep pace with
men, most of whom had undergone some military training as a result

of conscription. For example, Nancy Wake, who had walked across the Pyrenees, took twice as long as her male colleagues on an obstacle-ridden hike despite missing out half of the apparatuses.[57] While gender differences were often assumed and reinforced, resulting in discrimination against women, sometimes paradoxically, women could have difficulties when some distinctions were not recognised, as Wake's account suggests. In order to evade PT at dawn, Wake found it convenient to highlight her gender difference from her comrades by pretending to have stomach cramps due to her period.[58]

Despite assertions that gender was irrelevant, it shaped the experiences of both male and female students. Mixed training put additional pressure on men, who were unlikely to accept being beaten by women. Moreover, both the acknowledgement of gender differences, as demonstrated in Everett's testimony, and the lack of awareness of gendering practices, as indicated in Wake's experience, meant that gender dynamics shaped women's training at Arisaig. This pattern persisted during the subsequent stage of the training.

Trade training

Recruits were then sent on various courses to develop the specific skills needed to undertake the generally gendered role they had been allocated. There were courses on arranging reception committees, as well as on explosives, safe-breaking, forgery, Morse and coding. Wireless operating was the most complex training and students designated for this role underwent much longer training than those sent as couriers, saboteurs or organisers. This was the only trade course in which men and women trained together: the other courses mentioned above prepared male students for the roles of organiser or saboteur.

Yvonne Cormeau excelled at Morse and was allocated the role of wireless operator. However, she struggled with the mechanical part of the WT training as she claimed: 'I'm far from technically-minded.'[59] She recalled: 'There were about seven or eight of us. I was the only woman and there the poor Signals Sergeant was explaining everything as to how it worked. And I was looking blank at him because I'd never had lessons. My days at school, girls didn't get things about waves in the atmosphere.'[60] This is another example of women's training being impeded because gender differentiation in education at that time was being ignored.[61] Like most girls of her age in this period, Cormeau had not studied physics and thus struggled to understand the technical knowledge that repairing

WT sets required. After a few private lessons with her Signals Sergeant, Cormeau was able to grasp the technicalities, complete the WT training and embark upon parachute training.

Parachute training

Next, students moved on to Tatton Park on the edge of Ringway aerodrome near Manchester where they attended the Airborne Troops Parachute School. They were taught how to simulate landing by jumping from a tower and from a lorry travelling 30 miles an hour. They then progressed to jumping from a stationary barrage balloon tethered in the park and finally they jumped out of a Whitley aircraft both during the day and at night.

Although it might be presumed that men and women would be given the same parachute training, this was not the case. Pearl Witherington claimed: 'There was a difference there. The men had to do five jumps to be able to wear the wings. This I discovered when I came back. They did four training jumps and the operational jump that was five, but the women only did three and the fourth was in operation so we weren't allowed to wear the wings and this I thought was jolly awful but, anyway, it didn't stop me going.'[62] It could be surmised that because women were required to do fewer jumps than men, they were considered to be more proficient at it, needing less experience. However, as is evident in Witherington's statement, in which she articulates her irritation at this unnecessary differentiation between men and women, this had far-reaching consequences in that women were prevented from obtaining their parachute wings and thus were not afforded the same status and pay as male parachutists. It also meant they had less experience. Despite her annoyance, Witherington apparently just got on with the job. This disparity would not induce her to abandon her decision to join the organisation. The parachute wings were certainly prized: sixty years after receiving them, Gaston Cohen still has them, framed and mounted on his wall. Perhaps bestowing wings on women was considered unnecessary given that women would play no further role in the army after the war. It must also be remembered that, at this time, men received greater financial rewards for undertaking exactly the same occupations as women. Despite pushes for parity in wages during the Second World War by various groups of British female employees, such as those at the Rolls-Royce plant in Hillington, near Glasgow, this was only attained in 1970 with the passing of the Equal Pay Act. Whatever the reason for the disparity in training and payment, it is significant not only that Witherington recalled being annoyed when she learned of this differential treatment, but also that she wanted to have it on record at the Imperial War Museum where researchers could access her interview.

Representations of parachute jump training in the film *Carve Her Name with Pride* further illustrate the argument made previously that, initially, instructors had difficulties in adapting to female students. In the film, the parachute instructor is shown observing the two lead characters jumping from a tower. Szabo, who jumps competently, is followed by fellow student, Fraser, whose jump is less technically sound. The instructor berates him for not keeping his legs together and exclaims: 'Even the women are better than you are. That's something I thought I'd never say.'[63] The instructor is portrayed as registering surprise that women have proved themselves capable of undertaking parachuting. In fact, his praise of Szabo, and female students in general, is aimed not at them but rather it is articulated as an insult to Fraser. Representations of instructors in *Carve Her Name with Pride* generate and mobilise scepticism concerning women's ability to train alongside men. There is something of a progress narrative in the film's portrayal of Szabo, beginning with the combat instructor's exclamations of despair at her inability to defend herself during unarmed combat, leading to his restrained acknowledgement of Szabo's shooting expertise and culminating with the parachute instructor's indirect praise. In conformity with the war hero genre, Szabo is shown to be a competent student by the end of the training scenes. However, these scenes chart her difficulties and depict her overcoming discernible and gender-specific obstacles. This both confirms the sense that women were different and had problems in such crucial military activity, while also proving that despite the controversy concerning the recruitment of women, the SOE's decision to employ females was vindicated.

In *Carve Her Name with Pride*, Szabo is shown to be fully cognisant of the role that was expected of her, having been informed of this in the initial interview. This was not necessarily what actually occurred. Many recruits were halfway through their schooling before realising that they were not being trained for ordinary military or civilian jobs. Francis Cammaerts recalled that after six weeks of training he still did not know the nature of his prospective role: 'And still at that stage I had really no idea what was happening. Even when we went to Manchester and jumped out of an aeroplane I simply thought I'd been given to understand the notion that we might be needed in North Africa where the landings had taken place in November [1942].'[64] The basic training at Wanborough was similar to that which most army recruits experienced and parachute schooling at

Ringway implied an ordinary army unit that was training for an aerial assault. Although Cammaerts was not informed of the nature of the SOE, as a man training in combatant techniques he was able to speculate about the type of warfare in which he might soon be engaged. For those female students who had not been informed, finding out about their future role would have come as something of a shock, considering that most would not have entertained the idea of front line involvement. Although the wartime economy had necessitated certain changes which impacted upon women, as evidenced in their employment in munitions factories, occupying positions previously regarded as masculine and enlisting in the auxiliary services, few women would have considered that they would be recruited to work behind enemy lines in occupied countries. Someone who was alerted to the nature of the organisation during her recruitment interview was Pearl Witherington (Jepson joked that it was she who had interviewed him.[65]) She remembered a conversation between herself and Odette Wilen during the training:

> [Wilen] was on the same group ... She was very, very, very feminine. Of course there she didn't know what she was letting herself in for because one fine day we'd been blowing up things left, right and centre and she said, 'Pearl, I must ask you for some advice'. She said, 'What are we supposed to be doing?' I was so surprised and said, 'Don't you know?' 'Well', she said, 'no, I thought I was coming in to this because I was recruited as a bilingual secretary' ... So I said, 'Well, you'd better go and talk to Major Watt about this because that's not what we're doing.'[66]

Unfortunately, there is no record of Wilen's reaction when she was enlightened as to the nature of the organisation, but she successfully completed the training and was infiltrated into France. Why some recruits were informed of the SOE's role and others were not seems unclear. All students, however, were informed of the nature of the organisation when they moved to Beaulieu, which was known as 'the finishing school'.

'The finishing school'

Having undertaken parachute jumping, the students moved on to the Group B schools which were situated on Lord Montagu's estate at Beaulieu in the New Forest. This final course prepared them for living a clandestine life. Peter Lake noted: 'That's where you're told how to behave like a secret agent.'[67] There were five elements to Beaulieu. At Department A, students were trained in agent technique, personal security, organisation of circuits, methods of communication, recruitment and handling of agents. Instruction in passing techniques was a core element of the syllabus at Beaulieu and students were shown how to maintain their cover or, as Jacques Poirier claimed, 'how to disguise one's own personality'[68] in order to be inconspicuous. M. R. D. Foot noted: 'Agents had to be taught how to play a part, how to act their cover. To be one person in reality, and quite another in appearance – to *live* one's cover – was unusually hard, but vitally important: survival hinged on it ... It was a matter of becoming a new character, and knowing in advance how – in one's new character – one was going to behave in particular social settings.'[69] At Wanborough, the extent to which students had embraced French cultural habits was observed but it was during their time at Beaulieu that they were given advice on passing. For example, students were informed that, when they arrived in France, it was imperative that they found out about 'unprocurable articles (e.g. danger of ordering wrong drinks or cigarettes)' and 'new slang or colloquialisms brought about by war.'[70] Lectures also reminded students to: 'Avoid foreign words, tunes, manners etc. Avoid slang which has developed among your countrymen in Britain. Avoid showing knowledge or expressing views acquired in Britain. Conform with all new conditions which have arisen, observe new customs and acquire the language which has developed in your country.'[71] This training in passing was about ensuring that agents were up to date as far as French culture was concerned. It did not address habitus at the deeper level as this was something they were already expected to possess. SOE staff recognised that slippages in passing could occur and sought to alert students to aspects of their behaviour which might expose their clandestine identity. Those agents who were British nationals needed to reposition themselves through avoidance of phrases and behaviours which identified them as British: their dissimulations of Britishness were as crucial as their reproductions of a French identity.

Their training was so comprehensive that they were even given a preview of what it was like to be arrested.[72] Students were lectured on German interrogation techniques, as well as having a practical demonstration of these. During the night, each student was brusquely shaken awake and marched to an office, flanked by staff of the training schools dressed in Gestapo uniform. They were then subjected to a mock interrogation to test how well they endured questioning. In an Imperial War Museum lecture, Tony Brooks provided an account of the simulated examination:

> At 2 o'clock in the morning, I was tipped out of bed by a German soldier with a bayonet fix and a rifle and a tin hat and I recognised it was Kennedy the mess waiter ... [He] smacked me on the backside with a rifle butt with

terrific vigour … A very good instructor called Peter was dressed up as a German Sicherheitsdienst Officer and he said, 'What's your cover name?' and I gave it and he said, 'Right, sit down' and they had string around the leg of this stool and they whipped it away and I sat on the floor … He kept swearing at us in German.[73]

Despite the fact that students instantly identified the 'German officers' as their instructors, those involved in the mock questioning tried to make the role-play as realistic as possible. FANY Dorothy Temple played a part in the interrogations when she was stationed at Algiers. She recalled: 'We were supposed to giggle. I couldn't bring myself to do that. The point was, as they told me, the Gestapo had women standing by who'd do this. Laugh at them, jeer at them, and they've got to get used to it.'[74] Laughing women were used to 'unman' male prisoners, to strip them of their dignity and to fracture their morale. Temple disliked her role in the cross-examination, but her presence was necessary in order to replicate a Gestapo interrogation as closely as possible. There was an acknowledgement by the SOE staff then that German female clerks were used to observe interrogations and purposefully to mock male agents while they were being interrogated. Consequently, simulated interrogations of male students in Algiers incorporated laughing FANYs into the role-play. However, there appears to be no recognition that captured female agents might experience male derision, which could have strong sexual implications, and there was certainly nothing done to prepare them for this. Moreover, female students were unlikely to be subjected to the physical and verbal assault that male students, such as Tony Brooks, experienced.

The mock interrogation was the responsibility of Department A. Department B re-acclimatised students within wider society. While undertaking their courses at Wanborough, Arisaig and Ringway, students had been in relative isolation, but at Beaulieu they were encouraged to participate in the community. Bob Sheppard recalled: 'We used to go to church on a Sunday morning. We got back into life, to put us back into contact.'[75] Students were sent for several days on schemes during which they were to accomplish various tasks, such as setting explosive charges on railway lines or breaking into buildings and stealing documents.

It was the job of Pru Willoughby, who worked in the SOE's Counter-Espionage Department, to find the students accommodation for the week away from Beaulieu. She asserted that: 'This was really meant to be a sort of dummy experience of what they would find behind the lines. What they might find in their sort of lifestyle.'[76] Willoughby contacted the relevant regional office and informed them of the arrival and personal details of students on their schemes. Local police were given descriptions of the students, which encouraged them to adopt disguises. On this scheme, if they had the misfortune to be caught, they were to stick to their 'cover story' and try to be released without interference by the SOE. However, as a last resort, they could make a telephone call which would verify them and occasion their discharge. Thus, they were able to put into practise what they had learned at the various training schools while NCOs observed them and alerted them to their distinctive mannerisms that displayed a slippage between their real and purported identities. Brian Stonehouse was doing a radio scheme in Manchester, accompanied by an NCO. The officer noticed Stonehouse's distinctive gait and, according to Derrick Duesbury, informed him: 'You'll have to alter the way you walk, it's much too English. If you're going to France, you have to walk like a Frenchman does'.[77] Although this advice might appear somewhat histrionic, another agent, Guido Zembsch-Schreve, was alerted to his distinctive military gait by a friendly French gendarme.[78] This example not only suggests that ways of walking might be seen as embodied dispositions which could help or hinder agents' passing, but it also indicates the rather incidental (as opposed to systematic) way that the nurturing of appropriate habitus occurred.

Another element in male students' training to pass as ordinary French civilians was undertaken at Beaulieu. We have seen that at Wanborough, FANYs were used to ply male agents with alcohol to test whether they were irresponsibly garrulous. At Beaulieu, this was sometimes taken one step further. In an interview for the Imperial War Museum, Peter Lee, head of the Security Section, recalled that 'intelligence services of any country use women as agent provocateurs' and thus it was imperative that male students were tested 'to see whether they were susceptible to women's charms'.[79] Pru Willoughby recalled: 'I was in charge of a very nice girl who was a prostitute. We told this girl, Christine, to go to the pub and try and break this chap down and try and get him into bed. After the week was up, he came back to Baker Street and there was a committee of people to interview him about what had happened on this week and he found to his horror that there was this girl amongst the people.'[80] Christine could also detect whether they talked in their sleep and note in which language. Some students, however, outwitted the SOE's ploy to ensnare them. Bob Maloubier recollected his 'blind date' with an attractive woman whom he immediately realised was a plant. When they retired to his bedroom, he confronted her: 'We talked the matter over in my room. Anyway, she said, "Now what are we going to do?" "I'm going to kill you." [imitates gun and laughs] I said, "You're dead." We talked the matter over. I said, "Ok. You can tell the people that employ you that you came up to my room to extort information out of me and I killed you!"[81] Maloubier's involvement in the SOE did not prompt him to alter his exuberant life-style. Although this might be considered reckless, he was a native Frenchman and thus was highly unlikely to accidentally speak English in his sleep. By intimating that he could have killed the *agent provocateur*, Maloubier was able to enjoy her company while demonstrating that his security remained intact.

We have already seen that whereas male students' partiality for alcohol was scrutinised, this did not occur with female recruits. Similarly, it appears that only men's susceptibility to *agent provocateurs* was tested. It is interesting to reflect upon why women were not subjected to a similar test. Perhaps it was considered unlikely that women might engage in sexual relationships with local men or ungentlemanly to lecture women on this point. Certainly, there is no evidence to suggest that female agents did embark upon affairs with Frenchmen. However, perhaps it should have been anticipated that the stressful circumstances of living permanently in a false identity might have been conducive to forming close attachments with others that shared those anxieties. In fact, a number of women formed relationships with their SOE comrades. During the training, Eliane Plewman and Eric Cauchi, Sonya Butt and Guy d'Artois and Muriel Byck and an unnamed male agent identified as 'No. 15' in her personal file became lovers.[82] Relationships also occurred in the field between Odette Sansom and Peter Churchill, Andrée Borrel and Gilbert Norman, Sydney Hudson and Sonya Butt, as well as between Claude de Baissac and Mary Herbert who became pregnant. Presumably, there were also other attachments which have remained undisclosed. Assumptions that women would not be sexually active during this period would appear, then, to have been misguided and the decision to instruct only men on the dangers of forming relationships may have been imprudent.

The other departments at Beaulieu were Department C, which was responsible for teaching students about the German forces, in particular the Gestapo (Secret State Police), Wehrmacht (Army), Abwehr (Intelligence) and Sicherheitsdienst or SD (Security Service), as well as their different uniforms, knowledge of which was relevant to passing; Department D supervised the secret circulation of propaganda; and Department E focused on the use of codes, ciphers and secret inks. Together, they completed the training at Beaulieu.

Retrieving passing and gender

To recapitulate, gender was a significant factor at every stage of the students' schooling. As we have seen, at Wanborough, although both men and women's partiality for consuming alcohol was tested, women were more severely judged for drinking and inebriated men were presumed to be more susceptible to *agents provocateurs*. Moreover, trainees were allocated tasks along highly gender-specific lines and instructors may well have been intolerant of female students. While some enabled women to opt out of PT, others did not acknowledge gender differences which could lead to women struggling to compete against men in order to prove themselves. An instructor at Arisaig claimed that women were afforded no special considerations and thus they had to undertake the same physical rigours that men with prior army training found arduous, and one male student played upon fellow male trainees' expectations that women could not undertake either demanding physical exercise or leadership by placing the only female student in a position of responsibility. The only trade training that was undertaken by both men and women was wireless operating and women often struggled with the technical aspects of the course because of lack of experience and education. Women were required to do fewer jumps when stationed at Ringway, and thus were unable to receive the prized parachute wings, and at Beaulieu only male students' composure in spite of sexual derision during interrogations and susceptibility to *agents provocateurs* were tested.

My picture of the specific forms of gender relations in each phase of the SOE training contrasts with that which emerges in much of the historical literature. I have demonstrated that gender was relevant throughout the courses and shaped both men's and women's experiences. Despite this ubiquity, gender is often not addressed in either historical accounts of the training or in veterans' testimonies. Why have patterns of gender relations been ignored in accounts of training for the SOE? The problem in articulating the existence of gender differentiation in the training is made explicit in the following excerpt from an Imperial War Museum interview with Maurice Buckmaster, the head of F Section:

> *Interviewer* – Was there any training for women agents that was different to that what the men got?
> *Buckmaster* – No.
> *Interviewer* – It was exactly the same?
> *Buckmaster* –[*long pause*] Yes. We didn't make any differentiation.
>   They may have opted out of one thing or another which
>   they were entitled to do … I think the women did slightly

less weapon training than the men but it was up to the
instructor to decide that.[83]

Buckmaster hesitates in answering the interviewer's second question and
still avows that men and women undertook the same training. However,
he then goes on to amend his assessment. He initially claimed that staff
did not view men and women differently but that women might have
decided not to participate in some aspects of the course, as we have seen
was the case with Witherington and Wake. However, his final comment
suggests that decisions regarding who did what were taken by the instructors, rather than the students or the policy-makers.

Buckmaster's statement indicates the difficulties in claiming that the
training was differentiated by gender. The SOE policy-makers were
committed to a notion that the teams (organiser, wireless operator,
saboteur and courier) were functional combat units with no special needs
based on gender, age, background or any other differentiator. Yet agents
were not combat units: they were human beings with physical and discursive differences. Buckmaster's account moves between the reiteration of
formal policy and the necessity of day-to-day practices. It is likely that
Buckmaster does not want to assert that female students undertook an
easier training course because that would imply a criticism of them. Yet
it is clear that men and women did not receive *exactly* the same training
not only at the hands of individual instructors but as a matter of policy, as
in the case of parachute training.

This differentiation is referred to by a number of female agents who
record their dissatisfaction with aspects of the training in which they felt
they were not treated equally. Their accounts indicate elements of resistance. Both Cormeau and Witherington for example assert their annoyance at the 'discrimination' which was 'jolly awful'. However, they do not
consistently assert their right to equality as they also express pleasure
and relief that women were not expected to take on the role of saboteur
which would have involved killing. Moreover, despite making comments
referring to specific forms of gender differentiation, Witherington also
claimed that the training was undifferentiated by gender. In this regard,
the testimonies of agents are riddled with inconsistencies. It appears that
Witherington and Cormeau are contradicting themselves: saying on the
one hand that they were treated as equals, and, on the other, that they
experienced gender-specific discrimination. Their seemingly contradictory testimonies can be better understood when they are read as narratives of agency. Choice was paramount to Witherington's feelings about
the training. She had the option to undertake the same PT as the men but

chose not to, but she did not have the opportunity to win her parachute wings because of the limit on the number of jumps that women could perform. The complexity in the accounts concerning gender dynamics during the training is also related to the desires of female veterans to prove that they were not given any special treatment and undertook the same courses, while acknowledging that there were some differences which were beyond their control. They do not want to be underrated, seen as second-class agents, and they seek the recognition accorded their male counterparts.

Furthermore, the process of looking back and reflecting on their wartime training usually elicits positive recollections which leave little space for recalling discrimination. Much like remembering school days, agents generally recall their training period with affection. Most students, both male and female, approached the training as a fun activity, where they met new people, made friends and enjoyed themselves while working hard and learning new skills. All of the veterans I spoke to remembered the different aspects of their training with enthusiasm as the following statements indicate: Yvonne Baseden 'enjoyed every bit of it', Bob Sheppard noted that 'the team spirit was fantastic' and Cyril Watney 'enjoyed the training very much … we were all very friendly and happy and jolly'.[84]

Perhaps one explanation for this effusion of sentiment is that they are recalling the period directly before they were infiltrated into France and experienced grave dangers that made them anxious, as will be discussed in the next chapter. With the benefit of hindsight, veterans may compare the carefree abandon that characterised their months during the training with the unease and continual anxiety of being exposed that they experienced while operational. Emphasising the negative aspects of the courses, in which they were treated differently, such as being prevented from attaining their parachute wings, would tarnish female veterans' recollections of those halcyon days. Consequently, many de-emphasise gender. Another possible explanation is that gender did not seem to be important to the big issues at stake. These included communality, mutuality, solidarity and the common objectives that agents shared as people and as fighters in the war. Overall, the cause for which they were fighting and the identity their occupation bestowed were not gendered, even if, in some respects, the experience of undertaking the training was, both physically and discursively. This may explain why gender differences were rarely discussed and were dismissed with statements such as Everett's: 'The training for the women was the same as the training for the men' and Witherington's: 'We all did exactly the same thing'.[85]

While gender dynamics were pervasive throughout the training, not all aspects of the schooling were concerned with passing: the paramilitary, trade and parachute courses taught students practical skills. However, there was emphasis on passing at the first and last schools: during the preliminary course, lectures were given on how to maintain a low profile and students' drinking, sleeping and eating habits were observed in order to test assimilation into French culture, while at 'the finishing school' students were lectured on how to disguise their personality and the importance of avoiding British phrases and habits, were interrogated to test whether they maintained their cover under pressure and were sent on a scheme lasting several days. There was more emphasis on testing students' ability to pass, as demonstrated by the observation undertaken at Wanborough and the interrogations and schemes at Beaulieu, than on assisting students in their improvement and development of passing skills. Although the lectures did to a certain extent instruct students in how to effect passing, training was more about supporting students, as it was assumed that those who had been recruited and who had graduated from the initial course at Wanborough would have the requisite skills to assimilate into French culture. Trainees were urged to use the skills that the SOE instructors assumed that they already possessed. Nevertheless, students were also furnished with material provisions which assisted their assimilation.

Provisions for passing

After their training was completed, students returned to London, made a will and awaited the briefing in which they were given their operational details and were equipped with false documentation, 'cover names', 'field names' and well-rehearsed 'cover stories'. As in acting, the agents had to be 'in character' and the accoutrements of a false identity were integral to their performances.

Agents possessed a number of forged documents, including identity cards, birth certificates, ration cards and travel permits. The forged documentation was perhaps the most important tool in the construction of new identities and carrying documents under false names enabled agents to conceal their original identities and pass as French civilians. Agents were continually asked for documentation to verify who they were and these would be scrutinised. Perfect French accents or French looks would offer no protection to those whose identity cards and documents were not 'in order'. The personal details of new identities, as indicated on ration books and identity cards, had to be learned in order to aid passing.

As well as being allocated false documents, agents required 'cover names', which were printed on the forged documentation and by which neighbours and non-Resistance friends knew them, and 'field names' by which Resistance colleagues would know them. The use of 'field names' can be seen as another layer of protection, since they removed suspicion and distanced them from their cover identities. This distancing was even more acute when male agents adopted a female nom de guerre. Cyril Watney recollected: 'I chose a girl's name, Eustache.'[86] By hiding his own gender, Watney was able to take advantage of the cover that a woman's name provided. Paula Schwartz, in her study of female combatants, calls this borrowing by men of female names 'gender-scrambling' or 'gender-swapping' and she observes that this practice was widespread among French resisters.[87]

Students were also expected to prepare their own 'cover story', which would further strengthen their performances if they were stopped and questioned. Many tried to make them as realistic as possible: Yvonne Baseden, whose cover was a secretary, had been a shorthand typist before joining the SOE and Roger Landes, who had been a student in architecture, became an architect.[88] If questioned, their knowledge of their civilian professions would augment their 'cover stories' and improve their chances of passing. This realism extended to other aspects of 'cover stories'. Francis Cammaerts had suffered jaundice following his training and this was woven into his 'cover story'. He noted that 'the important thing was to keep a cover story as near the truth as possible.'[89]

Lectures helped students construct their 'cover stories'. They were told that their appearance and conduct must fit their cover and they were given some instruction relating to habitus, although only at the level of exhortation. For example: 'Documents, clothing, possessions etc must be suitable. Manners, tastes, bearing, accent, education and knowledge must accord with your ostensible personality.'[90] Students were also advised on their 'cover names': 'Always sign correctly and respond to it immediately.'[91]Instructors tried to equip students with the knowledge they deemed necessary to pass inconspicuously.

In addition to forged documents, agents were also supplied with items of clothing appropriate to the region in which they were to be operating, which would help them to blend in, to look as inconspicuous as possible and to improve the chances of being mis/taken as civilians. Agents dressed in a similar style to that which was popular among locals to sustain their attempts at passing. Failure to take account of national variations could cause a slippage to ensue between their identities. Refugees who flooded into Britain were one major source of continental attire. However, this source soon dried up. Another source was the SOE Camouflage Section, the Thatched Barn, whose employees adapted clothing to European specifications. May Shrewsbury, an ATS employee, worked there as a seamstress in the Prop department: 'We altered clothes and made them look right. Take anything out that looked English and put in French labels … Just generally make them so there was no sign of English on them. Changed buttons to put French ones on.'[92] Continental and English styles of clothing were quite dissimilar and a single item of clothing could expose agents. By removing English labels and buttons and replacing them with French ones, May Shrewsbury and her fellow seamstresses were facilitating agents' passing as French civilians. Claudia Pulver, who also worked at the Thatched Barn, discussed the differences between French and English styles:

> We started making shirts for them in the very Continental fashion, which was quite different to anything in England … We looked at the various collar shapes that would have been fashionable during the time, we looked at the way they were manufactured. We looked at the seams and there certainly was an enormous difference between the side seams that were made on the Continent and those that were made in England. We did what we called a French seam which was slightly different. The shape of the cuffs was different, the position of the buttonhole on the under-collar was entirely different and sometimes the plackets of a shirt were different.[93]

What is particularly striking here is the attention to detail that went into this production. Each article was made to the exact specifications of the country and region in which the agent was to be infiltrated. As well as having clothes made in the French style and a seemingly authentic label, the items had to be made to look old and used so as to appear authentic. Because both clothing and shoes were strictly rationed, new items looked suspicious and had to be 'dirtied down',[94] which effectively aged them.

In addition to clothing, an agent's hairstyle was also important to their image. Yvonne Baseden noted that her 'hair was cut specially'[95] and, indeed, all students were shown how to cut and style their hair in a contemporary French fashion. They were often given hair dyes to alter their appearance. It is quite remarkable how strongly national identity was signified by clothes and hair in the 1940s, in striking contrast to the twenty-first century, in which styles have become much less nationally distinctive under the influence of globalised markets. It is also remarkable how very constructed bodies were. In addition to visits to hairdressers and tailors, Harley Street dentists also played a part in perfecting agents' appearances, replacing British fillings with gold, as used by French dentists. Some female agents also recall the SOE staff in London giving advice on self-presentation. Yvonne Cormeau recollected: 'They said "please don't try too many dyeing of your hair or very noticeable make-ups and things like that because you'll fall foul at some time or other." Then "try and dress as they do locally as much as possible. If you're going to live in the country don't have manicure, don't have this, don't have that."'[96] The advice was to try to blend in and look inconspicuous, which, as chapter 6 will show, was one of a variety of strategies employed by female agents once in the field.

Although the clothing of the agent was a superficial part of the self-presentation through which they could easily be exposed, it did offer them some protection, not least because the visual is often taken as evidence of authenticity. Their 'French' appearance was read as a reliable signifier of their civilian status, masking their national identity.

Conclusion

An examination of the training of the students preparing for their employment as paramilitaries working behind enemy lines in occupied France reveals how ordinary men and women were transformed into agents with knowledge of subversive techniques and equipped with various aids to assist passing. Despite the necessity of passing, students had little training in how to accomplish this. What was regarded as the 'first qualification' at the recruitment interview was at least initially overlooked in favour of training in military combat, a role that many were not going to undertake. If the initial interview can be regarded as the first phase of vetting, then the training at Wanborough Manor, during which time they were observed, can be seen as a second phase and, once those who were deemed unsuitable had been rejected, instruction in passing was evidently considered relatively unnecessary. Those who had not been rejected had typically lived in France as children, had had a French education, contact with French people and married French nationals and thus had already developed an appropriate French habitus. Indeed, all of my interviewees, who survived the selection and filtration processes of the recruitment interview at Wanborough, had acquired a French habitus.

The virtual absence of instruction in passing is even more curious when we examine the strategies adopted by some female couriers and wireless operators. Couriering, especially, required them to be highly mobile and, accordingly, they needed to pass much more frequently than agents undertaking other roles. As chapter 6 will show, femininity was crucial to women's passing and yet there was no instruction about how female students might exploit the invisibility that they, as women, might benefit from. None of the female veterans I interviewed remembered being given any advice on making the most of the fact that they were women, which is surprising given that female agents' testimonies brim with tales of how they performed femininity either by wearing feminine clothing which was appropriate to the situation or by flirting with German soldiers. Thus, although staff at the training schools were conscious that other countries used female *agents provocateurs* to outwit agents and taught their male students to protect themselves from such activity, there appears to have been no plan for the SOE women to undertake training in how to perform such 'feminine' roles. Vera Atkins, F Section's Intelligence Officer, asserted: 'You wouldn't try and teach a woman how to behave in that way',[97] suggesting that it was considered 'natural'.

The absence of such obviously gender-differentiated training may have contributed to the claim that the training was undifferentiated by gender. As we have seen, this is problematic. Female veterans themselves assert that they were equal to their male colleagues and that the training was the same for women as it was for men. But, although many features of the schooling were undertaken by both men and women who trained together simultaneously, it becomes apparent that there were moments during the training when gender parity was suspended. Even some of the agents who assert that the training was undifferentiated by gender recollect moments when they eluded various aspects of the courses or felt that they were discriminated against. Claiming equality while confessing to circumventing the training syllabus or recalling prejudice appears contradictory. These apparent contradictions and complexities are not confined to accounts of the training: descriptions of emotions provoked by operational passing also appear incongruous, as the next chapter explains.

Notes

1 National Archives, HS 9/77/1, report by Lieut. Colonel Woolych, dated 25 August 1942.
2 IWM SA, 9925 Despaigne.
3 Personal interview with Derrick Duesbury (pseudonym).
4 National Archives, HS 9/11/1, report dated 20 November 1942.
5 National Archives, HS 9/11/1, report by Cpl Morris, 10 September 1942.
6 Personal interview with Nancy Wake.

7 Personal interview with Gervase Cowell.
8 Personal interview with Gervase Cowell.
9 Personal interview with Derrick Duesbury (pseudonym).
10 IWM SA, 9925 Despaigne.
11 Personal interview with Cyril Watney.
12 National Archives, HS 6/568.
13 Bourdieu, *Outline of a Theory of Practice*.
14 Personal interview with Bob Sheppard.
15 Personal interview with Gaston Cohen.
16 Butt, *Behind Enemy Lines* (Channel 4).
17 Personal interview with Claire Everett (pseudonym).
18 Bourdieu, *Sociology in Question*, p. 86.
19 Personal interview with Francis Cammaerts.
20 National Archives, HS 9/910/3.
21 Butt, *Behind Enemy Lines* (Channel 4).
22 Personal interview with Lise de Baissac.
23 National Archives, HS 9/165/8.
24 IWM SA, 8689 Cornioley.
25 Fitzsimons, *Nancy Wake*, p. 179.
26 Rake, *Rake's Progress*, p. 49.
27 Tickell, *Odette*, p. 103; Binney, *The Women Who Lived For Danger*, p. 7.
28 BFI film script 513981.
29 BFI film script 513981.
30 BFI film script 513981.
31 BFI film script 513981.
32 BFI film script 513981.
33 National Archives, HS 9/114/2.
34 National Archives, HS 9/10/2.
35 National Archives HS 9/457/6.
36 National Archives, HS 9/339/2.
37 Gleeson, *They Feared No Evil*, p. 18.
38 Personal interview with Claire Everett (pseudonym).
39 Personal interview with Yvonne Baseden.
40 National Archives, HS 6/576.
41 H. Kedward, *In Search of the Maquis: Rural Resistance in Southern France, 1942–1944* (Oxford: Clarendon Press, 1993), p. 272.
42 Personal interview with Francis Cammaerts.
43 IWM SA, 10447 Cornioley.
44 IWM SA, 8885; 7369 Cormeau.
45 IWM SA, 8689 Cornioley.
46 Personal interview with Yvonne Baseden.
47 Personal Interview with Nancy Wake.
48 Personal interview with Claire Everett (pseudonym).
49 IWM SA, 7369 Cormeau.

50 IWM SA, 8885 Cormeau.
51 Personal interview with Gaston Cohen.
52 A report on recruitment and training claimed that 1955 students of all nationalities were accepted for training in SOE schools in the UK between 15 December 1940 and 2 April 1942, while 202 were considered unsatisfactory and were returned to their units. Although fourteen students were sent to the Cooler, none of the F Section students were sent. National Archives, HS 8/371.
53 Personal interview with Gaston Cohen.
54 Personal interview with Claire Everett (pseudonym).
55 Ottoway, *Violette Szabo*, p. 55.
56 Personal interview with Eric Sheppard.
57 Braddon, *Nancy Wake*, p. 122.
58 Braddon, *Nancy Wake*, p.122.
59 IWM SA, 8885 Cormeau.
60 IWM SA, 7369 Cormeau.
61 See F. Hunt, *Gender and Policy in English Education: Schooling for Girls 1902–44* (Hemel Hempstead: Harvester Wheatsheaf, 1991).
62 IWM SA, 10447 Cornioley.
63 BFI film script 513981.
64 Personal interview with Francis Cammaerts.
65 IWM SA, 10447 Cornioley.
66 IWM SA, 10447 Cornioley.
67 Lake, *Churchill's Secret Army* (Channel 4).
68 Poirier, *The Giraffe Has a Long Neck*, p. 62.
69 Foot, *SOE: An Outline History*, p. 87.
70 National Archives, HS 7/55.
71 National Archives, HS 7/55.
72 The personal file of Guido Zembsch-Schreve contains his debriefing report completed after his return from Germany as a prisoner: 'Source commented that the interrogation exercises at Beaulieu were very valuable.' National Archives, HS9/1329/2.
73 IWM SA, 16568 Brooks.
74 Personal interview with Dorothy Temple.
75 Personal interview with Bob Sheppard.
76 Personal interview with Pru Willoughby.
77 Personal interview with Derrick Duesbury (pseudonym).
78 Zembsch-Schreve, *Pierre Lalande*.
79 IWM SA, 7493 Lee.
80 Personal interview with Pru Willoughby.
81 Personal interview with Bob Maloubier.
82 National Archives, HS 9/250/2.
83 IWM SA, 8680 Buckmaster.
84 Personal interviews with Yvonne Baseden, Bob Sheppard and Cyril Watney.

85 Personal interview with Claire Everett (pseudonym); IWM SA, 10447 Cornioley.
86 Personal interview with Cyril Watney.
87 P. Schwartz, 'Partisanes and Gender Politics in Vichy France', *French Historical Studies*, 16:1 (1989), p. 134.
88 Personal interviews with Yvonne Baseden and Roger Landes.
89 Personal interview with Francis Cammaerts.
90 National Archives, HS 7/55.
91 National Archives, HS 7/55.
92 Personal interview with May Shrewsbury.
93 Pulvey, *Secret Agent* (BBC2).
94 Personal interview with May Shrewsbury.
95 Telephone conversation with Yvonne Baseden.
96 IWM SA, 7369 Cormeau.
97 Personal interview with Vera Atkins.

4

'A jittery business':
representations of anxiousness
in personal and filmic accounts

Films such as *Odette* (1950) and *Carve Her Name with Pride* (1958) portray agents who engaged in clandestine war against the Nazi war machine as unflappable and psychologically strong. And yet both written and oral testimonies of SOE agents suggest that these are inaccurate depictions and that most agents were constantly plagued by self-doubt. The pressures of passing provoked a great deal of worry, generated by the threat of slippage and disclosure, as individuals were conscious of the penalties of failing to pass. This chapter explores these different types of accounts in order to examine the phenomenon of passing undertaken by SOE agents in the context of wartime France.

It would appear that within the narrative genres of oral history and autobiography, veterans feel that it is appropriate to recount their feelings of insecurity and apprehension. Oral history in particular often gives the researcher access to interviewees' emotions. Discussion of feelings of anxiety about not successfully passing as French civilians figure prominently in both male and female agents' testimonies. They mention their wartime concerns that they might say or do something which could undermine their attempt to inhabit other personae. This fissure between successfully passing and not quite accomplishing the performance can be labelled slippage. The passing subject in this context continually fears slipping from one identity to another and being discovered to be an impostor. To pass is to ward off failure, and yet passing is always haunted by and troubled by potential failure. Although most instances of passing occasions some loss of reputation or incurs penalties if revealed, the performances by SOE agents entailed considerable risk. Agents had far more at stake than other passing subjects because discovery could occasion captivity, persecution and execution. Furthermore, unlike in other contexts of passing, agents had to 'prove' their assumed identity on almost a daily basis: a consequence of living in an occupied country. Rather than just passing visually to an unsuspecting audience, agents often had to substantiate their attempts at passing with forged documentation and cover stories to a suspicious 'other'. Hence, the passing undertaken by SOE agents differs from that performed in many other situations, because in this context it involved great risk and was generally undertaken in view of a suspicious, observing audience. These performances were potentially plagued by anxiety.

Anxiousness can be seen to be a rational reaction which is triggered by some precipitating factor. While many psychiatrists, including Sigmund Freud, claim that anxiety is a *post*-event emotion, an unpleasurable state of tension which is triggered by something experienced in the past, in the context of civilian passing undertaken by SOE agents, the nervousness they endured was a sporadic sentiment brought on by, and experienced during, certain stressful situations. Roy Grinker asserted that anxiety is an 'indescribable foreboding or dread of personal doom'.[1] It is a consequence of the projection of the self into the future in anticipation of specific dangers. Anxiousness is thus experienced in the present but it is an emotion that perceives the future as threatening. Apprehension, occasioned by specific events, was the result of the anticipation of capture, torture and execution: a future that is envisaged as undesirable and unliveable.

This was experienced by men and women alike. In contrast, G. S Hall, writing in 1904, regarded fear as gendered. He claimed that 'the anxiety neurosis was relatively more common in women than men'.[2] The idea that women experience anxiety to a greater extent than men became very dominant in the twentieth century. The psychologists Ronald Kessler[3] and Lee Robins and Darrel Regier[4] invested in this discourse by concluding from their studies that anxiety, which they classified as an emotion-based disorder, was nearly twice as common in women as in men. However, in the context of agents passing as French civilians in occupied France, the evidence does not suggest that women did experience fear – and hence passing – differently from men.

The debut performance

Agents' unease about their military identities being exposed was heightened during their first attempt to pass across identity borders. Sentiments of concern about failing to pass feature significantly in agents' testimonies: Denis Rake for example, recollected that it was 'always [a] very trying phase in an agent's experience'[5] and Peter Churchill noted: 'The first few days are always a jittery business.'[6] The initial attempt at passing across identity borders, the debut performance, was the agents' first opportunity to assume their new identity and to check whether anyone would identify them as impostors.

All agents landed in France at night and they began their journey in the following days to the town or village where they would operate. Their appearance, accent and forged documents were immediately put to the test. Yvonne Baseden parachuted into a town near Toulouse in south-west France in 1944 and, carrying incriminating apparatus, she had to make a long journey by both bus and train to the Jura, near the Swiss border, where she was to operate. Her narrative recounting her first journey, which she perceived as the 'most worrying time I had in France',[7] explicitly conveys the anxiety and constant fear of exposure she experienced:

> We had to go from where we were, which was near Auch, which is north of the Pyrenees, to Marseille by bus and take the train from Marseille to Dijon and Dôle where we were going ... Naturally very anxious to get on with things ... I had my crystals [plugs which determined the frequency of the radio transmission] on me and my ciphers [codes concealing the meaning of radio messages] ... First we went by coach ... That was quite worrying in a way because it was the first time one travelled on public [transport] in occupied France and because it was a coach there was no other way out except the front door. Anyway, there was no trouble. We were stopped once or twice. They just glanced at the papers as we walked out and walked back into the coach ... Marseille was terrible of course because there were several hours to wait there. I think I waited about four hours on a bench and of course I was on my own ... It was very difficult because there were patrols in the station. Anyway, I got on the train and it's quite a long way to Lyon ... I got off at Lyon without trouble and got into Dôle. It took a day and a half.[8]

The couching of her feelings in such emotive words as 'difficult', 'anxious', 'terrible' and 'worrying' communicate Baseden's concern about disclosure. The length of this commentary reflects the length of the journey: it is long, drawn-out, marked by stages and infused with her fear, as was her travelling experience. Baseden's anxiety is multi-layered: she is restless and wants to start her mission, uneasy about carrying her wireless operating equipment, perturbed by the absence of an escape route from the bus and concerned about being subjected to document checks. Her agitation is heightened by the long, solitary delay at Marseille train station.

Furthermore, she was concerned that her appearance would betray her as she felt that she looked too English: 'Well, of course, that was something I was worried about in case it happened, which it didn't. One always thought you are so obviously from another world. I felt that it must be noticed that I was different to everybody else. Of course, I looked very French anyway, in those days particularly.'[9] Although she knew that her papers were good forgeries and that she possessed many of the traits that signified French nationality, such as brown hair and average height, she was still anxious that she would be detected and exposed as an impostor: 'You were conscious of being different in this group of people.'[10] She felt that her difference was marked and noticeable. She also felt alien to the culture, despite being half-French and having lived in France for most of her life, and thought that it was obvious to others that she originated 'from another world'.

Baseden's testimony suggests that passing as a French civilian required a consciousness about other people's perceptions of the performance. Readings of passing subjects were crucial to the success of the enactment. Consciousness of such readings – seeing oneself through the eyes of others – produced anxiety, but it was also crucial in facilitating passing. This implies that passing is dialogic in that there is a referential, external (imaginary) other who is incorporated in the preparation for passing. Mikhail Bakhtin claimed that a dialogic interaction with others is required before a coherent image of self is developed. In his discussion of the works of novelist Dostoevsky, he asserted: 'Consciousness never gravitates towards itself but is always found in intense relationship with another consciousness. Every experience, every thought of a character is internally dialogic, adorned with polemic, filled with struggle, or is on the contrary open to inspiration from outside itself – but it is not in any case concentrated simply on its own subject; it is accompanied by a continual sideways glance at another person.'[11] Bakhtin suggested that everything is dialogic: every person is continually performing identities and hoping that they will pass successfully. In this sense, all identities involve a form of passing that incorporates an imaginary other. Perception is thus never autonomous and non-referential, but rather is shaped through the acknowledgement of the existence and judgements of others. Passing subjects do not exist in a vacuum, but rather produce themselves in relation to an anticipated observer. It is not only preparations for passing which incorporate others. The success of each passing performance depends upon the evaluations of a reciprocating audience. Baseden critically examined herself in relation to other French civilians as well as evaluating herself through the eyes of German soldiers. It is this continual reference to others that emphasises the sense in which passing is dialogic.

The reliance on others' readings of their performances provoked unease about whether they would be successful and for what length of time. A further concern of Baseden's, which highlights the dialogic nature of passing, was that she was conscious that she might inadvertently speak in English while asleep and be overheard by her German travelling companions who would recognise her as a British agent. Consequently, 'it was difficult to relax or even fall asleep'.[12] However, it was not only talking in English while sleeping which was a concern. Some agents found that in a moment of concentration lapse, they accidentally conversed in English. Roger Landes recalled: 'The first night when we landed, we were sleeping in the mayor's house. In the morning, he knocked on the door and I said to him, "Enter, come in."'[13] Although Landes was French, he had lived in England since 1938 and had been accustomed to conversing in English. On this occasion, the mistake greatly alarmed Landes and undermined his self-confidence.

Landes was not the only agent to inadvertently slip into speaking in English. On her first bus journey, Anne-Marie Walters said 'please'[14] and Jacques Poirier made an error when purchasing a train ticket on his first day in France: 'Was I tired or simply absent-minded? Whichever, I made my first mistake at the station. I walked up to the guichet [ticket office] and said, in English, "A single to Brive, please." "*Que dites-vous?*" [What did you say?] demanded the woman behind the window. I quickly pulled myself together. "*Un billet pour Brive, s'il vous plaît, madame.*" And to think I'd just spent nearly six months learning the tradecraft of a secret agent!'[15] Some agents found it difficult to shed the customs appropriate to British habitus when they were in France, such as slipping into speaking in English. That agents of French nationality unintentionally did this, as well as British-born agents, suggests that this was probably a result of speaking English while living in Britain for long periods during their training and while waiting to be infiltrated into France. Thus, moving between different situations or 'fields' in which different types of performances were appropriate could be problematic. Agents were manifesting previous experience of acculturation by instinctively speaking in English, which suggests that habitus is durable and deep-rooted, and once acquired not readily displaced. Despite rigorous training and close monitoring by their instructors, slips such as these occurred and were potentially life-threatening. The speaking of English while passing as a French civilian is, then, an example of slippage as their behaviour did not precisely fit the identities they assumed. Rather, a fracturing occurred, revealing other identities. This disparity or slippage, triggered by a number of factors, such as exhaustion or negligence, jeopardised their endeavours at passing.

In addition to the fear of speaking English, the credibility of forged documents was cause for concern. Denis Rake recalled his first contact with authority in his autobiography. He recounts an episode when Vichy police were inspecting his forged (and thus unregistered) identity card: 'I must admit that I was more than a little bit nervous. It wasn't that I had no confidence in SOE's forging department, but I think that every agent in similar circumstances must wonder whether his papers will pass examination by a supposed expert.'[16] Certainly, many agents recall similar feelings of apprehension. Peter Churchill experienced acute anxiety when his papers underwent their first inspection. Churchill, who continued to conceal his identity in his autobiography by writing in the third person, recalled: 'Michel felt as though he were advancing to his doom, like a bullock in one of the Chicago meat-packing yards ... He moved forward, hoping that his affected look of indifference did not belie his real feelings. With jelly in his knees, he handed up his ticket.'[17] This quotation explicitly highlights the performance required to execute passing since feelings of unease had to be masked by composure. Despite his display of indifference and apathy, he was extremely nervous. On another occasion, Churchill recalled that 'the calm manner that he affected was an artificial façade that covered up his real mercurial nature.'[18] Agents therefore had to obscure their fear, as well as their British and paramilitary identities. These examples illustrate the inside/outside dichotomy which was commonly experienced by most agents: the internal fear hidden by the affected composure inscribed upon the external body. Indeed, the contrived look of apathy that screens unsteady nerves is crucial to passing: by erasing signs of anxiety, the passing subject is more likely to be successful. However, traces of fear may still be discernible despite the façade and this anxiety leakage or slippage is a clue to the deception. Occasionally, agents were unable to mask their unease, which was manifested upon the body. In his autobiography, Richard Heslop recalled his first encounter with security checks: 'On the way to the station I went through my cover story, for I was about to go through my first police identity check. Naturally, I was frightened. Would the documents, prepared in London, be good enough? Were the official stamps the right ones? Was the paper the right kind? My stomach tightened up, and I could feel sweat come into the palms of my hands.'[19] Heslop invoked the term 'naturally' which indicates that he considered his anxiety to be an inevitable reaction to circumstances of acute danger. By posing such questions about practical considerations relevant to his circumstances, he indicated how he had been assessing his chances of passing successfully. He also mentioned some physical symptoms of his fear: his tightening stomach and sweaty palms. Corporeal indications of anxiety mentioned in the SOE accounts include quickening heartbeat, nausea, sweating and restricted breathing. Anxiety could thus have a distinct bodily expression as well as taking the form of intensive introspection.

Forged identity cards were not the only form of document that could cause the new agent concern. In order to purchase food at restaurants, it was imperative to provide coupons from a ration book filled with tickets for cheese, fats, bread and meat. It was a complicated process remembering which coupons to submit and this greatly troubled some agents. Peter Churchill recalled the first occasion in which he had to do this: 'He gave the correct coupons out of his own ration book as though he had done it a thousand times. He was delighted to see that no one, not even the waiter, looked at him as though he was anything other than another Frenchman. He was beginning to feel [sic] his feet.'[20] Churchill's affected display of nonchalance, pretending that he had undertaken this mundane routine on a daily basis, assisted his passing.

A further cause for concern was the presence of German soldiers. Many agents recall their first sighting of enemy forces and remember it as an occasion when they evaluated their chances of passing. We have already seen that Baseden found the initial sighting particularly disconcerting. Devereaux Rochester was also disturbed by the sudden presence of German soldiers: 'My heart flipped and started to thud against my ribs. I also felt a little sick.'[21] Denis Rake recalled: 'This was the first time I had seen the whites of the enemy's eyes, and it really startled me ... I went to a nearby window and leaned out, gulping in air in an effort to quieten my pounding heart and to bring back the colour to my cheeks, for I was certain that I had gone as white as a sheet.'[22]

References to feelings of dislocation are also rife within personal accounts recalling encounters with German soldiers. Roger Landes remembered feeling anxious on the first morning after his return to France: 'You feel a bit strange. The day after when I had to walk from the village to the station there w[ere] German patrols coming opposite on the road and I got the feeling I had a board on me, "English parachutist."'[23] Landes reports that he internalised his unease, feeling that his difference was emblazoned upon his body. Similarly, Anne-Marie Walters asserted:

'The next day I walked self-consciously about Condom ... I imagined I stuck out like a sore thumb ... It took me nearly three weeks to shake off this form of self-consciousness and to get over the idea that I had "British agent" written all over my face.'[24] Walters' statement emphasises that agents were conscious that others validated their performances, which is further indication that passing was dialogic. Like Yvonne Baseden and Roger Landes, who both feared that they were marked as British agents, Walters felt that other people would notice that she was different. Despite the fact that Walters, Baseden and Landes all had French mothers, they were concerned that they would be recognised as foreigners. Reports of feelings of not belonging are prevalent in these accounts: Baseden indicated that she felt that she was from 'another world' and 'different to everybody else', Landes felt 'strange' and Walters believed that she 'stuck out like a sore thumb'. They did not look discernibly different but they sensed that they were. Moreover, their discomfort was always related to the presence of German soldiers: they were all in close proximity to soldiers in the specific episodes when they recalled their markedness. Peter Churchill illustrates this feeling of conspicuousness when he wrote in his autobiography: 'You almost imagine that neon lights are blinking from your forehead and proclaiming, on and off, "Made in England".'[25] Churchill was concerned that he literally could be read as an agent.

There were, then, dual problems of passing: being detected as a foreigner and as an agent. The heightened threat of disclosure, provoked by the presence of German soldiers, precipitated their feelings of difference. Three agents invoke almost exactly the same metaphor to indicate their feelings of markedness, sensing that their British national identity was written on their bodies. Walter's reference to 'British agent' being inscribed on her face, Landes' board emblazoned with 'English parachutist' and Churchill's neon lights flashing 'Made in England' from his forehead emphasise their feelings of dislocation, of not fitting in and of being conspicuous when encountering German soldiers. This suggests that the body can be viewed as a text or a surface on which identity is inscribed. Others read identities that are written upon the surface of the body. The metaphors of reading and writing are useful in further highlighting the dialogic nature of passing.

Most agents who recall feeling anxious at specific moments remember experiencing a surge of confidence when they successfully passed. Henri Diacono for example, recollected:

When I got on the train, I saw a German soldier for the first time so that was a little bit of a shock ... looked at him the way he looked at me and I found that I wasn't something special. I was like all other Frenchmen and I was very relaxed ... My attitude was normal, people didn't think I was a spy, they just thought I was a fellow like the others, so that makes you more and more confident all the time. After that we took the tube, still more Germans and I felt more and more comfortable and not worried at all.[26]

The speed with which Diacono became comfortable with seeing German soldiers is striking. Despite the initial shock, he soon became accustomed to this sight, and by the end of his first day in France, he felt at ease. His confidence was increased also by his awareness that he looked like other Frenchmen. Unlike Baseden, Walters, Landes and Churchill, who were conscious of being different and thought that other travellers would detect that they were not French civilians, Diacono was reassured by the soldier's disinterest in him. His shock was quickly replaced by reassurance.

Many agents gained self-assurance from these initial encounters with soldiers at controls, ticket operators at train stations and waiters in restaurants. That they had passed successfully on the first occasion increased their belief that they could blend into crowds and be mis/taken for ordinary French civilians. For example, Anne-Marie Walters noted: 'I had lost the sensation of being an outlaw.'[27] Gaston Cohen, who recollected that 'the first time I saw a German soldier, I was not very happy about it, a bit scared in fact', asserted that 'after a while it didn't bother me. I used to go on the Champs-Elysées and it was full of Germans in uniform.'[28] Sonya Butt also recalled her increased confidence: 'After being there a week, it was just a way of life. The first time I saw Germans in uniform, walking up and down the street, I was petrified. But then you get used to it and you get used to how you have to behave with them.'[29] However, this new-found assurance might have dangerous repercussions. An SOE file comments on the dangers of this replacement of unease with confidence: 'Many of the members were frightened at the beginning as they felt they were conspicuous, and always being followed, but [in] a few weeks, when nothing had happened, they quickly regained their self-confidence and in some cases became careless.'[30] Successful passing enhanced self-assurance which was, to a certain extent, psychologically cumulative: the self-belief acquired from each successful performance contributed to the likely success of subsequent passing attempts. This would suggest that passing was not a set of isolated accomplishments that neither added to nor was enhanced by other performances. However, because confidence was partially cumulative, the success of daily passing could result in agents' becoming blasé and imprudent. Thus, although confidence gained from successful passing might have strengthened future passing attempts, it may also have induced complacency. Because of the pressures of living a clandestine life, many agents began to disregard the advice they had been given during training. Consequently, some agents were captured. If complacency led to capture, then fear may well have improved agents' performance of passing as it kept them alert to various dangers. Moderate anxiety could, then, increase efficiency by being energising and fruitful (as noted by a study on male soldiers in the Second World War.[31])

There were, then, a number of different patterns and consequences of passing during this debut performance which emerged: the successful pass could encourage self-assurance enabling them to overcome this initial unease, could lead to over-confidence and complacency, or could have very little effect on nerves.

Anxious passing

Some agents continued to experience anxiety throughout their time in France. This ongoing unease is summed up by Cyril Watney: 'One was kind of frightened. One worries about things. It's difficult'.[32] He remembered that he had been troubled by the everyday, commonplace habits that could give him away. Trying to pass as French civilians generated considerable unease, which lasted, for some, throughout their operational time in France. Richard Heslop claimed that 'every checkpoint [was] a major anxiety'[33] and, similarly, Jacques Poirier recalled that 'every roadblock was an ordeal. The Germans would have done better to check our pulse-rate than our papers!'[34] Poirier's somewhat flippant but nevertheless perceptive remark suggests that, whereas papers could be forged to appear authentic, an individual's emotions were harder to fabricate.

'Cover stories', which were crucial to passing, were another source of ongoing unease. Yvonne Baseden remembered never feeling comfortable with hers: 'I was very much at sea with my cover story. You know, it worried me because I didn't know very much about it because they'd given me the right papers and explained to me what I was, secretary, and left it to me, on whatever the occasion, to fill in. So that was very worrying. I was very worried about that side of the job, more than any other, I think.'[35] Baseden's role as a wireless operator, the most dangerous job a resister could undertake with an expected 'life' of six weeks, was less of a concern than the unease she experienced at feeling so unprepared with her cover story. She invokes the term 'worried' three times in this short extract, when referring to the paucity of her cover story.

Despite having been operational in France for a considerable period of time, some agents still experienced unease. It could be explained by the fact that the penalties for failing to pass were so harsh, but the extreme difficulty of the task must also be considered. Peter Churchill describes the pressures that agents experienced. He mentions the 'mounting tension' which was 'an integral part of our lives', the 'daily fears, upsets and worries of his job', 'the stress of so many thwarting disappointments' and the 'state of jumpiness resulting from the many shocks and frights he had suffered over so long a period.'[36] The unremitting tension had an effect on his nerves and this was not even alleviated when he was asleep: 'The cumulative effect of more than sixty days of ... frustrations, of living a spurious existence, distrusting everyone on principle, constantly working out plausible reasons for being where he had no business to be and returning at the end of the long day to the loneliness of his flat where all the daily problems tended to grow out of all proportion and where sleep – when it finally came – was crowded with nightmares of captivity.'[37]

Anxiousness seems a reasonable reaction to life-threatening incidents. My assumptions about the pressures of a clandestine role prompted me to ask the interviewees questions about whether their appearance, false documents or the presence of German soldiers concerned them. Somewhat surprisingly, some agents claimed in their testimonies that they did not feel unduly perturbed and managed to operate in France without fear. Bob Sheppard recollected: 'As far as I'm concerned, no worry. I was not worried at all'[38] and Bob Maloubier claimed: 'I wasn't stressed at all.'[39] When I asked him if he was concerned about his false documents, he dismissively replied 'psffft! No problem'. André Watt remarked: 'I must say that I was never worried ... and I talked to Collins [Gaston Cohen] the other day and he said exactly the same; he said he was never worried or never afraid.'[40]

It might be surmised that it was only male agents who asserted they were not unduly concerned, given that courage has traditionally been regarded as a masculine virtue. However, testimonies of some female agents also indicate a lack of fear, which suggests that anxiety was not gender-specific. Françine Agazarian, who operated in Paris as a courier, recalled a train journey she made when she first arrived in France. She was surrounded by German soldiers while carrying blank identity cards, numerous forged ration cards, radio crystals, a revolver, ammunition and a considerable amount of French francs. She recollected: 'The ludicrousness of the situation somehow eliminated any thought of danger. In any case, I believe none of us in the field ever gave one thought to danger. Germans were everywhere in Paris; one absorbed the sight of them and went on with the job of living as ordinarily as possible and applying oneself to one's job.'[41] Agazarian was not the only female agent to deny feelings of anxiety. Speaking on a film which she produced herself about her life and wartime work, Nancy Wake claimed: 'I never had time to worry and I must admit some people don't believe me. I never was afraid and sometimes I think that people probably think I'm mad or that I'm telling lies but I can honestly say I was never afraid. I was too busy to be afraid.'[42] Heidegger claimed that it is the approach of something unwanted which is 'not yet within striking distance, but is coming closer' which provokes fear[43] and we have seen that many agents reported experiencing nerves while awaiting imminent document checks or in the presence of German soldiers. It would thus seem to be the delay, in which the passing subject has time to imagine their fate, which produces anxiety. Wake, however, recalled that she was too preoccupied to feel anxious. She suggests that her single-minded focus on the task in hand suspended the fear of discovery, arrest and torture, which was kept on the periphery of her consciousness. Moreover, Wake is conscious that her assertion of fearlessness has led others to conclude that she is untruthful, because it seems implausible that she was unafraid. This may be because courage is often gendered as a masculine attribute and anxiety is feminised.

Lise de Baissac reconstructed her wartime emotions in similar terms to those of Wake and Watt: 'You know that you are in danger all the time but you always think that you will go through. I have never been afraid really that I should be caught. It never occurred to me. I think that we're all like that. If you're frightened you can't do anything.'[44] The repetition of the words 'never afraid' pervade the accounts of Watt, Wake, and de Baissac, which are in stark contrast to the testimonies cited earlier. Using Penny Summerfield's dichotomy of heroic and stoic accounts,[45] these testimonies could be characterised as the former as their recollections about wartime dangers are heroically dismissive and nonchalant. However, some agents who constructed heroic narratives about themselves were not consistently unafraid. For example, in spite of her assertion of optimism concerning her future liberty, de Baissac confesses to having felt anxious on an occasion when retreating German soldiers, who had requisitioned her flat in Normandy, were sitting on her sleeping bag made out of her parachute: 'I tried to keep my dignity but inside I was very frightened. When I asked the man to get up and let me take my bag, I was really anxious to leave the place.'[46] In her narration of this episode, she utilises the inside/outside dichotomy that was identified earlier: she masks her ill ease with other emotions. Despite her earlier assertion that anxiety was disabling, hampering the effectiveness of agents and making them liable to arrest, she recalled an occasion when she managed to perform convincingly despite her fear.

In my oral history interview with her, de Baissac narrated several occasions in which she experienced anxiety, which suggests that her operational passing was infused with episodes of uneasiness: '[The landlady] asked for my papers and that was my first blow, little bit of heart-breaking ... I still remember that. That was really one of the difficult things. It's still there.'[47] The account of this incident provoked similar feelings to that experienced sixty years ago.

De Baissac was recalled to London when a double agent penetrated her circuit and she was in grave danger. She remembered waiting for the plane to arrive: 'It is a bit of nerves, you know, will the plane come, will it? As I say, I'm not a nervous person, anxious ... It seems to me, it's part of the work, of life.'[48] When she returned to France, she was received by a reception committee and taken by bicycle to a nearby safe house. However, an injury sustained during a refresher course impeded her cycling and she fell behind: 'I was a right long way back and I had to follow them ... they had turned left or right. I couldn't see. Luckily, I turned right and it was there that I found them. Had I turned left I don't know what would have happened to me ... But that was really frightening. I still remember that ... Perhaps, it's the most difficult moment of all my missions. Should I turn right or left?'[49]

On another occasion, when she was in Normandy she was carrying radio parts under the belt of her dress when she was stopped and searched. She remembered: 'I was very, very frightened. He touched everything and he let us free. That was once when I really was frightened.'[50]

De Baissac's account is interesting on several levels. Firstly, despite her assertion that she did not experience nerves, de Baissac spoke at length about several moments of fretfulness. There are, therefore, fractures in her narration of fearlessness. She repeated four times during the interview that she is an optimist and not of a nervous disposition. Yet without prompting, she revealed feelings of uneasiness on four separate occasions. Secondly, after three of the incidents, she implies that it was the only occasion in which she experienced nerves and was thereby exceptional: 'that was really *one* of the difficult things', 'perhaps, it's *the* most difficult moment of all my missions' and 'that was *once* when I really was frightened'. And the one time that she does not mention the uniqueness of her sentiments, she devalues her anxiety by claiming 'it's part of the work', thus reiterating that it is a logical and normal response to circumstances of acute danger and thus not worth dwelling upon in her personal testimony. Hence, not only would it seem that there is something at stake in claiming composure, but also de Baissac's account is heroic in spite of, or perhaps even because of, her admissions of anxiety. The general tone of de Baissac's reconstruction of her wartime emotions is one of fearlessness and optimism, and yet there are leakages in her heroic account. This slippage between her avowal of never feeling afraid of capture and her admissions of anxiety on hazardous occasions suggests that testimonies are imbued with contradictions, tensions and contestations. These accounts cannot be classified simply as polarised as either heroic narratives (demonstrated by the absence of anxiety) or stoic (defined by the disclosure of anxiety). This fluidity between heroic and stoic standpoints employed by the same people suggests that veterans may adopt different subject positions at different junctures.

How might we account for the variation in agents' recollections of their experiences of unease? Sydney Hudson claimed: 'I think some people, in a natural stupidity, just feel that they are not going to be caught. Perhaps it's something to do with the genes or the adrenaline. You can have adrenaline addiction.'[51] Hudson referred to a biological predisposition towards composure which might explain why some agents experienced fear, while others did not. Kenneth Strongman, a psychologist researching human emotions, noted: 'Anxiety-producing stimuli do not have similar effects on everybody: some seem to be habitually more anxious than others, reacting more strongly to situations which would not be productive of anxiety in others.'[52] This would suggest that individuals react differently in similar circumstances. Some psychologists have tried to establish a causal link between parents who suffer from anxiety and children who inherit this trait, which could explain why some agents experienced fear and others did not.[53] However, there is much debate and a high degree of scepticism about purely biological explanations for predispositions towards anxiety. It seems more likely that a complex combination of factors explains why some people were more prone to nerves than others. There may be other explanations which are linked to the cultural image of agents and other public representations. As in all forms of oral history and autobiography, there is a temporal gap between the experience and the reconstruction of the experience. During the intervening period, the individual is exposed to various cultural forms which may inform their own narration, such as other veterans' auto/biographies, television documentaries, fiction and film.

Filmic representations

Historian Graham Dawson, who examined the cultural imaginings of the soldier hero of adventure in his study of masculinity and British national identity, remarked that 'heroes are made, not by their deeds, but by the stories that are told about them.'[54] Having shown that some agents claim that they did not suffer from apprehension at all, I want to suggest that narratives denying fear may be a post-war re-reading of the period rather than an 'accurate' account of their feelings at the time of operation. Some may reconstruct their emotions, throwing a much more heroic light upon their sentiments. Admitting to feelings of trepidation might tarnish the myth of the heroic agent that has been built up in the public's consciousness. Biographies and melodramatic films have played a major part in the myth-making process which has established a specific, almost one-dimensional, archetypal imaging of agents. We shall now turn from an analysis of accounts of anxiety which seemingly have no gender-specificity to a very explicit gender focus in a discussion of the portrayal of Odette Sansom and Violette Szabo in film.

The film *Odette*, which premiered in 1950, was based on the biography of Odette Sansom by Jerrard Tickell which was published in 1949. It starred Anna Neagle in the title role, with Trevor Howard as Peter Churchill, Sansom's organiser, and Peter Ustinov as the group's wireless operator, Alec Rabinovitch. Despite the war ending five years previously, material deprivations continued to be experienced in 1950 when the film was released. Rationing for example was still enforced. The British public needed reminding why the war had been necessary and why they continued to endure these privations. According to Josie Dolan, *Odette* served such a function: 'Rather than offering a utopian escape from continuing bleakness of material shortages, *Odette* offers a dystopian vision of German occupation, the narrowly escaped fate.'[55] The construction of the lead character, a young mother who leaves her children in Britain to fight the Nazis in occupied France, is central to this reminder that the war had been fought to preserve freedom.

In the film, Sansom is represented as composed and seemingly undaunted by the dangers surrounding her. Her first task as a courier is to visit Marseille. She is shown visibly bracing herself as she walks past soldiers in uniform, with a determined expression, elevated chin and her head held high, apparently in proud defiance. To confirm her ability to pass, one of the soldiers she overtakes turns around with an admiring (rather than a suspicious) glance at her. This scene serves to emphasise

2 Anna Neagle, as Odette Sansom, successfully passing an identity card check.
Film still from *Odette*, 1950.

the potency of alluring femininity in facilitating passing, the readings
of others and the male gaze. She is then shown negotiating an identity
check in which she looks the soldier directly in the eye (see Figure 2).
She does, however, fiddle with her gloves while she is awaiting the return
of her identity card, which demonstrates her discomfort. This, however,
is the only indication of nerves in the film which, incidentally, is not
mentioned in the film script, and this is recouped in the next scene when

her organiser says to the wireless operator, 'She's got guts, determination and common sense.'[56] Sansom's resilience is thus depicted and then
emphasised immediately by the words of her admiring organiser in the
subsequent scene. Moreover, in the three scenes which intersect with
Sansom's mission in Marseille, her organiser is shown to be in a state
of nervous tension and concerned for her safety: he restlessly paces up
and down, anxiously looks at his watch, continually lights cigarettes in
order to calm his nerves and looks out of the window expectantly for her
return. When she does arrive, he is sitting on a couch waiting for her: he
is overwrought, on edge and this is clearly evidenced in his facial expressions. He informs her: 'I don't mind telling you I've been worried sick.'[57]
The typically gendered image of a wife awaiting her husband's return is
thus reversed as Churchill is portrayed in a conventionally feminine role,
passively waiting for Sansom to return, suggesting the new configuration
of gender roles provoked by the Second World War. Conventionally, the
male role is a protective one but the film destabilises this by showing that
Sansom is exposed to danger while Churchill is safe.

However, it is not merely her lack of anxiety which contributes to this
construction. The heroic myth of Odette is consolidated in the remainder
of the film by emphasising her leadership skills, physical strength, single-
mindedness and courage. Her organising aptitude is demonstrated after
Churchill's departure, when she assumes command of the group. She is
also shown to be mentally astute when a double agent and an Abwehr
agent who poses as a German defector penetrate the group. She immediately becomes suspicious and informs everyone to disperse.

The 'Odette legend' is further developed by the depiction of her physical
strength. She is shown rowing across Lake Annecy single-handedly to
meet the leader of the Maquis and to pass on instructions. This is not
the only physical feat that she accomplishes: in preparation for Churchill's return by parachute, a bonfire must be built to guide the plane to
the dropping zone which is 6,000 feet up a mountain. There are three
long frames, which last 37 seconds in total, of a solitary figure dragging
branches behind her in the snow. The scenic backdrop for Sansom's feat
is a range of snow-capped mountain peaks in the distance, which serves
to highlight her isolation and emphasises a key theme in the film: that of
a lone woman battling against the elements. Physical obstacles are easily
overcome by her single-minded determination to succeed. Sansom is
thus depicted as a larger than life character and this is emphasised by the
representation of her physical capabilities which are deemed exceptional,
especially for a woman.

The representation of Sansom's courage also contributes to the construction of the Odette myth. When both Churchill and Sansom are arrested on the evening after his return, she is shown managing to divert attention towards herself: 'He was not the head of the circuit. I was. It was I who persuaded him to come to France. What he did here, and it was very little, he did under my influence.'[58] She is also represented as deluding her interrogators into believing that Churchill was both her husband and the British Prime Minster's nephew. Her ability to think calmly and quickly in a moment of acute pressure, sacrificing herself to save her organiser, is portrayed as resulting in her own mistreatment. In case the audience has not grasped the heroism of Sansom, the film reiterates it emphatically. Having been given the death penalty twice, the heroine then audaciously remarks that they will have to decide for which charge to execute her as she can only be killed once. Notably, after she departs the screen, the camera remains fixed on the admiring, respectful gaze of the high-ranking officer who had previously ordered that she be tortured.

Thus not only is Sansom portrayed as assured and unperturbed, with only one small fracture in her composure, which is immediately redeemed in the next scene, but also a heroic image of her is constructed through the characterisation: her ability to manage the circuit in Churchill's absence, her physical and mental strength and her bravery. It is this depiction which has constructed the 'Odette legend'. This is not to say that Sansom was not like this 'in reality', but rather it is to highlight that the representation of her in the film mobilises a construction of her self-assurance in order to portray her as a heroine. However, in a post-war interview, Sansom herself in fact asserted: 'I was not confident in myself to do a marvellous job, that I never was'.[59] This suggests that, in contrast to her heroic image in film and print, she did lack confidence in her ability to do the work. This has been entirely erased in the filmic portrayal, thereby enhancing Sansom's heroism.

Similarly, as the title suggests, *Carve Her Name with Pride* (1958), which starred Virginia McKenna in the title role, constructs courier Violette Szabo in a heroic light. On her first day in France, Szabo is shown taking a journey on a crowded train. A German officer invites her to share his compartment and she seems completely at ease chatting to him and answering his many penetrating questions which test her cover story. Her apparently relaxed manner results in the officers showing photographs of their children to her. She allows the official to arrange her accommodation and agrees to meet him for supper, an appointment she fails to keep. She does not appear flustered by the presence of numerous German officers

3 Virginia McKenna, as Violette Szabo, heroically sacrificing herself to ensure the safety of her colleague Jacques Dufour, whose retreat she is covering by firing on advancing German soldiers. Film still from *Carve Her Name with Pride*, 1958.

and nor does she look apprehensive during her first identity document check in which she is portrayed as relaxed and level-headed.

The characterisation of Szabo as composed is not the only factor establishing her heroic legend. Her courage and single-mindedness are exemplified in the portrayal of her volunteering for a dangerous operation immediately upon her return to France for a second mission. The film shows her and a fellow resister being ambushed by a division of SS crack troops while in the country. They manage to evade their pursuers for a short time but during the escape Szabo twists her ankle, weakened as a result of a bad parachute jump during training, and cannot proceed. She selflessly urges her Resistance colleague, Jacques Dufour, to leave her behind. While covering his retreat, she is shown shooting five soldiers (see Figure 3). Even when she is wounded she still manages to fire accurately, killing another before her ammunition runs out and she gives herself up. In a similar scene to that in *Odette*, Szabo's heroism is underlined by the enemy's admiration: a smiling, high-ranking officer congratulates her performance: 'You put up a good fight, Mademoiselle. Cigarette?'[60]

Szabo's selflessness is further depicted in a sequence portraying a train journey from Paris to Germany, when the RAF strafes the train. In the chaos Szabo and fellow SOE agent Denise Bloch, who are chained together, decide to escape. However, they forego the opportunity upon hearing the wailing requests for water from the male prisoners in the next carriage. These scenes, which highlight her gallantry in foregoing assistance from Dufour when she fell, choosing instead to cover his retreat, and her selfless act of distributing water to the men instead of escaping, echo the sacrifice that Sansom makes in her shifting the blame and attention from Churchill on to herself. Both films thus utilise similar conventions in order to portray Sansom and Szabo in a heroically sacrificial light.

The most dramatic depiction of Szabo occurs in the filmic representation of Ravensbrück concentration camp and is constructed as her 'finest hour'. When a female guard informs Szabo and fellow SOE agents Denise Bloch and Lilian Rolfe that they are to accompany her, they realise that the time has come for their execution. Both women look to Szabo for support and strength. As the emotive music builds to a crescendo, the three of them are shown being taken to the execution pit. Not one is shown as being tearful or asking for a reprieve. As the voice-over names the three women in turn, the camera focuses on each as they raise their faces defiantly and look resolutely at their executioners. As the camera rests on Szabo, it lingers in particular on her dry eyes. The camera then pans away from the three women, the bullet shots penetrate the eerie silence and the camera focuses on the clouds. The iridescent sun, which breaks expeditiously, serves to suggest an acceleration of time as well as a portent of peace: their souls have ascended to heaven and the war will shortly be over. These final scenes consolidate the construction of Szabo as a heroine.

What makes this film particularly interesting, however, is that this is a more nuanced illustration of the emotions experienced by agents than in

Odette. Not only do we witness psychological strength but there are also moments of uncertainty and anxiety. For example, prior to her departure to France, she confides in her organiser: 'I get frightened ... I'm just afraid of being afraid.'[61] In this scene, a crack in Szabo's composure is represented in which she is depicted as eager to accomplish her mission successfully but afraid that anxiety will prevent her.

A second representation of Szabo's unease follows the completion of her first mission when she returns to England. She is shown confiding to her organiser: 'Won't it be wonderful to wake up in the morning without that tight feeling in the stomach?'[62] Despite this articulation of anxiety, the film offers no portrayal of Szabo's fear throughout her operational mission. There are no depictions of anxiety and this absence enhances the representation of heroism. This serves to suggest that Szabo concealed her nerves behind a mask of composure. Subtly hinting at feelings of apprehension without depicting them, this film seems to provide a more realistic illustration of agents' experiences than the representation of Sansom in *Odette*, while maintaining a heroic construction of Szabo.

A third representation of her discomposure can be found in the interrogation scene. The interrogating officer is shown shining a spotlight into her heavy eyes and asking for her poem to break her code. This is the point in the film when she is depicted at her lowest. Deprived of sleep for 32 hours, she slips into a fantasy, imagining she is with her husband. She smiles, her eyes glaze over dreamily and it appears that she is on the brink of repeating her poem as her mouth moves. In her fantasy, she says in dialogue with her dead husband, 'I want to say it'. However, the daydream evaporates and in response to the request for the poem, she states emphatically, 'I hate you'. She is then pictured in her dark cell, which reinforces her isolation and despair, weeping, seemingly having lost hope, when Bloch and Rolfe enter and comfort her. Rather than undermining the heroic myth, this depiction of discomposure strengthens it as her agitation heightens the tragedy and reminds the audience that, despite her almost superhuman bravery, she is just a woman.

Despite the heroic characterisation of Szabo, there are moments in which she is portrayed in a less heroic light. There are ambiguities in the film that permit the representation of her concerns. These portrayals of cracks in her composure seem necessary in order to be overcome and moments of fragility and self-doubt are always shown as redeemed immediately by a show of moral and psychological strength. For example, the scenes when Szabo is shown to be emotionally vulnerable during and after her interrogation are succeeded by scenes of her selflessly distributing water on the train to Germany and of her psychological strength during the execution scene.

Both *Odette* and *Carve Her Name with Pride* depict the female lead in a heroic fashion. Both use filmic conventions to signify heroism, including uplifted face, elevated chin, steely eyes and determined expression. Sacrifice is a key theme developed in both films. The heroines are shown to use their acumen to extract themselves from dangerous situations. Their brave defiance is shown as commanding respect from high-ranking German officials and the calmness and psychological strength of both Sansom and Szabo are depicted in contrast with images of less composed agents.

The filmic representations of Sansom and Szabo have fashioned the public imagination and established them as iconic figures in Britain. They have become a focus for the cultural imaginings of the heroic national figure of the British agent, which is manifested in the way that their forenames have become part of popular knowledge. They have become the subject of veneration, remaining two of the enduring examples of female bravery associated with the Second World War. While the representations of these figures in these popular films have shaped the public's perception of the SOE, they may also have influenced veterans' perceptions of wartime emotions. For veterans to admit to feelings of discomposure and nervousness in their testimonies might undermine this heroic legend around the SOE. Indeed, many veterans wanted to protect the reputation of the organisation and appeared unwilling to mention anything critical or salacious in their accounts. This protectiveness extends also to specific agents. Susan Ottoway, author of a biography of Szabo, encountered this tendency to safeguard and she found that this hampered her research:

> The book and the film, *Carve Her Name with Pride*, have both shown [Szabo] as being an almost perfect being and the little band of her supporters still describe her in superlatives; even Odette Hallowes called her 'the bravest of us all'. Perhaps they are frightened that another book about their idol might destroy the myth. Perhaps it will. The woman that I discovered in my research was much less perfect than she had been portrayed, but certainly much more interesting and real.[63]

Odette Sansom's (later Hallowes') character assessment of Szabo is particularly interesting in view of the fact that she never met her and thus her appraisal is grounded on second-hand accounts, such as Minney's biography and the film. This illustrates that even SOE veterans may be influenced by myths and that they too have a stake in preserving them. Sansom's role in sustaining the legend is also interesting given that she became involved in manufacturing her own public image: she is the subject of a biography and a film with which she cooperated. The film ends with a written declaration by Sansom, confirming the film's authenticity. She acted as an adviser for this film as well as for *Carve Her Name with Pride*. She is not the only one to become involved in the process of making the SOE into a legend: Buckmaster, F Section's head, plays himself and attests to the film's authenticity in his introduction to *Odette*; Peter Churchill, Sansom's organiser, also makes an appearance as a local resister; and Harry Rée and Jacqueline Nearne featured in *School for Danger* (1947), a film based loosely on their SOE experiences. It is thus very difficult to separate myth from 'reality' in analysing representations of the SOE.

One consequence of veterans' stake in preserving the legend might be that some have suppressed memories of feeling afraid and reconstruct their recollections in a more fearless and valiant manner to align their own wartime experiences with the myth of the heroic agent. That veterans' testimonies are informed by filmic representations suggests that a 'cultural circuit' is in operation. Alistair Thomson's work on the ANZACs (Australian and New Zealand Army Corps) explored the relationship between personal narratives and the 'public legend' of the Corps. He noted that the public myth of the ANZACs was created in part by the media producing films such as *Gallipoli* (1981) starring Mel Gibson.[64] The result was the creation of a standardised ANZAC identity which did not accommodate accounts that were at variance with this myth. Thomson noted that this homogenous ANZAC legend influenced veterans who punctuate their narratives with 'familiar anecdotes' in order to fit their recollections into the dominant collective memory of the Corps: 'The memories of working-class diggers had become entangled with the legend of their lives … Veterans had adopted and used the ANZAC legend because it was resonant and useful in their own remembering.'[65]

It is possible to trace a 'cultural circuit' around representations of the SOE. The film *Odette*, for example, is based upon the biography by Tickell and the testimony of Sansom herself. The public account is thus informed by personal testimonies. However, this cultural construction does not end here because popular representations may play a role in individual testimonies. As the characterisation of Odette Sansom was the dominant cultural construction of SOE agents, later modified, but essentially upheld by the portrayal of Violette Szabo in *Carve Her Name with Pride*, this representation might have influenced veterans' memories. Television documentaries of the last five years, the novel *Charlotte Gray* and the subsequent film (2002), illustrate that this circuit is ongoing.

Like the ANZAC legend, the SOE mythology glosses over awkward questions and issues. For example, the training reports of both Sansom and Szabo are less than complimentary[66] but this is not depicted. As a result of filmic constructions of Sansom and Szabo, a standardised tale of F Section agents began to be conveyed, which left little room for testimonies that were inconsistent with this heroic myth. The accounts mentioned earlier in this chapter which refute feelings of anxiety might, then, be read in the light of these films.

De Baissac commented fairly positively on the film *Odette*: 'It was quite a good film ... I think that after all, it has given an idea to the public ... Quite pleased with Odette doing it.'[67] De Baissac's account suggests that she thought that the film was an accurate portrayal of SOE agents' experiences in France and something which the public should know about. In an interview for a book which was published in the 1970s, she was less enthusiastic about filmic representation: 'Films and novels have made people think of an agent's work as glamorous. But, believe me, our job was, above all, sheer hard work.'[68] Similarly, Bob Maloubier, who had been a colleague of both Violette Szabo and Jacques Dufour and later served alongside Dufour in Force 136 in the Far East, recalled: 'It's confused. Nothing to do with her real life anyway. This is why Buckmaster told me, "Don't go and see it, it's awful." He said, "You're in the picture. You're supposed to be the head of a brothel!" It is just bullshit. Incredible.'[69] Claire Everett asserted: '*Carve Her Name with Pride* was glamorised a bit and *Odette* was, I think, too. They're not realistic. They should be factual. But probably it wouldn't sell, you see, if it was factual.'[70] Organiser Francis Cammaerts was also critical of over-romanticisation and the extent to which agents have been venerated: 'The lives of almost all agents who have come into publicity at all has been terribly romanticised.'[71] Moreover, he argued that the focus on agents is misleading in suggesting that veterans, like himself, were one-person armies outwitting the Germans single-handedly, whereas a more realistic account would have emphasised the bravery of others: 'The people who got all the publicity have been the great heroines ... These films have been too one-person-centred, you know heroes and heroines ... but there were so many ordinary housewives who don't get into the picture.'[72] Cammaerts talked at length about the contribution of housewives and their subsequent omission from Resistance historiography. He claimed that films focus on individual bravery and not collective action. This emphasis on individualism creates various notions of heroism: the maverick individual fighting the might of the Nazi war machine single-handedly is constructed as the epitome of heroism. Indeed, he turned down the opportunity to have his story televised:

I had a long, long correspondence with an American television firm in the early 50s. They asked me to do a programme about my arrest and release and I said, 'Provided you stick by facts, I'm perfectly happy to cooperate.' They sent me text, eight times, ten times, and I had to send them back with a red pen through everything saying it's completely untrue. Finally, the maker rang me up ... and said, 'Our bosses have got a formula and there must be so much sex, so much violence, so much explosion.' I said, 'I can't have my story nominally told as a fairy tale, full of inaccuracies.'[73]

Many SOE veterans, then, did not want to identify as heroes and did not invest in the discourse of heroism presented in these films. Many felt they had nothing interesting to say, which may suggest that they were judging their wartime experiences and emotions against those of others represented heroically in film and auto/biography. For example, Sydney Hudson remarked: 'I can't believe that there is much which I can contribute to your research,'[74] and Claire Everett protested: 'My contribution was so minute compared to other people. I don't think I can tell you that much, I really don't.'[75] Others, however, wanted to 'set the record straight' and have actively tried to escape the over-romanticisation and mythologising of SOE agents. Pearl Witherington maintained: 'I don't consider such an experience needs romancing and any of the books I have read which do so do not bring out the stark facts of life as they should be learned. I want to help historians get the right idea of what we went through as agents.'[76] There appears to be a distancing from the construction of the heroic agent depicted in film and auto/biography in this statement. Wither-ington suggested that the portrayal of agents in both published and filmic accounts is inaccurate and misrepresents agents' experiences. Similarly, Claire Everett was critical of *Charlotte Gray*:

The scenery was beautiful, the acting was great but I thought the story was – they could have done something with so much more substance to it. There's no way with the training we had that we would have breached security the way she did and this business of going to look for her lover or her boyfriend or whatever! And the mission that SOE gave her was to carry a bunch of detonators! It belittled all of our training, all of the work you know that SOE was doing. I thought it was just frivolous.[77]

These comments suggest that the 'cultural circuit' operates in complex ways. Rather than simply informing veterans' narratives so that they reconstruct their memories in a heroic light which does not tarnish or undermine the myth of the British agent, popular representations may be critically reflected upon, and often challenged.

Thomson's oral history interviews with ANZAC veterans offered an opportunity for his subjects to reconstruct their wartime experiences in terms which were previously marginalised and obscured from the historical record. Similarly, it is possible that my research enabled some agents to reflect about aspects of their experience which have been neglected and virtually censored because of the potency of the heroic myth.

Conclusion

The representations of agents in written, oral and filmic accounts portraying passing and fear are diverse and complex. Passing and anxiety are intimately connected since passing is generally haunted by the fear of failure and exposure. Reminiscences about anxiousness indicate that passing takes a dialogic form: agents were conscious that their performances required external ratification in order to be successful and thus there was an incorporation of the other as well as resistance as they tried to subvert the readings of others.

Whereas some veterans feel that it is appropriate to recount their feelings of insecurity in oral history interviews and auto/biographical accounts, it was not acceptable to portray agents in *Odette* and *Carve Her Name with Pride* in this manner. Thus, representations of emotions in the testimonies of veterans and filmic accounts may be quite different. Most agents are likely to have experienced nerves and it is important to analyse this in order to understand the lived experience of passing and to comprehend how they negotiated tensions. Undertaking such analysis contests the filmic image of the unflappable SOE agent, what we might call the 'Odette myth'. In the making of Sansom and Szabo into popular national heroic figures, the fear that many agents experienced is denied. There are significant contradictions which need to be explored so that the prevalence of self-doubt can be recuperated, and the iconic image of the heroic agent can be demystified. In the next two chapters, I shall address the unspectacular and quotidian efforts that agents made to undertake their work, and the gendered complexities of their endeavours.

Notes

1 R. Grinker, 'The Psychosomatic Aspects of Anxiety', in A. Simon et al. (eds), *The Physiology of Emotions* (Illinois: Springfield, 1961).

2 G. S. Hall, *Adolescence*, 1:4 (1904), p. 285.

3 R. Kessler et al., 'Lifetime and 12–month Prevalence of DSM-III-R Psychiatric Disorders in the United States: Results from the National Comorbidity Survey', *Archives of General Psychiatry*, 51 (1994). They concluded that 30.5

per cent of adult women had experienced an episode of major anxiety, compared to 19.2 per cent of men.

4   L. Robins and D. Regier, *Psychiatric Disorders in America: The Epidemiologic Catchment Area Study* (New York: Free Press, 1991). They found that 10.2 per cent of women and 5.2 per cent of men experienced anxiety.
5   Rake, *Rake's Progress*, p. 113.
6   Churchill, *Duel of Wits*, p. 160.
7   Baseden, *Secret Agent* (BBC2).
8   Personal interview with Yvonne Baseden.
9   Personal interview with Yvonne Baseden.
10 Baseden, *Secret Agent* (BBC2).
11 M. Bakhtin, *Problems of Dostoevsky's Poetics* (Manchester: Manchester University Press, 1984), p. 32.
12 Baseden, *Secret Agent* (BBC2).
13 Landes, *Secret Agent* (BBC2).
14 Walters, *Moondrop to Gascony*, p. 49.
15 Poirier, *The Giraffe Has a Long Neck*, p. 71.
16 Rake, *Rake's Progress*, p.103.
17 Churchill, *Of Their Own Choice*, p. 107.
18 Churchill, *Duel of Wits*, p. 183.
19 Heslop, *Xavier*, p. 53.
20 Churchill, *Of Their Own Choice*, p. 130.
21 Rochester, *Full Moon to France*, p. 119.
22 Rake, *Rake's Progress*, p. 100.
23 Landes, *Secret Agent* (BBC2).
24 Walters, *Moondrop to Gascony*, p. 36.
25 Churchill, *Duel of Wits*, p. 180.
26 Diacono, *Secret Agent* (BBC2).
27 Walters, *Moondrop to Gascony*, p. 136.
28 Personal interview with Gaston Cohen.
29 Butt, *Behind Enemy Lines* (Channel 4).
30 National Archives, HS 6/568.
31 R. Grinker and J. Spiegel, *Men Under Stress* (Philadelphia: Blakiston, 1945).
32 Personal interview with Cyril Watney.
33 Heslop, *Xavier*, p. 231.
34 Poirier, *The Giraffe Has a Long Neck*, p. 77.
35 Personal interview with Yvonne Baseden.
36 Churchill, *Duel of Wits*, p. 7; p. 7; p. 183; p. 249; p. 296.
37 Churchill, *Duel of Wits*, p. 166.
38 Personal interview with Bob Sheppard.
39 Personal interview with Bob Maloubier.
40 Watt, *Churchill's Secret Army* (Channel 4).
41 Letter cited in Jones, *A Quiet Courage*, p. 63.
42 *The Story of Nancy Wake: Codenamed The White Mouse.*

43 M. Heidegger, *Being and Time* (Oxford: Basil Blackwell, 1962).

44 De Baissac, *Behind Enemy Lines* (Channel 4).

45 Summerfield, *Reconstructing Women's Wartime Lives*, pp. 82–104, especially p. 103.

46 De Baissac, *Behind Enemy Lines* (Channel 4).

47 Personal interview with Lise de Baissac.

48 Personal interview with Lise de Baissac.

49 Personal interview with Lise de Baissac.

50 Personal interview with Lise de Baissac.

51 Personal interview with Sydney Hudson.

52 K. Strongman, *The Psychology of Emotion* (Chichester: John Wiley and Sons, 1987), p. 203.

53 E. Slater and J. Shields, 'Genetic Aspects of Anxiety', in M. Lader (ed.), *Studies of Anxiety* (Ashford: Headley Brothers, 1967).

54 Dawson, *Soldier Heroes*, p. 188.

55 J. Dolan, 'National Heroines: Representing Femininity and the Past in Popular Film and Literature, 1930–1955' (Ph.D. thesis, Lancaster University, 1997), pp. 189–90.

56 BFI film script 58909.

57 BFI film script 58909.

58 BFI film script 58909.

59 IWM SA, 9478 Hallowes.

60 BFI film script S13981.

61 BFI film script S13981.

62 BFI film script S13981.

63 Ottoway, *Violette Szabo*, p. 2.

64 Thomson, *Anzac Memories*.

65 Thomson, *Anzac Memories*, p. 7.

66 For example, Szabo's personal file includes a report dated 8 October 1943 which stated: 'After a certain amount of doubt, esp. at the beginning of the course, I have come to the conclusion that this student is temperamentally unsuitable for this work.' National Archives, HS 9/1435.

67 Personal interview with Lise de Baissac.

68 Cited in Gleeson, *They Feared No Evil*, p. 91.

69 Personal interview with Bob Maloubier.

70 Personal interview with Claire Everett (pseudonym).

71 Cammaerts, *Behind Enemy Lines* (Channel 4).

72 Personal interview with Francis Cammaerts.

73 Personal interview with Francis Cammaerts.

74 Correspondence with Sydney Hudson.

75 Personal interview with Claire Everett (pseudonym).

76 Correspondence with Pearl Witherington.

77 Personal interview with Claire Everett (pseudonym).

5

'Living a different life': performing 'heroic' and 'stoic' masculinities

In the previous chapter, it was noted that while commemorative films and fictional novels depict agents' work as glamorous and exciting, narratives of both male and female agents frequently recount the concerns that they had. While some continued to experience fear, many apparently managed to overcome their nerves and in time gained satisfaction from successfully passing. The next two chapters will continue to analyse operational passing by investigating the gendered nature of these performances: agents were not simply passing as French civilians, they were performing particular types of French masculinity and femininity which were appropriate to the situations in which they found themselves. The gendered dynamics embodied in their performances were an important element of their success. This chapter synthesises the understandings of both passing and gender which, hitherto, have mainly been discussed separately, in order to explore the ways in which many male agents chose to play upon dominant ideas of masculinity in their enactments.

'The heroes': 'hegemonic masculinity'

It was not feasible for agents to retain their British paramilitary identities. As SOE agent Francis Cammaerts noted: 'You were living a different life, that's to say you were a different person and you had to think of being a different person.'[1] Consequently, they had to construct a cover which concealed their status so that they would not be arrested. Moreover, they had to live in a manner which was in keeping with their cover stories. Thus, not only were agents passing but also they were compelled to embody the persona of their cover identity as Cammaerts makes explicit. SOE agents had to select from a repertoire of behaviours that which they deemed suitable to both their cover status and locale. They pursued different tactics to facilitate passing. In their testimonies, some male agents recollect trying to act in keeping with their cover as ordinary young bachelors. Such behaviour might be seen to be associated with 'hegemonic masculinity'. Bob Connell invokes the concept of 'hegemony', originally used by Antonio Gramsci in his discussion of class relations, to analyse masculinity. Connell asserted that 'hegemonic masculinity' is 'not a fixed character type, always and everywhere the same. It is, rather, the masculinity that occupies the hegemonic position in a given pattern of gender relations, a position always contestable'.[2] 'Hegemonic masculinity' is, then, a specific configuration of gender practice that is culturally exalted. In wartime France, as in many other contexts, drinking and 'womanising' were key elements of 'hegemonic masculinity'. This is not to say that the hegemonic mode is the most common form of masculinity, but rather that in many ways it is the most respected for men of a particular age group. Accordingly, it could be productive for male agents to perform a mode of masculinity which might be perceived as normative for young Frenchmen. For some this was a deliberate choice, while for others it was less conscious.

Two forms of expression crucial to 'hegemonic masculinity' in the context of wartime France will be examined: extravagant pleasure-seeking and heterosexual relationships. Some agents believed the best way to pass as ordinary civilians was to lead active lives so as not to draw attention to themselves as loners. André Watt, for example, visited nightclubs, black-market restaurants, theatres and cinemas frequently. When he was asked how he spent his days when he was not involved in wireless work, Watt replied: 'Was ordinary. You go to a restaurant for lunch and you go to the cinema ... I would see Dericourt [SOE Air Liaison Officer who organised Lysander operations] about once a week and ... we used to go to black-market restaurants and have good lunches. Once or twice we went out in the evening with his wife to a nightclub. Yes, several times actually.'[3] Watt also dined out and visited the theatre with fellow SOE agents Julienne and Jean Besnard, whom he saw two or three times a week.[4] M. R. D. Foot noted that Watt 'concealed his fervour behind a gullible or even foppish appearance ... An appearance of elegant ease served admirably for cover in a circuit of this particular kind.'[5] To the unsuspecting observer, Watt, who enjoyed drinking champagne and cognac, was something of a Parisian playboy. In this persona, he was unlikely to be suspected of engaging in clandestine activities. This could then be an effective cover.

It would appear that in spite of his clandestine work as a wireless operator, Watt experienced little disruption to his 'normal' (pre-SOE) life. He wrote: 'I didn't really consider these activities [dining in black-market restaurants and visiting nightclubs, cinemas and the theatre] "high living" but normal and amusing.'[6] Watt had been raised in Paris and decided to resume his usual habits upon returning to the capital in 1943 after his training in Britain. Other agents also recommended old pastimes. Denis Rake, a pre-war circus entertainer, managed to get some engagements in restaurants and nightspots which 'helped me to face the abnormality of my secret life much more calmly than I would otherwise have done.'[7]

Watt and Rake endured little disruption to their ordinary, pre-SOE lives by continuing to visit nightclubs. Not all agents, however, adopted this lifestyle. When I asked Sydney Hudson what kind of life he lived, he replied: 'About medium profile I would say. Certainly not nightlife. But black-market restaurants and all that sort of thing.'[8] Thus, although he did not condone the extravagant lifestyle of agents such as Watt, Hudson did visit black-market restaurants which German soldiers frequented as 'that was about the safest place.'[9] He remarked that he did this in part to maintain his cover. Dining frequently at local restaurants was integral to the localised performance of what could be considered 'hegemonic masculinity'. It resulted in Hudson becoming a familiar figure in the community. Moreover, he was keeping with the behaviour of other young male civilians and, to a certain degree, this would have protected him.

However, dining out could raise suspicions, considering that most men and women, who were earning about 1,800 to 2,500 francs a month, could not afford the 800 francs required for a black-market meal and patronising restaurants could jeopardise agents' freedom as the PROSPER disaster indicated. The hub of the Paris-based PROSPER network, Francis Suttill, Andrée Borrel and Gilbert Norman, ignored the security rules taught them at Beaulieu. Not only did they socialise in a Montmartre nightclub where, on one occasion, according to M. R. D. Foot, Suttill and Borrel demonstrated their Sten guns, but the 'almost inseparable trio' also used to meet daily with Jack Agazarian, the second PROSPER wireless operator, to eat lunch in black-market restaurants frequented by high-ranking German officers and to play poker in local cafés in the evenings. Foot states that they did this out of a 'desire for companionship with people who could share with them the secret of their identity and their mission.'[10] As noted previously, agents often found it both stressful and exhausting to lead a double life and the comfort provided by those who shared these pressures should not be underestimated. However, this could lead to the penetration of the organisation. The PROSPER circuit's lax security resulted in disaster. Gestapo agents photographed both Suttill and Norman when they were in a café and all three were captured and executed. Referring to the PROSPER group, Andy Forbes, an SOE enthusiast, wrote: 'Those who eluded capture were seldom those who were seen dining together in black-market restaurants, talking things over in English!'[11] Certainly, PROSPER was not the only group to make this mistake. Foot claimed: 'The whole high command of PRUNUS – six or seven people – were gathered round a single table [in a black-market restaurant in Toulouse] finishing an excellent dinner and chattering away in English. This was riding for a fall; and they fell.'[12]

Agents who worked together tended to patronise the same places and thus if one was captured, the Gestapo found it relatively easy to arrest their comrades. Frequenting black-market restaurants and cafés could therefore be quite dangerous as the following statement of Gaston Cohen, wireless operator to a sub-circuit of PROSPER, illustrates:

> I went to black-market restaurants. Well, in Paris there was no other way. I used to go near the Champs-Elysées to have a steak. There were Germans there as well. And we had our own little restaurant the other side of the Champs-Elysées. They were arrested of course. And then we had our own bistro this side of Paris. A lot of the chaps would call there of course. I think Prosper [Suttill] used to go there. The day I said I was going up there, one of the agents came on a bicycle and said, 'Are you coming for lunch?' I said, 'No'. And I didn't go and the Germans were waiting at the bistro.[13]

With the exception of Sydney Hudson and Denis Rake, all of the agents mentioned above were operational in Paris. Frequenting restaurants and cafés in the capital was not regarded as unduly dangerous, despite the threat of arrest Cohen noted. Adopting a high-profile existence meant that agents could pass as typical Parisians doing their best to ignore the strictures of rationing and the occupation. Moreover, it would appear that agents were not discouraged by SOE Headquarters from enjoying these pastimes as, according to Maurice Buckmaster, head of F Section, briefing officers in London 'informed agents on which days they could have meat in a restaurant [and on] which days and at what times cinemas were open.'[14]

Living an extravagant lifestyle in small towns and rural villages would, however, have been inappropriate as it would have made agents conspicuous. Bob Maloubier, a saboteur who was based in Rouen, recollected:

In Rouen, we tried not to attract attention. We didn't go to bars, nightclubs, black-market restaurants which would have round-ups from time to time. There behind the Atlantic Wall, Germans were all over and very strict. We kept a low profile, looking like ordinary Frenchmen, courteous with the occupier, smiling and even sometimes cracking jokes with them in rough German. With Philippe [Liewer, his organiser], I went to Paris from time to time for a weekend just to relax. A much more relaxed city. We played the part of wealthy businessmen. So Liewer and I ate at black market restaurants, went to nightclubs, met girls. Money opened all doors. It was quite safe.[15]

German presence was much stronger in the 'Forbidden Zone', which was adjacent to Great Britain, than in other parts of France. Because of the heightened German presence, Maloubier had much more contact with Germans than other agents might have had. Although he was aware that his lifestyle had to be relatively low-key in Rouen so as not to draw attention to himself, Maloubier and his organiser Philippe Liewer did have opportunities to socialise. Such excursions provided opportunities to release tension generated by the pressures of the job and to enjoy the high life, without excessively jeopardising security. They were protected by the relative anonymity which characterised the highly-populated capital and thus they were free to pursue rather decadent activities that would have made them conspicuous in the much closer-knit community of Rouen. There was, then, a recognition of the context-dependent suitability of normative masculine personae and they adjusted their behaviour accordingly.

Thus, a number of male agents, in particular those based in Paris, frequently performed what can be regarded as 'hegemonic masculinity' by dining at black-market restaurants, associating with other men and even frequenting nightclubs and cinemas. Denis Rake asserted that this was because 'being an agent or saboteur isn't living a secrecy life all the time. In fact, the greater part of the time consists of living a quite public life.'[16] Here, Rake invoked the idea of dual lives. Indeed, many of the agents in their testimonies reflect on the duality of their operational life in France, noting that in addition to their identity as clandestine operatives for a British organisation, they also intermittently took on cover personae enabling them to pass as ordinary French civilians. These parallel personae were also noted by SOE agent Guido Zembsch-Schreve: 'It is impossible to have a normal life because it's entirely a dual life. For certain things, for certain occasions, you have to put up a front.'[17] Zembsch-Schreve recalled that he slipped between two identities. He also explored this duality in his autobiography: 'Anyone leading a double life of an agent must wear a cloak of normality and behave in keeping with his age.'[18] Zembsch-Schreve asserted that, in order to pass as a French civilian, it was necessary to conceal clandestine identities with masks of ordinariness. This statement makes explicit the performance undertaken in passing. Although it might have been impossible for the agent to *live* a normal existence, it was imperative that a *performance* of normality was undertaken to facilitate passing. Rake and Zembsch-Schreve both formulate their strategies for living in occupied France in terms of duality and normality. Passing involved moving between the so called 'authentic' identity and the new persona the passing subject embodied, compelling them to lead a double life. As we have seen, one way of building up a cover persona which was consistent with the profile of local Frenchmen was to frequent black-market restaurants.

Another strategy adopted by some of the male agents was to have a girlfriend as this was considered customary for young Frenchmen. As noted, Bob Maloubier recalled meeting women and enjoying brief affairs while in Paris with his organiser Philippe Liewer. 'Hegemonic masculinity' in this context, as in others, was emphatically heterosexual. Hence, being seen accompanied by a young woman was consistent with hegemonic masculinity and, as such, was a way of passing. Peter Churchill, who was based in the south of France, remarked in his autobiography: 'There's no better cover to be had in this country than to be seen in the company of a girl … just the right sort of impression to give.'[19] Guido Zembsch-Schreve also believed that a female companion made the ideal cover: 'A normal young bachelor should also have a social life. A girlfriend was essential not only to my façade but also to my mental well-being, so I had to find myself one.'[20] He succeeded in finding a girlfriend and remarked that it was a conscious strategy: 'To put up a front, to be able apparently to be a normal human being who was running around with a girl … I go out with a girl … in order that people see me with a girl and that's a normal thing. Otherwise people might start to think. In order to maintain cover.'[21] Zembsch-Schreve considered that a girlfriend, an explicit marker of his sexuality, would sustain his civilian persona and help to build his personality profile. His repeated use of the word 'normal' in the two statements quoted above suggests that he regarded heterosexuality as normative. Moreover, he used language which signifies compulsion: a bachelor *'should'* have a social life, a girlfriend was *'essential'*, he *'had'* to find one, which all suggest that heterosexuality was obligatory. This has particular resonances with Bob Connell's employment of the term 'compulsory heterosexuality' coined by Adrienne Rich to analyse the position of women.[22] Connell used the term with reference to men, on whom 'compulsory heterosexuality' is also enforced, with the implication that to 'do' masculinity correctly is to be seen to be heterosexual.[23]

Zembsch-Schreve thought that, in addition to bolstering his cover, a woman was crucial for his mental health. We have seen that most agents experienced anxiety and the solitude of the job intensified this unease. Peter Churchill, for example, stated that 'returning at the end of the long day to the loneliness of his flat' did not ease the 'mounting tension'.[24] His relationship with Odette Sansom provided intimate companionship, support and solidarity: 'Her moral courage and fearlessness were like a fountain of strength upon which I was to draw on many a future occasion of black despair.'[25] Similarly, Sydney Hudson noted: 'Well, I must say, of course, that many times, a comrade, by this, an extremely beautiful young woman, sparks one up a bit to say the least.'[26] Girlfriends helped male agents to overcome loneliness and this fortified them for their Resistance role.

While Zembsch-Schreve claimed that heterosexual relationships sustained his cover and alleviated the tension, other agents were less explicit about their reasons for forming relationships with women. Rather than stating that it was a strategy to uphold their cover, some implied it was purely for pleasure. When I asked Bob Maloubier if he had had a relationship with a woman, he indignantly replied: 'A woman? We were twenty!' As well as having relationships with three civilian women in London during the training, he claimed that he also had girlfriends in Paris, one of whom was the niece of a German Colonel whom he met: 'She said, "This is my uncle!" He bowed the German way, I did so too, and we shook hands! No problem.'[27] Maloubier continually emphasised promiscuity and nerve. Throughout the interview, and specifically at moments when he was reconstructing tense situations such as the above, he declared 'no problem'. His reconstruction of his wartime experiences conformed to the heroic narrative in that he denied fear, but there is evidence in his account that he avoided risks. For example, he explained that he had been careful that none of his girlfriends found out about his clandestine work; they thought he was a publicity agent called Bob Mortier. Thus, it becomes apparent that, behind his fearless image, there was a recurring assessment of risk going on: 'no problem' precisely recognises the possibility that there could be a problem.

Maloubier asserted that brief relationships only occurred in Paris, where he went with his organiser for weekend breaks to relax, and 'definitely not' in Rouen, where he was based. Thus, he did not have girlfriends in order to sustain his cover, as Zembsch-Schreve did, but rather for personal pleasure. Maloubier was conscious of what was considered appropriate in Rouen and consequently when he was there he did not socialise in local black-market restaurants or embark upon affairs with civilian women. This is further evidence of Maloubier's consideration of risk.

Some agents had affairs with women involved in the Resistance. Despite being warned by a senior RAF officer the night he was leaving England about lapses in security caused by relationships with women – 'many a slip up on a pillow slip!' – Gaston Cohen also had several girlfriends:

> *Cohen:* I didn't do that sort of thing [on my first mission in Paris]. The second time I used to do that, on my second op in Marseille.
> *Pattinson:* You had a girlfriend in Marseille?
> *Cohen:* A few! [laughs] Most of them were couriers.[28]

Unlike Maloubier and Zembsch-Schreve whose girlfriends were civilians, Cohen's relationships were with women who were also engaged in clandestine work. As a wireless operator, his contact with others was strictly limited and those he did see were couriers who came to deliver or collect messages, who were usually women. It is perhaps unsurprising that he formed close attachments with women who both shared his anti-Nazi beliefs and the pressures of the job. Francis Cammaerts recognised that the hazardous nature of the task made it conducive to forming close alliances: 'When you are in danger, you tend to cling to the person you're nearest.'[29] Cammaerts was referring not only to sexual relationships but also to intimate friendships based on mutuality, solidarity and shared objectives. This might explain not only why sexual relationships were common among resisters but also why the members of the central command of the PROSPER circuit mentioned above became almost inseparable.

A number of male agents, then, had girlfriends but they had very different reasons for embarking upon sexual relationships. Some, such as Guido Zembsch-Schreve, asserted that girlfriends upheld their cover and were necessary for their mental health to help them alleviate the stresses and anxieties of living clandestinely. Others, such as Bob Maloubier and Gaston Cohen, emphasised their youth and claimed that brief affairs with women were purely pleasurable and not strategic. It is striking that there are no accounts of female agents who claimed to have either formed relationships to sustain their performance of their cover identity or for their own personal enjoyment. Some female agents did form intimate attachments with male SOE colleagues either during training or while in France but it was rare for women to embark upon relationships with civilian men once in the field. This suggests that established patterns of masculine and feminine distinctions were at play in this context. What was considered appropriate for men was not necessarily suitable for women.

One way of performing masculinity was, as we have seen, to engage in heterosexual relationships and to be proud of it. Many of the 'heroes' affirmed in their testimonies that they were heterosexually active and some regarded this as part of their cover. Homosexual relationships, on the other hand, were much more ambiguous and could be highly dangerous given the homophobic culture in which agents operated. In his autobiography, Denis Rake wrote candidly about his relationships with men, including a brief sexual affair with a German soldier. It appears that this encounter was undertaken for pleasure and not part of any cover strategy.[30]

There seems to have been a recognition among some male agents that excessive performances of normative masculinity could lead to trouble and there are a few examples of organisers who dismissed agents who were either promiscuous or drank too much. Francis Cammaerts asserted: 'I had an agent sent to me who was a terrible womaniser and he got chucked out of every centre he went to for chasing the wives. They didn't want to know about that sort of thing.'[31] This agent was not the only one whose behaviour was irresponsible. Bob Maloubier remarked: 'I came as the replacement to Gabriel Chartrand, a Canadian who was a bit too keen on nightclubs and their hostesses. After a drink or two, he talked too much with an awful Canadian accent. Liewer had him flown back to the UK.'[32] It is likely that Chartrand's highly conspicuous behaviour was a factor influencing Maloubier's and Liewer's decision not to socialise in Rouen. There would appear, then, to be a fine line between what was considered appropriate masculine behaviour and what was regarded as too extreme to facilitate passing.

'The stoics'

While some performances of masculinity can be considered hegemonic, others clearly cannot. Some male agents thought that frequenting black-market restaurants and nightclubs constituted a security risk and they pursued a strategy of avoiding such social contact and heterosexual relationships because they considered such engagements too risky. The pursuit of more security-conscious lifestyles appears to be at a distance from the hyper-masculine behaviour mentioned above. Robert Boiteux recalled that he had adopted a low profile and was determined not to attend social events because of dangers to personal security. When the Newton brothers invited him to a party before they left the field, having completed their SOE mission, he declined, informing them that he did not attend parties:

> Alright, I'm a bloody square but I'm still here and they were caught. They had a party and made so much noise, the neighbours called the police and they were taken away. They eventually finished up in Mauthausen [concentration camp]. Of course, they went through Klaus Barbie [Gestapo interrogator nicknamed the 'Butcher of Lyon' who was renowned for his brutality] who beat them up a bit. How security-minded I was, that was my biggest, strongest point. That's why I'm still here. I wouldn't go to parties. I wouldn't go with women even.[33]

This statement can be regarded as somewhat stoical in that it expresses a resistance towards the construction of heroic narratives. The rather defensive tone at the beginning of this statement is particularly striking in that Boiteux is seemingly fending off criticisms of his decision not to socialise. He believed that his circumspect behaviour or 'security', which involved not going to celebrations and forming relationships, saved his life. He indicates that he was continually assessing risk. The final sentence of this statement, and in particular the word 'even', is striking in that it serves to suggest that being with women was something 'natural' but that, in these circumstances, it was contrary to his personal security rules.

Boiteux was not the only agent to feel that security was more important than socialising. Kenneth MacKenzie noted: 'Once I was over in France, I never had any close relationships with any women at all. It was quite hard at times, admittedly, but that's one thing, there's a responsibility. I wouldn't take that risk.'[34] MacKenzie implies that he had the opportunity and desire to engage in heterosexual relationships but chose not to. In some agents' testimonies, then, there is both reference to the normality of heterosexual relationships and to the hardship and/or necessity of foregoing these as potentially dangerous.

Some agents remarked that they had not patronised black-market restaurants. Cyril Watney claimed that 'I never felt that way inclined … you've got to be very, very careful'[35] and Francis Cammaerts asserted: 'Serious failures were very often because the agents led too high-level forms of life … I believed you had to keep a very low profile, and there were some agents who enjoyed leading a rather high profile, who used the black-market restaurants and places where the Germans used.'[36] Cammaerts is critical of agents who jeopardised their safety by frequenting restaurants patronised by German soldiers. To him, avoiding such sites was basic security practice. In contrast to the extravagant lifestyles of some agents, Cammaerts used to stroll around attractive French villages in order to unwind. He noted: 'Avignon was one of the towns I loved dearly, and went to frequently. Antibes, Nice, Marseille, Valence, these were all towns I knew well and I wandered round.'[37] At his debriefing interview after his first mission, he noted: 'Another point that should be impressed on students is the probability of boredom. They must be prepared to spend many hours alone, often in an uninviting bedroom, with nothing to do but read a book.'[38] Cammaerts was not the only veteran to assert that conspicuous socialising was totally inappropriate: many agents were of the same opinion. Organiser Maurice Dupont stipulated to his colleagues that 'cafés were out of bounds for ordinary rendezvous' and that 'two members of the organisation were not allowed to go out together without necessity'.[39] Jacques Poirier claimed: 'The risk ... even when you go for lunch, you never know what's going to happen ... It was terribly risky.'[40] There was, then, a recognition by some agents that mundane acts such as eating and drinking in cafés and restaurants could be hazardous and that taking unnecessary risks was highly irresponsible. For this reason, Poirier also refused to allow his WT operator Ralph Beauclerk to become involved in other aspects of resisting, such as training maquisards in weapons and undertaking sabotage missions: 'The most important thing in all our organisation is a radio man because without a radio man I could not have any contact with London. Therefore, I kept him really, practically, like in jail ... We got more freedom ... I was feeling a bit sorry for him.'[41]

Whereas Poirier met up with comrades in the maquis and recollected that 'the excitement was absolutely fabulous ... I must say it was a fantastic emotion',[42] Ralph Beauclerk, Poirier's wireless operator, had quite a different experience. His testimony is that of a frustrated hero who longed for more action, but it also contains an element of stoicism in that he endured circumstances which were not of his choosing. When he was not engaged in encoding, decoding and transmitting, Beauclerk became restless as the following statement suggests:

I read books ... I had nothing to do the rest of the time [when not wireless operating] ... I seldom went out. I went out for walks but not very often ... It was very boring. I was bored. I was longing to get into some action. I tried to get Jacques [Poirier] to take me with him somewhere but he wouldn't do it. I was longing to get into action actually. I wanted to see a bit of excitement ... He was a strict disciplinarian. I didn't revolt but I got furious ... I was bored. Here I was in the middle of an exciting job and seeing nothing of what was happening. I never had any encounter with the Germans. I wanted to see the Maquis in the skin but he wouldn't risk it … I was disappointed. I was frustrated. I felt that I could do more than I actually did. I longed to be involved a little bit with active operations … My role was only as a wireless operator … I suppose I had no right to expect anything else but that's just what I wanted. I was frustrated and Jacques, I think, understood that. I made it clear to him several times that I longed why can't he take me out … and so I had a frustrated war, but it was still very exciting.[43]

Beauclerk felt that although he was central to the circuit's work, reporting to London about their activities, demanding arms and arranging drops, he was on the periphery, not meeting other members of the group and not being allowed to participate in more active resistance work. His testimony is shot through with a sense of frustration that because he was cooped up he did not see any action. This is evidenced in his repetition of the words 'frustrated', mentioned three times, and 'longing', said four times, as well as the pithy, staccato sentences, such as 'I seldom went out', 'I was bored' and 'I was disappointed'. Beauclerk's account of his struggle to cope with isolation and his yearning to be more active may be connected with his desire to perform particular modes of masculinity. Selwyn Jepson, the recruiting officer for F Section, believed that men were less suited to solitary work than women as they 'usually want a mate with them. Men don't work alone. Their lives tend to be always in company with other men.'[44] In stating that men like companionship, Jepson challenges the gendered stereotype of men as autonomous. Certainly, Beauclerk longed for the company of other men and the excitement that involvement in a close-knit group entailed.

Whereas other agents remember the camaraderie that existed between Resistance colleagues and the adrenaline rush from encounters with German soldiers, Beauclerk did not as he was closeted in his safe house and rarely ventured outside. He struggled to make sense of his feelings about his contribution and his account of his role is intensely ambivalent: he felt that he could have done more. His contradictory statement at the end of this quotation, in which he asserted that his war was both 'frustrating' and 'exciting', illustrates his ambivalence: he recognises the heroism and romanticism of being a combatant working behind enemy lines and yet feels that he missed out on some aspects of that experience. Looking back on his wartime work, he cannot narrate exciting tales as some saboteurs might. His retrospective dissatisfaction concerning his passivity and inaction may well have been the result of his failure to live up to normative notions of masculinity prevailing during the Second

World War or after. War is often perceived as a masculine pursuit and the clandestine role of saboteur might be regarded as the epitome of masculinity. Indeed, Bob Maloubier recollected that when he showed an aptitude for wireless operating during his training, colleague Eliane Plewman warned him:

'You know that if you're too good, you'll be taken on as a wireless operator. Wireless operators usually don't do anything at all. They stay in, in hiding. The others do some type of sabotage, they go round, they form reception committees for parachute. Basically [if you become a wireless operator] you'll be in a remote place. It's very dangerous too.' So my skill just left me all of a sudden! I wanted more excitement. Definitely, more excitement. I wanted to see action, not to be confined. So I was made a saboteur. I enjoyed blowing things up, power and industrial plants, railway lines and bridges by the dozen.[45]

This statement makes explicit Maloubier's desire for action and his daredevil, masculine bravado, which is encapsulated in the final sentence, as well as his knowledge of the inactive and isolated life of a wireless operator, which would appear to be borne out by Beauclerk's account. In contrast to the role of the heroic saboteur, Maloubier perceived wireless operating as tedious and unglamorous.

The perceived passivity of wireless operating might be a result of the fact that work which is conventionally viewed as not heroic is often undertaken by women and is attributed a lower status. The gendered division of labour which operated within the SOE exacerbated this: women undertook the role of wireless operator but were prevented from becoming saboteurs. Thus the role of saboteur possessed a higher status precisely because women were prohibited from carrying out this work. Unlike sabotage, which was considered active, destructive, under-taken outdoors and requiring scientific knowledge, wireless operating in contrast was regarded as passive, constructive, usually carried out in the private arena and required dexterity and patience, which are tradi-tionally regarded as feminine skills. Indeed, Bob Connell claimed that modes of masculinity which are not hegemonic are often 'symboli-cally assimilated to femininity'.[46] He used the terms 'subordinated' and 'marginalised' masculinities to refer to modes which were less culturally valued and provided an example of a homosexual (Adam Singer) who was ridiculed for throwing a ball 'like a girl' to illustrate that subordi-nated masculinities are often perceived as 'feminine' because such modes appear to be at a distance from normative masculine behaviour. It is, then, perhaps unsurprising that Beauclerk was negative about his rather passive contribution. While other veterans recall comradeship and adrenaline stimulated by tense excitement, Beauclerk presents them as an acknowledged and regretted absence. He craved for that kind of activity but he did not experience it and he felt somewhat cheated by the fact that despite undertaking a risky job, he had none of the compensations which others experienced. Where he got his sense of what he was missing is unclear. Perhaps it was from Poirier, or from the messages about parachute drops that he passed on, or possibly it was a matter of hindsight: his retrospective knowledge of what others achieved, gleaned from published memoirs and heroic constructions of agents in films, led him to re-evaluate his experiences. His memories have little in common with those of Richard Heslop, for example, whose autobiography is entitled *Xavier: The Famous British Agent's Dramatic Account of His Work in the French Resistance* or the biography of Roger Landes, *Aristide: Warlord of the Resistance*, which conjure images of heroic masculine activity. Even the titles of these representations are indicative of heroic engagement.

The previous chapter showed that some agents who deny feelings of anxiety may have been influenced by the heroic representation of the British agent in films and auto/biographies: that is to say a 'cultural circuit' is in operation which informs their testimonies. For Beauclerk, however, there was a disjuncture between his personal memories and the heroic portrayal of SOE agents in most films and auto/biographies. Moreover, Poirier does mention that Beauclerk was very quiet and never complained about his inactivity. That Poirier does not remember Beauclerk being unhappy about his limited role might suggest that Beauclerk's sentiments of frustration emerged after the Second World War. Conversely, Beauclerk might have felt at the time that he was missing out: in the interview he remarks that he was privately irritated and informed Poirier of his frustration and longing to be more actively involved in other Resistance activities. It is thus unclear how much at the time he felt that he was missing out. Possibly post-war accounts have intensified Beauclerk's feelings of disappointment. What is interesting is that he represents his wartime memories as tainted with a disillusionment and with a striking awareness of the distance between the image of what heroic agents experienced and his memory of what he did.

Beauclerk had a very clear image of what he considered to be heroic activity. Was this yearning for more excitement restricted to men or had some women also longed for greater activity? SOE agent Philippe de Vomécourt believed that women were more focused on the task assigned to them than men: 'They showed more single-mindedness in their duties' and were 'less liable to be found where they ought not to be – they did not feel so tempted to attend parachutings, for example.'[47] Vomécourt suggested that male agents in comparison tended to covet a more active life. An SOE report also claimed that many male agents were unsuited to solitude: 'Because of the specialised nature of their work, WT operators led a very quiet, if not lonely existence and it was found, on examination of agents' case histories, that many active young men were employed in France on this task for which they were technically, but not temperamentally, qualified.'[48] The dynamic image of the heroic British male agent is confirmed by the inclusion of the adjective 'active' here. The author of this report implied that WT was 'women's work'. Men's temperamental unsuitability is in spite of the fact that technical proficiency and scientific knowledge were (and often still are) regarded as masculine (albeit a mode of 'nerdish' masculinity). From this perspective, then, wireless operating was not consistent with 'hegemonic masculinity'.

Women, on the other hand, were considered to have a suitable disposition for WT work and, certainly, many female agents were content with such responsibility. Yvonne Baseden, for example, was satisfied, but this was because, in addition to her role as a wireless operator, she participated in many other tasks, such as teaching new recruits how to use arms and searching the countryside for suitable dropping grounds: 'Usually the radio operator stayed in her little corner except for the odd occasion when you went to one group and showed them how to use some particular material ... I was very fortunate because I was able to go around and that's why I didn't feel isolated because I was involved in all the different types of things we had to do.'[49] Baseden hinted at the frustration that she would have felt if she had been confined to wireless operating, which would suggest that it was not just men who craved activity, comradeship and involvement. Indeed, there are also accounts of women who recall yearning for more excitement. Lise de Baissac, who was sent into the field as a reception officer, recalled wanting to do more for the war effort: 'I thought it wasn't enough to receive agents from the sky and put them on their way, for it was very little. So I started to have a little more action ... It wasn't enough. I wanted to do a little more. I started to find fields where I could have received weapons ... I just wanted to be a little more active.'[50]

By reading Beauclerk's account alongside Baseden's and de Baissac's, one can avoid falling too easily into an argument based on gender polarity, as do de Vomécourt and the author of the SOE report. Despite their conclusions that the desire to be more active was gendered, it can be seen that there were women who were just as eager as men to be more active in the

Resistance. Both de Baissac and Beauclerk were impatient to extend their Resistance activities, but unlike de Baissac who worked alone and could choose to undertake more work, Beauclerk was constrained by Poirier who did not want to jeopardise the circuit.

Beauclerk does, however, recollect one interesting episode. This occurred on 14 July 1944 when forty or fifty planes flew over the area of France in which he was operating during daylight hours and dropped over four hundred containers. The night before the operation, Beauclerk needed to contact England:

> We were on our way at night travelling in a Citroën and we stopped at a house, just at random on the side of the road. We broke our way into the house, forced the door and we had guns. We told the occupants, 'Go and sit down over there. Don't do anything' and we cut the telephone [line]. I had my set with me and I laid it out, put an aerial up … and I sent the message to them that everything, the groups are ready, everything is prepared, the op is on … This was one occasion when I was able to play a fairly important part and most probably the most important part of all in a way. I had to be in touch with the Home Station.[51]

The tone of this narrative is in sharp contrast to that quoted previously. The pace of this description of events is brisk and, unlike the earlier statement with its epigrammatic sentences, these are much longer and run on, serving to signify Beauclerk's exhilaration. Moreover, this statement conforms to the typical conventions of the heroic narrative: rather than reflecting on how he felt, as in the statement describing his boredom and frustration, the account is action-based and violent. Moreover, Beauclerk recalled feeling integrated into a team: his role as wireless operator meant that he was crucial to this particular operation. This would seem to recall a moment in which he was actively participating in a public setting, with weapons, and he recognised that he was crucial to the operation. However, even the recollection of the only action in which he played a significant part is tainted as he subsequently noted: 'I didn't see much of the operation'. Thus, despite playing a crucial role in the preparation of the daylight drop, Beauclerk's part in the operation itself was minimal and this change in role is evidenced in his account as he retreats into using concise sentences once more.

Beauclerk's minor role in the action is in direct contrast to the part played by Yvonne Baseden whose circuit received hundreds of containers in operation CADILLAC, the first daylight drop on 26 June 1944. Not only did she have a crucial role in preparing the operation but she was also ensconced in a ditch at the edge of the field as the aircraft came overhead. She recalled: 'I found a sort of culvert where I could be in with my radio, yet open in the field and so I sat there with my radio and established contact with England and to guide the planes in ... It was incredible. I was jumping around, waving madly to them!'[52] She interspersed this heroic reconstruction of the events with terms such as 'wonderful', 'marvellous', 'extraordinary', 'incredible' and 'exciting'. Unlike Beauclerk's testimony, Baseden's account of such events conformed to the conventions of a heroic narrative.

This examination of agents' accounts has facilitated an analysis of their different constructions of wartime masculinities. While a tone of disrespect can be detected in 'heroic' narratives, disapproval can be perceived in 'stoic' accounts. The different strategies pursued by male agents might be accounted for by considering their age and pre-SOE lifestyles. Maloubier was only twenty when he joined the organisation and was parachuted back into France, and Cohen and Zembsch-Schreve were both in their early twenties. All three were single and actively heterosexual and chose to pursue a way of life which was similar to their pre-SOE lifestyle. Francis Cammaerts, on the other hand, was slightly older and married with children, which might account for why he was disinclined to lead a high-profile lifestyle which entailed great risk. However, differences in age fail to account for why Cyril Watney, who was born in 1922, the year before Maloubier, preferred to lead a quiet life, focusing solely upon his WT work or why Sydney Hudson, who was in his thirties, chose to frequent black-market restaurants. Ultimately, every agent was an individual with different notions of security and each chose to pursue a lifestyle which suited their personalities.

Disguise: transforming masculinities

When the identity of SOE agents became known to the Gestapo, perhaps because individuals had been observed frequenting nightclubs and black-market restaurants as Francis Suttill had, they often needed to alter their appearance so that they could continue with their work without attracting the attention of German soldiers. If posters with either visual images or written descriptions of agents were displayed around the city, town or village in which they operated (as occurred with Bob Maloubier in Rouen), agents found it necessary to change their appearance. There were some techniques which agents could employ: 'Several agents used minor disguise with success, such as growing moustaches, using glasses, parting hair differently.'[53] SOE's exhibition room at the Natural History

4 Agents' passing encounters were made credible by disguises, sustaining and lending authenticity to their gendered performances. Photographs from the SOE exhibition or 'Demonstration Room' at Natural History Museum.

Museum included examples of how this might be achieved (see Figure 4). Dyeing hair was one way of altering appearances. Alfred Newton, one of the brothers of whom Robert Boiteux disapproved, had to alter his appearance as his biographer explained:

> In order to be able to move about the city freely, he decided on a complete change of personality. A friendly hairdresser gave him a permanent wave, but when it was done it looked too artificial. He washed his hair in soap flakes several times to get out the thick grease with which it was darkened. When it had dried it was back to its original light brown shade and frizzled like the back of a sheep. He trimmed his newly-grown moustache to pencil thinness, dyed it with Bohémienne's [a courier] mascara, brushed his eyebrows the wrong way and donned a pair of horn-rimmed spectacles.[54]

The usefulness of disguise in affecting particular styles of masculinity is evidenced in the above example: Newton constructed a totally different image and his confidence resulted in his increased use of public space.

Alfred Newton was not the only agent who increased his mobility by utilising disguise. Bob Sheppard had been arrested immediately upon arrival in France when he landed by parachute on the roof of a gendarmerie. Following his escape, he felt compelled to alter his appearance:

'After an arrest and an escape I had to change entirely and my chief of réseaux called "Nicholas", Robert Boiteux, decided to dye my hair black. So instead of [blond] waves, I had black hair like Tino Rossi or the singers at the time. And apparently it changed my appearance completely; the way of dressing and the way of doing my hair.'[55] Changing from blond waves to straight black hair meant that Sheppard did not fit the description of him which had been circulated by the authorities. Moreover, it enabled him to conceal his distinctive English appearance and look more like the stereotypical Frenchman.

Growing facial hair was another technique for transforming appearance. Gaston Cohen, who escaped the widespread penetration and arrest of members of the PROSPER circuit, returned to France on his second operation with a newly-grown moustache. Not only did this alter his appearance in case any of those captured had divulged information about him during interrogations, but also he considered a moustache to be typically French. Photographs taken before his return to France, which were used on his identity documents, show him with a moustache. This contrasts with Kenneth MacKenzie who felt compelled to shave off his moustache: 'No other Frenchman at that time wore a moustache. I would be really advertising a British officer so I had to cut my moustache off. Very sad!'[56] These contrasting strategies for disguise may have been related to regional differences: Cohen operated in Paris and Mackenzie in rural Malon.

Some agents had several identity papers, each with a different photograph, as the following report, concerning Paul d'Istria who operated in Corsica, suggests: 'Informant often changed his appearance, and had photos taken in his various disguises for his identity cards. Sometimes he was clean-shaven, sometimes badly shaven, he would grow a moustache, he wore his hair sometimes long, sometimes short, he placed great reliance on change of clothes, and stated that the change from beret to a felt hat, or from light to dark clothing, can effect a very useful disguise.'[57] Subtle alterations in clothing, hair and facial hair resulted in this agent outwitting his pursuers. It could be argued that women had even greater opportunities to change their appearance than men. Whereas male agents were restricted to growing facial hair or changing the colour of their hair to effect an alteration, women had comparatively more options. In addition to dyeing their hair, women could also style it in many different ways because women's hair was typically much longer than men's. Like d'Istria, Muriel Byck possessed several identity papers bearing different photographs of herself. Her organiser, Philippe de Vomécourt, recorded in his autobiography: 'Muriel was provided with three different photographs of herself for identity papers, each of them projecting an apparently separate person, by the adoption of a changed hairstyle. By drawing back her hair from her forehead, or by fluffing it out, untidily, she could assume different identities in an emergency. And she would have the identity papers, bearing the appropriate photograph of herself, to aid the transformation.'[58] Changing the length, colour and style of hair enabled female agents to perform different modes of femininity and were utilised to great effect.

There were also more drastic measures for transforming agents' appearances as the following statement by Jack Thomas, the biographer of the Newton brothers, illustrates: 'A man can alter his appearance considerably in a number of ways. He can dye his hair, disguise the colour of his eyes with contact lenses, change the shape of his nose or chin by plastic surgery.'[59] Such radical measures as cosmetic surgery were unlikely once in the field, but there is evidence that some agents, whose appearance was either well-known to the Gestapo or especially conspicuous, underwent surgery in London. For example, George Langelaan had his ears pinned back and a piece of thigh bone added to his chin.[60] There is, then, much confirmation in agents' testimonies of the importance of physical disguise in transforming the presentation of masculinity and, in so doing, assisting passing.

Conclusion

This analysis of male agents' retrospective constructions of their lifestyles in wartime France and of the ways in which they chose to pass emphasises their investments in particular kinds of gendered performances. They were not merely imitating French civilians but were performing French civilian masculinities, choosing from a repertoire of masculinities those which they considered appropriate to their cover stories. Although students had been lectured during their training on the necessity of keeping a low profile in order to pass successfully as French, some agents adopted very extravagant lifestyles. Veterans who represent their wartime lifestyles in this way might be regarded as producing heroic narratives as their accounts conform to the typical conventions of the genre by downplaying danger, and emphasising bravado and their commitment to the greater cause. Unsurprisingly, 'the heroes' identified in this chapter, including Sydney Hudson, Gaston Cohen, André Watt and Bob Maloubier, also featured in the previous chapter as heroic for denying fear.

Male agents who led comparatively more risky lifestyles were generally those who claimed that they had not experienced anxiety. Perhaps being unburdened by anxiety gave them the confidence to enjoy a more extravagant existence. This would suggest that lack of anxiety and high living go together as ways of telling the story and living the life.

However, not all male agents adopted lifestyles that conformed to hegemonic masculinity. Instead of trying to pass as stereotypical Frenchmen, some agents opted for a very secluded existence to reduce the risk of exposure, while others who had solitude thrust upon them were frustrated by their inactivity and yearned for more involvement. Their accounts are less heroic in tone and correspond more with the emblematic conventions of the stoic testimony in that they are characterised by endurance of circumstances not chosen by the protagonist. Furthermore, some of 'the stoics' identified in this chapter, in particular Cyril Watney and Jacques Poirier who disapproved of agents who led high-profile existences, also featured in the previous chapter as stoically enduring sentiments of anxiety.

Male agents thus adopted a number of strategies and had a varied range of experiences of being an agent which emerge from representations of their wartime selves. Female agents, as we shall see in the next chapter, adopted very different strategies from those pursued by their male counterparts and had to police their conduct to a much greater extent.

Notes

1 Cammaerts, *Secret Agent* (BBC2).
2 Connell, *Masculinities*, p. 76.
3 Watt, *Churchill's Secret Army* (Channel 4). Similar remarks were made by Watt in personal correspondence.
4 Correspondence with André Watt.
5 Foot, *SOE in France*, p. 294.
6 Correspondence with André Watt.
7 Rake, *Rake's Progress*, p. 111.
8 Personal interview with Sydney Hudson.
9 Personal interview with Sydney Hudson.
10 Foot, *SOE in France*, p. 198; p. 310.
11 A. Forbes, 'The Princess who would be Spy', available online at: www.the-south-asian.com/Sept2001/Noor%20Inayat%20Khan1.htm [Accessed 2002].
12 Foot, *SOE in France*, p. 274.
13 Personal interview with Gaston Cohen.

14 M. Buckmaster, *They Fought Alone: The Story of British Agents in France* (London: The Popular Book Club, 1959), p. 127.
15 Personal interview with Bob Maloubier.
16 Rake, *Rake's Progress*, pp. 205–6.
17 Zembsch-Schreve, *Secret Agent* (BBC2).
18 Zembsch-Schreve, *Pierre Lalande*, p. 95.
19 Churchill, *Of Their Own Choice*, p. 151.
20 Zembsch-Schreve, *Pierre Lalande*. p. 95.
21 Zembsch-Schreve, *Secret Agent* (BBC2).
22 Rich, 'Compulsory Heterosexuality and the Lesbian Continuum'.
23 Connell, *Masculinities*, p. 70.
24 Churchill, *Duel of Wits*, p. 166; p. 7.
25 Churchill, *The Spirit in the Cage*, p. 21.
26 Personal interview with Sydney Hudson.
27 Personal interview with Bob Maloubier.
28 Personal interview with Gaston Cohen.
29 Personal interview with Francis Cammaerts.
30 Rake, *Rake's Progress*, p. 143.
31 Personal interview with Francis Cammaerts.
32 Personal interview with Bob Maloubier.
33 IWM SA, 9851 Boiteux-Burdett.
34 IWM SA, 18154 MacKenzie.
35 Personal interview with Cyril Watney.
36 Cammaerts, *Churchill's Secret Army* (Channel 4).
37 Personal interview with Francis Cammaerts.
38 National Archives, HS 9/258/5.
39 National Archives, HS 6/569.
40 Poirier, *Churchill's Secret Army* (Channel 4).
41 Poirier, *Churchill's Secret Army* (Channel 4).
42 Poirier, *Churchill's Secret Army* (Channel 4).
43 Beauclerk, *Churchill's Secret Army* (Channel 4).
44 IWM SA, 9331 Jepson.
45 Personal interview with Bob Maloubier.
46 B. Connell, *The Men and the Boys* (Cambridge: Polity, 2000), p. 31.
47 De Vomécourt, *Who Lived to See the Day*, p. 211.
48 National Archives, HS 7/66.
49 Personal interview with Yvonne Baseden.
50 De Baissac, *Behind Enemy Lines* (Channel 4).
51 Beauclerk, *Churchill's Secret Army* (Channel 4).
52 Personal interview with Yvonne Baseden.
53 National Archives, HS 7/135.
54 Thomas, *No Banners*, p. 212.
55 Personal interview with Bob Sheppard.
56 IWM SA, 18154 MacKenzie.

57 National Archives, HS 6/573.
58 De Vomécourt, *Who Lived to See the Day*, p. 170.
59 Thomas, *No Banners*, p. 134.
60 Langelaan, *Knights of Floating Silk*, p. 82. See also L. Bell, *Sabotage: The Story Of Lt-Col J. Elder Wills* (London: T. Werner Laurie Limited, 1957), pp. 57–8.

6

'The best disguise': performing femininities for clandestine purposes

In the previous chapter, various accounts of different wartime masculinities were analysed. Male agents made investments in particular kinds of gendered performances by emulating civilian men in order to facilitate their successful passing as ordinary French nationals. Like their male counterparts, female agents also recall the importance of behaviour appropriate for the region in which they were operating. They undertook specifically feminine performances by mobilising conventionally attractive appearance and appropriate conduct which usually made it possible for them to undertake the hazardous role of couriering.

The gendering of courier work

A gendered division of labour was developed within the SOE with women being sent into the field only as wireless operators and couriers, thus preserving the 'combat taboo'. SOE files state that women were allocated the role of courier in Resistance networks for very gender-specific reasons: it was believed that women possessed skills and attributes that made them more suitable for this work. An excerpt from an SOE file from 1944 on operations in Holland offers a number of explanations as to why this was the case: 'Girl couriers were used extensively, because it was a fact that women were rarely stopped at controls; and only during the period immediately before the Liberation – and even then rarely – were they searched. They were seldom picked up in mass arrests. They provided excellent cover for their movements about the country by visiting friends, carrying out shopping expeditions and later, foraging the country for food.'[1]

It was assumed that women were unlikely to be suspected of being engaged in the Resistance in France as well as in Holland. Thus, an SOE file concerning France reported: 'The advantage of women couriers was that they passed controls with much more ease than men.'[2] Duncan Stuart, Gervase Cowell's replacement as the SOE Adviser at the Foreign Office (1997–2002), also provided support for the notion that women were better equipped for courier work in France: 'Women were regarded as more suitable for the role of courier … since they attracted less attention from the various security forces than did men, were cooler and more adept at talking their way out of trouble at check points and, indeed, could use their femininity to help them in tight spots.'[3] Stuart asserted that women were more inventive, being capable of conjuring ingenious cover stories to extract them from dangerous situations. This is confirmed by veterans' testimonies which overflow with tales of how resourcefulness enabled female agents to evade capture. For example, when Christine Granville (née Krystina Gizycka) was confronted with a German patrol while carrying an SOE escape map printed on silk, she took the map out of her bag and tied it around her head like a scarf. This was consistent with the appearance of women in the 1940s and was thus considered appropriate behaviour in this specific historical context. The 'naturalness' of this action for a woman resulted in the soldiers paying no attention to her headdress. Another example of a female agent's inventiveness is provided in Peter Churchill's autobiography where he recounts a conversation he had had with Odette Sansom, codenamed 'Lise'. She told him that she had been stopped by German soldiers after the curfew while she was searching for suitable landing grounds for arms drops: '"[There was] one really stiff control where the sergeant brought out the Duty Officer. I pulled a big yarn about tearing through the night in order to see my very sick child in a Cannes nursing home. When I saw him still hesitate I turned on a few tears and that fixed him." "Congratulations, Lise! A man could never have got away with it."'[4] Churchill noted that Sansom remained calm when confronted by an awkward situation, quickly devised a plausible explanation for her violation of the curfew and played upon stereotypes of feminine emotion to conceal the real reason for her late-night excursion.

Testimonies of veterans indicate a widespread belief that women possessed certain skills, such as resourcefulness and composure, which were useful for undertaking clandestine work. What is particularly striking is that they perceived these specific skills of femininity as timeless, innate capacities of women, rather than seeing them as specific to this period and to the nature of their work. Resourcefulness does not have a history of being gendered as feminine; however, post-war testimonies feminise ingenuity in relation, for example, to the wartime constraints imposed upon European housewives, such as rationing. This period abounds with tales of how ingenious women were: they provided meals with limited ingredients, washed clothes without soap and used foodstuffs, such as gravy browning powder, to produce the effect of stockinged legs. Such testimonies tend not to acknowledge that it is the nature of the task which genders composure, inventiveness and linguistic ability as feminine. The fact that women were employed as couriers and experienced encounters with German soldiers at snap controls, often on a daily basis, meant that women had more opportunities to be inventive.

By contrast, several wartime accounts indicate that male agents were less resourceful and inventive than their female colleagues. For example, an episode described in the biography of SOE agents Henry and Alfred Newton illustrates the latter's inability to remain composed when he came across a snap control in Le Puy while sitting in the back of a truck loaded with weapons: 'Squatting on the tarpaulin covering their arsenal, Alfred tried desperately to make up his mind what to do … The harder Alfred searched for inspiration, the more jelly-like his brain seemed to become … a fear-strangled, high-pitched voice, which Alfred realised with horror was his own, piped up, "We're carrying submachine guns, hand grenades and enough explosive to blow half your town to hell and back."'[5] This quotation makes explicit Newton's agitation and highlights his inability to remain calm. Rather than attempting to invent a plausible excuse, Newton found himself involuntarily trying to bluff his way out by acting the part of the comedian, saying something which was so outrageous that it could not possibly be true. Not only was his retort to the guard ironic, it was doubly so given that what he said was truthful. His strategy was, nevertheless, successful as the soldier on duty at the snap control did not perceive Newton's discomfort and unease and waved the truck on without searching the contents. On one level, this example illustrates the perception that male agents were less adept than their female colleagues at inventing plausible stories under pressure. However, this example also suggests that men and women invented the types of stories that were appropriate to their gender: while Sansom fabricated a story about her ill children, Newton made a wisecrack.

A further asset alluded to in the SOE files was that, unlike men, women were less susceptible to being rounded up and deported to Germany for employment purposes. On 4 September 1942, Pierre Laval, the first minister of Pétain, the head of state who pursued a collaborationist policy from Vichy, introduced the Service du Travail Obligatoire, or STO, which made it compulsory for men aged between twenty and twenty-three to be directed into work in Germany. Consequently, it was hazardous for young men to be engaged in courier work because this would have entailed daily encounters with German soldiers, any of which could have resulted in their deportation. Women, however, could move about unhampered by this threat.

Furthermore, women were not regarded with the same mistrust as men. Groups of men who were not engaged in work looked suspicious. This was partly because it was generally assumed that 'terrorists' were male and it was a few years into the war before it was recognised that women could be resisters as well. For this reason, some male organisers specifically requested a female colleague: Francis Cammaerts recalled that his decision to ask headquarters for a woman was 'for the reason that it was easier for them to get around'[6] and Sydney Hudson noted: 'That's why I originally asked for a woman. I knew when Muriel Byck was dropped with George [Jones, his wireless operator] and me and we went into Issoudun. Well, there we were, two men and a girl, nobody took any notice of us at all. Then, I thought, well, it is really much better to be accompanied by a woman and that was how I asked for one as well as a man. So they gave me Sonya.'[7]

Why were female agents beyond suspicion? Nazi views of ideal German femininity may shed light on the Nazi attitude towards French women. German women were largely seen in the context of the home, a contained, private sphere isolated from the outside world, whereas men were located in the public arena of work, politics, science and the military. Central to this 'separate spheres' thinking is the glorification of domesticated femininity: women's activities were to be largely limited to 'Kinder, Kirche und Küche' (Children, Church and Kitchen). A natalist backlash occurred and motherhood, which was understood to be women's ideal primary occupation, acquired increasingly national and racial associations in the pursuit of an Aryan race. Because of the pervasiveness of an ideology which placed women firmly in the home, it was not surprising that German soldiers were slow to realise that young, attractive women were politicised and involved in the Resistance and, moreover, that they were exploiting this misconception.

Female agents were able to make use of the gender tags of childcare and shopping to cover their clandestine activities. For example, Nancy Wake cycled over 500 kms in 72 hours in search of a wireless operator, hoping that she would be mis/taken for a French housewife performing her domestic chores: 'I cycled to the local markets and filled my string bag with all the fruit and vegetables I could buy without food coupons, hoping that I would pass for a housewife out shopping'.[8] Wake reproduced the gendered division of labour of that time and setting, but performing these domestic functions for a military cause altered their meaning in that they became quasi-military acts in themselves. It was vital to maintain the feminine identification of the cover task, in order to conceal the military character of the clandestine ones. In this sense, she was, in effect, protected from being read as a suspected 'terrorist' because of the very fact that she was a woman and also because of the conventional tasks assigned to women. The repeated miscalculation by German soldiers concerning the improbability that women were involved in clandestine operations was effectively exploited by the SOE.

Not only did shopping give female agents a reason for being out of the home, but also shopping baskets could hide weapons and radio parts. An SOE report noted: 'Messages and packages were concealed in bicycle frames, shopping baskets, hand-bags, the lining of clothes or round the waist under the clothes.'[9] Testimonies of SOE agents reveal that women did indeed conceal incriminating material in their baggage and upon their person: the bag belonging to Yvonne Cormeau had a false bottom under which she secreted documents and radio parts and Lise de Baissac strapped radio parts underneath the belt on her dress.[10] The masculine connotations of the Resistance materials they conveyed were thus literally cloaked in femininity. Evidence from both written and oral testimonies suggests that female agents routinely used both clothing and the trappings of femininity to smuggle documents and equipment in order to conceal their role as couriers. Moreover, there is evidence to suggest that male agents encouraged their female colleagues to exploit the trappings of femininity. Richard Heslop recalled: 'A few hiding-places [for messages] I suggested were, under the soles of stockings, in a powder compact, or, if the girl had long hair, in her hair.'[11]

In addition to this, until the latter stages of the war, German soldiers on guard at checkpoints were male, and female agents frequently record consciously and deliberately performing femininity in their presence. Female agents' appearances and behaviours could contribute to images of civilian femininity that would place them beyond suspicion. They strategically used their knowledge of conventional gender relations and their awareness of the potency of feminine performances.

Femininity as appearance

Female agents frequently note in their testimonies that clothing was vital to their performances. They assumed the dress of ordinary housewives, rural peasant women or aristocratic socialites according to their circumstances. In each case, they either assumed the disguise in order to blend in, be inconspicuous and pass unnoticed, or to stand out and be observed. Clothing was thus utilised as a tool for concealment or, conversely, for exposure. There were therefore numerous strategies that agents could pursue. Different circumstances called for performances of different types of femininity. On some occasions, urban glamour was opted for. In her study of white working-class women in late twentieth-century Britain, Beverley Skeggs defined glamour as an amalgam of sexuality, femininity, desirability and respectability and noted the work which goes into performing glamour appropriately so as to avoid being read as 'rough', 'common' or 'tarty'.[12] Skeggs found that clothing was crucial in women's strategies to dissimulate their working-class identities. Clothing can provide a repertoire of status symbols, signifying, as well as distinguishing, between classes. However, in the 1940s, clothing was rationed in most European countries and items were perpetually recycled. Lise de Baissac recollected: 'In France, they were wearing very old things. Everybody wore all sorts of things and not particularly elegant. Old clothes were taken out of cupboards. Clothing was in very short supply, rationed and expensive.'[13] A different kind of glamour was in operation in the Second World War. As a consequence of rationing, there was also an element of austerity.

Glamour was a means by which female agents could assert their difference from other women as 'glamour', according to Skeggs, 'offers the ability to appear as something different from the mundane'.[14] A smart, elegant appearance may have implied that they were of high social standing given that sophistication and poise have class connotations. The interaction between gender and class meant that glamorous, attractive women were often read as middle-class. Indeed, agents were advised by SOE staff to use class-specific signals. An SOE file commented: 'It was found an advantage for couriers to travel first class as this gave them more prestige with train controls.'[15] Another SOE file noted: 'Much more attention is paid to those travelling third class than first. The least risk is incurred in first class. This is because Germans and big businessmen travel this way and the police etc. don't want to annoy them.'[16] Passengers seated in first class were less likely to have their luggage subjected to thorough searches, perhaps because German soldiers were unlikely to perceive first class travellers as 'terrorists'. Agents' accounts testify to the respect for social status that was instilled within German soldiers. Reflecting on her treatment by German officials, Odette Sansom asserted: 'In those days I called them a "race de valets". I think if you treated them in a certain way, as if they were almost your servants, they had a type of respect for you.'[17] Sansom believed that the observance of social hierarchy was fundamental to German national identity. Consequently, invoking middle-classness could be an effective passing strategy. This was useful, not only because conventionally attractive, respectable-looking women were generally regarded as middle-class but also because displays of femininity were seen as indicative of inner character. On both counts, glamorous women were unlikely to be suspected of being involved in the Resistance.

This miscalculation was exploited mercilessly. An excerpt from the second biography of Nancy Wake emphasises her consciousness about the potency of sexual allure:

> Nancy's past experience had taught her that not only does sexual attraction not recognise national borders nor political divisions – meaning she had often been ogled by the very guards meant to check her – but the innate warmth and intimacy of that attraction was a great soother of possible suspicions. If she got it right, it had to seem beyond the range of possibilities for the Germans between her and her destination, that such an attractive young woman could be on a mission specifically devoted to bringing them carnage and destruction in the very near future. That, at least, is the factor Nancy intended to play to the hilt and she spent the twenty-four hours before departure rustling up the most attractive outfit she could get.[18]

Narrative accounts, then, suggest that female agents found it productive to accentuate their physical appearance. Many women recognised that it was important to present themselves as feminine as their appearance may have had a considerable influence on how they were received by German soldiers on guard at stations and at checkpoints. Wake, who encountered numerous German-patrolled checkpoints on her arduous bicycle ride, recalled: 'I would just look over to the officer, flutter my eyelashes and say, "Do you want to search *moi*?" And they would laugh flirtatiously, "No, Mademoiselle, you carry on."'[19] According to John Berger, women must survey themselves precisely because others survey them:

> She [referring to women generally] has to survey everything she is and everything she does because how she appears to others, and ultimately how she appears to men, is of crucial importance for what is normally thought of as the success of her life … Men act and women appear. Men look at women. Women watch themselves being looked at … [Woman is] an object

of vision: a sight ... Men survey women before treating them. Consequently, how a woman appears to a man can determine how she will be treated.[20]

Anticipating the impact of their appearance, female agents surveyed themselves, were conscious of how they appeared and presented themselves in particular ways so as to appear attractive to men. These were heterosexual performances in that they were oriented towards male pleasure and were dependent upon male soldiers' sexual approval in order to be successful. Presumably, their displays of femininity would not have been so effective if performed in the presence of homosexual or female soldiers.

However, in contrast to the various beneficial effects of performing glamour, it could lead to negative consequences. Such appearances did not always protect female agents from discovery and some women were arrested despite such strategies. Indeed, the performance of feminine glamour could be highly ambiguous in that, although it might protect women from suspicion, it could also draw too much unwanted attention to agents as they worked. Didi Nearne recalled one occasion when she was sitting on a train with her radio set in a suitcase:

> There was this German soldier who kept looking at me and smiling, so I smiled back. Then I was looking through the window and he said, 'Cigarette, Mademoiselle?' And I said, 'No, thank you, I don't smoke.' And my hands, you see, were stained with nicotine. You could make mistakes like that. He was looking at me and he said 'What is in your suitcase?' So I said, 'Oh – c'est un phonographe, savez, de la musique', and he said, 'Oh, oui' and he was looking at me and I thought Oh la la, I must get out quickly.[21]

The soldier's interest in her, coupled with his inquisitiveness about her suitcase containing the radio set, unsettled Nearne as it was difficult to judge whether he was paying attention to her as an attractive young woman or because he suspected her of engaging in illegal activities. Thus, on the one hand, the fact that they were women meant that they were unlikely to be read as 'terrorists'. However, on the other hand, the attention they attracted as glamorous women, which they could do little about, made them more suspect than they would otherwise have been. Deliberate performances of femininity were, then, by no means unproblematic.

Occasionally, female agents attracted a different kind of attention which was most unwanted. Shortly after parts of France had been liberated, Claire Everett, a twenty-year-old courier, embarked upon a new role with her organiser going back and forth across the lines and providing the Americans with intelligence. Everett, who carried their American papers in a secret pocket in her girdle, was sexually assaulted by two German soldiers:

I heard this marching behind me and I turned around and there were these two guys so I just smiled at them and went on my way and they followed me in and they raped me. One held me down. My first instinct was to put up a fight and then I thought no, I can't. I've got these papers. If I put up a fight, they're going to overpower me and then they'll probably strip me and we'd be in a worse mess than we already are in. I've just got to let them do it and get on with it ... Anyway, it was quite an experience! But they didn't get my papers! [laughs][22]

Although being female and conventionally attractive have been recognised as advantages in both contemporary and post-war accounts, it was not necessarily a major benefit since they could induce unwanted attention as Claire Everett's experience shows.

Some female agents were less eager to court danger for the greater protection that it might offer. In some instances, a less glamorous performance meant that female agents were not noticed and they merged into the background. If glamour is correlated with visibility, mundaneness resulted in relative concealment. For those who wanted to be comparatively invisible, it may have been necessary to downplay femininity so as not to attract attention. In order to be as inconspicuous as possible, Yvonne Baseden wore a very casual, plain grey skirt and a blue blouse: 'The idea was to blend in somehow.'[23] She did not wear any make-up and styled her hair in a very simple way in order not to invite attention. When Diana Rowden was concerned for her safety following the circulation of an accurate description of her by the French authorities, she changed the colour and style of her hair, disposed of all the clothing she possessed and borrowed clothes of a more modest fashion in order to construct a different identity so that she would not be recognised.

Displays of ordinariness were only successful in specific contexts and agents had to carefully select the correct style for the situation. Upon visiting a larger town, Anne-Marie Walters realised that her appearance was unsuitably casual. In her autobiography, she wrote: 'I discarded my beret, it was all right in a small town like Condom, but in Agen women wore high, complicated hair styles and even more complicated ear-rings.'[24] She was conscious of the regional particularity of hairstyles. However, this had not always been the case: when she first arrived in France, George Starr, her organiser, advised her that her hairstyle was inappropriate for the country village where she was based: 'You'd better not do your hair swept up across the back like this. Women in the country towns round here wear it very high in front and down at the back ... Your clothes are not very suitable for this region either.'[25] Walters' clothing was considered inappropriate because she had been allocated clothes for a city, rather than for rural villages. Fashion differences between cities, towns and country villages meant that agents had to be aware of these variations in order to blend in, to look as inconspicuous as possible and be mis/taken as civilians.

Similarly, female agents had to be aware of the jewellery which ordinary French women wore. Yvonne Cormeau arrived in France without any jewellery but soon noticed that 'every woman, even in the country districts, always wore a necklace or bracelet, or ornament of some kind'.[26] She managed to find a few small articles of jewellery to sustain her performance of rural French femininity. However, to complicate matters, Cormeau also found that peasant women did not wear certain items of jewellery: 'I was asked to look after the cows, take them out in the morning and bring them back at sunset ... Before going, the farmer's wife had told me, "Don't wear a watch. No woman who looks after cows would be able to afford a watch."'[27] Cormeau's statement illustrates that forms of femininity could be both regionally- and class-specific. She mobilised localised forms of femininity, in this case through not wearing jewellery. While it would have been unfitting for Cormeau to wear a watch whilst cowherding as this might have exposed her, it was equally perilous not to have any jewellery in localities where women routinely wore necklaces and bracelets. Jewellery was thus a crucial element in the appearance of women in rural France at this time.

Another important aspect to blending in was giving up smoking. Like many British women in the 1940s, Cormeau was a heavy smoker. In France, however, cigarettes were scarce and could only be found on the black-market at exorbitant prices. As Cormeau was operating in a rural peasant village and her cover meant that she was unlikely to be able to afford tobacco, she had to give up smoking so as not to draw attention to herself.[28] Starr, Cormeau's organiser, also warned Anne-Marie Walters: 'Mind YOU never smoke in public: women smoke so little here that you would be picked out right away.'[29] He was clearly conscious of both cultural and regional differences and was awake to the demands of habitus. Paddy O'Sullivan was also advised by her organiser Edmund Mayer (codenamed 'Barthelemy') that her smoking could expose her. Her debriefing file claimed: 'Informant is a very heavy smoker and most French girls do not smoke, or if they do, they could not afford to keep packets of cigarettes which were a terrible price in France. It would have looked very suspicious if informant had smoked too much in public places and was told not to by Bartelmy [sic].'[30] Female agents were required to conform to French gendered smoking patterns as part of their displays of ordinariness.

Undertaking performances that totally lacked glamour was another strategy employed by some agents. On one occasion when Nancy Wake needed to adopt a disguise in order not to be recognised, she chose to dress in antiquated and outmoded clothing and to pass as a middle-aged peasant. In her autobiography, she wrote:

> I borrowed a long white piqué dress [a close-textured fabric made from silk, cotton or spun rayon woven with ribs going lengthways] which must have been fashionable before World War 1 ... I was ... looking like a real country bumpkin, wet hair pulled back tight, no make-up, an old-fashioned dress, and wearing a pair of the farmer's old boots ... Our cart and the produce were inspected several times by the Germans as we entered Aurillac; they did not give me a second look, even their first glance was rather disdainful. I did not blame them. I did not look very fetching.[31]

In his biography of Wake, Russell Braddon asserted that the dress, which dated from 1890, was borrowed from an elderly lady. He wrote: 'The Germans questioned him [the farmer] and searched his vegetables, but they showed no interest at all in his revolting-looking daughter'.[32] Wake's performance of unglamorous femininity was effective in that her drab appearance meant that she was comparatively invisible. Her one-off performance of a peasant farmer's daughter, which effected obscurity, contrasts with the attention that performances of middle-class femininity received. For many of the agents, the codes of middle-class femininity became associated with visibility, while those of working-class femininity were linked to invisibility. (Yet, as we have seen, third-class passengers on trains were more likely to be searched than first-class.) In her peasant attire, with her hair deliberately lank and without any trace of make-up, Wake was read as uncouth and unrefined. Her lack of glamour held no fascination for the guards on duty at the controls and, as a result, she was less noticeable, enabling her to pass successfully.

Stereotypes of the alluring female spy seducing her enemy, epitomised by Mata Hari, the Dutch-born exotic dancer and courtesan who worked for both the French and the Germans during the First World War, might suggest that performances of glamour would always work and were the key to passing as the cases of conventionally attractive women who were not suspected of engaging in paramilitary tasks suggests. Although this was sometimes the case, there is also evidence to suggest that in some instances glamour would have been inappropriate and unsuccessful. Indeed, auto/biographical evidence suggests that almost every type of femininity was employed by female agents to pass: glamour, quotidian, lack of glamour, chic/urban and peasant/rural femininities. Agents had to select what they and their colleagues believed to be the most suitable performance of femininity for the specific circumstances in which they were working because choosing inappropriate modes of femininity could have led to capture. Appearance was thus crucial in constructing different identities and, although the objective was to pass as a law-abiding civilian woman, the strategies to effect this were diverse.

Femininity as conduct

Female agents also found that crucial to their heterosexual perform-ances, which hinged upon the effect of the physical appearance of female agents on German soldiers, were both flirtation and physical frailty. Theorist Susan Brownmiller asserted: 'Feminine armour is never metal or muscle but, paradoxically, an exaggeration of physical vulnerability that is reassuring (unthreatening) to men'.[33] Memoirs, biographies and oral histories of veterans provide numerous tales of female agents who stimu-lated chivalrous behaviour from German soldiers, who unknowingly transported suitcases containing radio sets and weapons across borders or past checkpoints. The slight physique and attractive appearance of Claire Everett enabled her to take advantage of the conventional correlation of femininity with physical weakness. On numerous occasions, German soldiers assisted her from trains and carried her bags through controls: 'Ask for help if you want to bring your suitcase down. Don't try and do it by yourself if there's a German chap there. Ask him, "Would you mind bringing down my heavy suitcase for me?" It just seemed the natural thing to do'.[34] The naturalness of this mundane strategy was confirmed in my interview with Lise de Baissac, who recalled: 'Once in a train, a German officer helped me to put my suitcase on the rack and I had things in it. But I mean it was part of ordinary life. It was not important'.[35]

The SOE files also referred to German soldiers' unconscious assistance in conveying Resistance materials: 'In most cases women were used for this work [couriering] as German controls were generally less strict with them than with men. Especially during the first two years of the occupa-tion, there are many examples of German officers and NCOs unwittingly assisting women couriers through controls by carrying the compromising material for them'.[36]

There is an interesting tension between the performance of physical frailty and the mental strength that such performances required in order to be successful. Agents' performances of fragility suggest that they were exactly what they were not; they *did* fragility when it was thought to be necessary or useful in order to accomplish their tasks in relative safety and not because they *were* fragile. There is a contradiction at the heart of such performances: female agents' power could ironically be vested in performances of physical weakness. Duping German soldiers into assisting with bags was made possible by female agents' invoking traditional feminine behaviour by demonstrating helplessness and reliance on others, combined with a feminine appearance. By asking a German soldier to carry her baggage, a female agent elicited traditionally masculine behaviour from the soldier. Paradoxically, the much-used strategy of requesting assistance from German guards overturned conventional gender norms, despite seemingly reinforcing them.

How their performances were interpreted were to a certain degree out of their control. German soldiers might recognise that these were performances and thus their displays were gambles which did not guarantee protection. A retrospective analysis of the performances of femininity recollected by women who survived the war suggests that these enactments were always successful and yet it is important to emphasise that, at the moment of undertaking these displays, female agents did not know whether they were going to be effective or not. Their selection of a mode of femininity from a vast range was a risk but it was considered by most as worth the gamble because it offered greater opportunities to pass.

Flirtation was a further strategy employed by female agents. Their flirtatious behaviour was consolidated by the signifiers of ideal femininity: hair, clothing and appearance. Beverley Skeggs claimed that flirtation involves an amalgam of the reproduction of conventional femininity (in particular passivity, helplessness and reliance on others), the stretching of traditional femininity (exemplified by the direct engaging in conversation), and the reproduction of heterosexuality.[37] Displays of physical weakness, active seeking of assistance and heterosexual appearance and behaviour facilitated their flirtation with German guards. Many performances involved the projection of conventionally feminine appearance and heterosexual flirtation that could turn precarious situations to women's advantage. Richard Heslop recollected in his autobiography: 'It is wonderful what a flashing eye or a cheeky smile can do to evade a search or a dangerous moment.'[38] A friendly disposition coupled with an attractive appearance could certainly disarm soldiers much more effectively than the strategies employed by male agents, as Claire Everett explained:

> You just react to the moment and think, I'll get by alright with a nice smile.
> I just sort of smiled and waved to them. All the time. Women could get
> by with a smile and do things that men couldn't and no matter what you

had hidden in your handbag or your bicycle bag, if you had a nice smile, you know, just give them a little wink. It just happened constantly, all the time. So I got away with it. It becomes sort of second nature … You did that [flirted] automatically. Absolutely. That was just par for the course. Just sort of went into the role automatically, just quite naturally.[39]

Written accounts of SOE agents' wartime experiences also relate episodes of flirtatious encounters with German soldiers, as the following extract from the biography of Nancy Wake illustrated: "'I played the part of a giddy Frenchwoman who didn't give a bugger what happened in the war", Nancy recalls frankly. "I was a *good-time girl*. I used to give Germans a date sometimes, sometimes three or four if I was away on a long trip and give them a little bit of hope. I played the part – I should have been an actress."'[40] Wake was not the only agent to arrange meetings with German soldiers in order to successfully negotiate checkpoints. Beryl Escott illustrates the successful use of flirtation in her narration of an episode involving Paddy O'Sullivan. She was cycling down a country lane with her radio set in her bicycle basket when she observed two German soldiers at a checkpoint:

> Putting on her most sunny and beguiling smile, she rode boldly up to the two men, one of whom liked the look of her advanced some way up the road to meet her. She stopped and leaning on her bike, chatted animatedly with him. Flattered by her friendly attitude, he asked her to meet him for a drink … the other German awaited her, and while he examined her papers, she laid herself out to be just as delightful to him, consequently so bemusing him also that he completely forgot to examine her case, while excited by the notion of making his own assignation with her for that same evening … It had been a very close shave, only carried off by consummate acting and the brazen use of her charms.[41]

The exchange between the German soldiers and O'Sullivan illustrates the powerful and effective use of conventionally feminine appearance, coupled with appropriate feminine behaviour. Escott's couching of the episode in terms of 'putting on', 'carried off', 'consummate acting' and 'brazen use' emphasises the performative nature of femininity and illuminates O'Sullivan's agency. She made this explicit elsewhere: 'All the girls would have found it difficult to carry out their missions unless they had been consummate actresses, studying each new person that they were to become and slipping into it like a character on the stage.'[42] O'Sullivan's show of femininity was an acting out of a performance which protected her from a potentially dangerous situation. She took the initiative by cycling confidently up to the German soldiers and actively seeking their attention. She played on the soldiers' heterosexual interest in her, enabling her to avert their gaze from her basket containing the wireless set and to outwit them.

The tactic of accepting engagements with German soldiers when in precarious situations has also been captured in filmic accounts of agents' experiences. The film *Carve Her Name with Pride* depicts the heroine accepting two dinner invitations with an Oberstführer, a high-ranking German official, neither of which she keeps.[43] The treatment of feminine performances in the documentary *School for Danger*, starring SOE agents, Harry Rée and Jacqueline Nearne as Felix and Cat, is quite different to that in *Carve Her Name with Pride*:

> *Cat* – The police were searching luggage at the station. They made me open my suitcases.
> *Felix* – Gosh -what did you do?
> *Cat* – I tried sex appeal.
> *Felix* – Did it work?
> *Cat* – No, it was a complete flop! I had to open it.
> *Felix* – What about the WT set?
> *Cat* – I told them with a sweet smile that it was an X-ray machine.
> *Felix* – It must have been a very sweet smile for them to have swallowed that![44]

In contrast to other related texts, such as SOE documents and auto/biographies, which identify successful performances of femininity, this documentary downplays their effectiveness. The audience does not witness Cat's performance first-hand but rather we see a reconstruction of the event when she informs Felix. This serves to de-emphasise her strategy, which is further dismissed by her claim that her performance was unsuccessful; she was compelled to open her suitcase despite her feminine performance. Nevertheless, it could be argued that her enactment of femininity was successful in that her smile stimulated a reaction and she was able to persuade the policeman that her suitcase contained a piece of medical apparatus. There is, then, ambivalence to this aspect of the SOE image in *School for Danger*. The documentary offered a down-to-earth, unglamorous account of the SOE which also omitted the romance between the two central characters that later audiences of *Odette*, *Carve Her Name with Pride* and, more recently, *Charlotte Gray* have come to expect.[45] That *School for Danger* was the official, government-sanctioned documentary of the SOE's F Section might suggest that acknowledgement of feminine performances was considered unsuitable for public consumption. Yet the performance of Cat's flirtation was evidently too central to the construction of a female agent for the documentary to dismiss altogether.

Both filmic and personal accounts, then, suggest that female agents found it productive to flirt and be responsive to German soldiers' advances in an attempt to avoid potentially dangerous situations. However, undertaking a flirtatious performance was not infallible and, on some occasions, female agents were arrested in spite of their enactments. Courier Sonya Butt, who had found flirting highly productive on numerous occasions, discovered that her flirtatious manner did not save her from imprisonment. As she was walking down a country road in mid-1944, she was stopped by two German soldiers who demanded to see her papers. Despite 'flashing her most charming smile',[46] she was taken to a cell while her papers were checked. After several hours, she was released without an explanation. This episode indicates that a smile was not necessarily a safeguard against arrest and suggests that the heightened sensitivity on the part of Germans, due to the increasing possibility of defeat, meant that by 1944 women were no longer entirely beyond suspicion: the 'natural' cover they possessed had ceased to be an unqualified advantage by this point.

Non-feminine norm

Female agents selected from these various strategies to assist their passing as civilian women. These special displays of femininity were intermittent and transitory, only undertaken when situations necessitated, as Yvonne Baseden made clear: 'It only came to the fore when it was necessary. I didn't live like that all the time. I popped in and out of it when I had to, which wasn't very often.'[47] So what was the 'reality' when female agents were not performing femininity in order to pass? Were there other kinds of gender performance that female agents undertook?

Nancy Wake, who on occasions performed drab peasant femininity as well as glamour, lived among seven thousand male comrades on the hillsides of the Auvergne, wearing khaki trousers, shirt, tie and beret, as well as army boots. Evenings were spent sitting round the fire, swigging whisky, having drinking competitions (which she asserted that she always won), swearing, raucously singing and playing cards with her male colleagues. This was certainly no place for deliberate performances of femininity. During the daytime, she would go on reconnaissance, ambush German troops or train men in weapons. On one occasion, Wake attacked the local Gestapo Headquarters at Montluçon, running into the room throwing her grenades before retreating. Wake also played a prominent role in the blowing up of a bridge over the Allier river. With the explosives strapped to them, she and four men climbed down the struts of the bridge to set the explosives in place. Wake also participated in sabotaging an armaments and munitions store in Mont Mouchet. When she went to disable a sentry, he heard her and a struggle ensued. His bayonet penetrated her arm but this did not impede her as she used her bare hands to kill him. She told me:

> Tardivat [a Resistance colleague] said, 'She is the most feminine woman I have ever met in my life, but in battle she's worth ten men'. So I changed. I was feminine but fighting. All I wanted to do was to kill Germans. I didn't give a bugger about them, to kill Germans. Didn't care about it. I hated, I loathed the Germans. I loathed them. As far as I was concerned, the only good one was a dead one and I don't care what anybody thinks of me. A dead German![48]

Wake's assertion that she was 'feminine but fighting' emphasises that femininity could also be belligerent. She dispels the myth that women are innately pacifist by asserting that she relished killing German soldiers and experienced no remorse for doing so. Her admission of hatred and loathing for the Germans and the manner in which it was said were quite startling. The unequivocal remark 'the only good one was a dead one' was spoken without passion, in a cool, calculated manner. From 'I hated, I loathed the Germans' to 'I don't care what anybody thinks of me', Wake's voice remained dispassionate and deliberate. The short, emphatic 'a dead German!' at the end of this statement, accompanied by a decisive nod of the head, gave closure to the topic of conversation. She appears to have had no moral compunction about ending the lives of dozens of Germans and states that other people's assessment of her ruthlessness had no effect upon her. Wake's lived reality was thus more in keeping with what is conventionally regarded as masculine behaviour.

Although Wake was by no means representative of the female agents, her experiences illustrate that, while enactments of femininity were infrequent performances contrived to facilitate passing, the everyday 'reality' required something closer to masculine performances from her. The actuality for female wireless operators, such as Yvonne Baseden and Yvonne Cormeau, was much more mundane than the tense excitement provoked by performing femininity in such ways: hours sat at the radio coding, decoding, receiving and transmitting messages were more typical of their usual daily work. For them, the inconspicuous conduct of tedious technical work demanded little in the way of deliberate performances of gender identities. Their task was simply to do their job and pass in the local community with as little fuss as possible.

Conclusion

An examination of textual accounts makes apparent that femininities, which were strategic and empowering, could be mobilised by female agents to avert discovery and to facilitate passing: for many, femininity was, indeed, the 'best disguise'. Different circumstances called for performances of different types of femininity. On some occasions, female agents courted danger for the greater protection it might offer: drawing attention to their chic, urban appearance and flirtatious behaviour and thereby attracting the attention of German soldiers in order that the enemy would unwittingly give protection and safe passage. However, it was not always appropriate to opt for urban glamour and, in other situations, understated displays of rural femininity or even unglamorous, peasant femininity were considered more appropriate to blending into the surrounding scene and being less visible. Female agents therefore had to be very adept at choosing the guise of femininity that they would display: how they comported themselves, their posture, accent, behaviour, clothing and hairstyle were all crucial in the performance of specific modes of femininity, but were not necessarily appropriate to all situations.

The gendered passing performances enacted by both male and female combatants which the last two chapters have examined had life and death consequences. The success of these strategies became even more crucial following captivity, as the next chapter demonstrates.

Notes

1 National Archives, HS 7/66.
2 National Archives, HS 7/66.
3 Correspondence with Duncan Stuart.
4 Churchill, *Duel of Wits*, p. 206.
5 Thomas, *No Banners*, p. 174.
6 Personal interview with Francis Cammaerts.
7 Personal interview with Sydney Hudson.
8 Wake, *The Autobiography of the Woman the Gestapo Called The White Mouse*, p. 134. Wake was critical of the bedraggled appearance of the actress who played her in the Australian mini-series: 'Looking as she did, that girl would *never* have got through the German control points!' E. Grice, 'Return of the White Mouse', *Daily Telegraph*, 7 June 1994.
9 National Archives, HS 7/66.
10 Personal interview with Lise de Baissac.
11 Heslop, *Xavier*, p. 165.

12 B. Skeggs, *Formations of Class and Gender: Becoming Respectable* (London: Sage, 1997), p. 110.

13 Personal interview with Lise de Baissac.

14 Skeggs, *Formations*, p. 110.

15 National Archives, HS 7/66.

16 National Archives, HS 9/314.

17 IWM SA, 9478 Hallowes.

18 Fitzsimons, *Nancy Wake*, pp. 236–7.

19 Fitzsimons, *Nancy Wake*, p. 239. Author's emphasis.

20 J. Berger, *Ways of Seeing* (London: BBC, 1975), p. 46.

21 Jones, *A Quiet Courage*, pp. 232–3.

22 Personal interview with Claire Everett (pseudonym).

23 Personal interview with Yvonne Baseden.

24 Walters, *Moondrop to Gascony*, p. 52.

25 Walters, *Moondrop to Gascony*, p. 44.

26 HS 6/568, National Archives.

27 7369 Cormeau, IWM SA.

28 National Archives, HS 6/568.

29 Walters, *Moondrop to Gascony*, p. 35.

30 National Archives, HS 6/576.

31 Wake, *The White Mouse*, pp. 132–3.

32 Braddon, *Nancy Wake*, pp. 182–3.

33 S. Brownmiller, *Femininity* (London: Hamish Hamilton Ltd, 1984), p. 51.

34 Personal interview with Claire Everett (pseudonym).

35 Personal interview with Lise de Baissac.

36 National Archives, HS 7/66.

37 Skeggs, *Formations*, p. 128.

38 Heslop, *Xavier*, p. 165.

39 Personal interview with Claire Everett (pseudonym).

40 Fitzsimons, *Nancy Wake*, p. 111. Author's emphasis.

41 Escott, *Mission Improbable*, pp. 169–70.

42 Escott, *Mission Improbable*, p. 232.

43 BFI film script S13981.

44 Film script, Box 10 Item 5, Thurold Dickinson Collection, BFI.

45 The omission of the romantic plot was also noticed by at least one contemporary reviewer: 'They recklessly disobey the first commandment in the Goldwyn Decalogue, and neither kiss nor show the faintest sign of wishing to kiss.' R. Mortimer, *The New Statesman and Nation* (15 February 1947).

46 Escott, *Mission Improbable*, p. 211.

47 Personal interview with Yvonne Baseden.

48 Personal interview with Nancy Wake.

7

'Pretending at once':
passing performances in captivity

This chapter analyses veterans' retrospective reconstructions of their captivity, which offers an opportunity to explore the experiences of those whose passing was exposed. Analysis of the penalties levied on those who assume alternative personae and are found out is crucial in order to be able to fully understand the risks that were run by passing subjects. Of the 441 male agents sent to France, over one hundred were arrested and incarcerated in French prisons and seventeen of the thirty-nine women experienced long-term captivity. Agents were captured as a result of bad security, bad luck, betrayal and direction-finding technology. Interestingly, there is little evidence to suggest that SOE agents were captured because they made an error which caused a slippage in their attempts at passing and exposed their British paramilitary identities. Because ninety-three agents who were infiltrated into France never returned, the circumstances of the arrest of many of those who were captured are unknown. It is impossible therefore to know whether many agents were arrested as a result of slips in passing. The only example found was an account provided by Maurice Buckmaster of an incident in which one agent accidentally looked right when crossing a busy road. Traffic braked, she stumbled back on to the kerb and unwittingly became the centre of attention. Unluckily, an astute Gestapo agent had witnessed her blunder, deduced the reason for her actions and arrested her.[1] As there are no other references to this incident and the identity of the agent to whom Buckmaster is referring is not disclosed, this might simply be a cautionary tale or apocryphal story to alert the post-war public of the dangers to which SOE agents were exposed. That only one reference could be found

Table 1 Fate of F Section agents deported to concentration camps

	Men	Women	Total
Sent to France	441	39	480
Total number deported	104	15	119
Survived camps	23	3	26
Total number of deaths in captivity	81	12	93
Died as a result of treatment received in captivity	12	2	14
Executed	69	10	79

Source: Calculated from the 'Roll of Honour' in John Sainsbury, *The F Section Memorial* (London: Hart Books, 1992).

to a passing indiscretion leading to arrest might suggest that the passing in itself was successful. This may have been due to the filtering process of recruitment, the instructions of the SOE trainers and headquarters staff, the corrective shock of initial passing errors such as speaking in English and the advice offered in the field by established agents and resisters. It might also have been due to the quality of the performances of the agents themselves.

Following arrest, some prisoners were fortunate to escape or be released: Blanche Charlet managed to escape from Castres prison with fifty-one inmates on 16 September 1943; Sydney Hudson broke out from his French-run prison in Villeneuve-sur-Lot with about fifty others on 3 January 1944 having been imprisoned for fifteen months; Arthur Staggs was released in February 1944 because of lack of evidence and was told by the Gestapo: 'We thought that you were a British parachutist!';[2] Mary Herbert, who had had a baby with her SOE organiser, which put a stop to her clandestine work, was released after two months because of the lack of evidence to link her with the previous (SOE) occupant of the flat at which she was staying; and Francis Cammaerts was released three hours before his execution in the summer of 1944 when his courier Christine Granville audaciously told the German officer in charge that she was a British agent, asserted that the Americans, whose arrival was imminent, would arrest him as a war criminal and demanded to know how much the release of Cammaerts would cost. However, these few examples are exceptional and in total, 119 agents were deported from French prisons to concentration camps. Ninety-three of these deportees did not survive incarceration, fourteen of whom died from malnutrition, starvation and disease as a result of the conditions of the camps. Yvonne Rudellat, for example, witnessed Belsen's liberation on 15 April 1945 but was one of the 14,000 people who died of starvation and typhus in the following week while awaiting repatriation. Seventy-nine agents were executed either by being shot, given lethal injections of phenol or garrotted on a piece of piano wire which prolonged suffocation. Of the 119 sent to the camps, only three women and twenty-three men returned.

Passing during captivity

The importance of SOE agents being mis/taken for French civilians so that they could do their clandestine work without being arrested has been emphasised throughout. Following their capture, it might be presumed that they no longer needed to conceal the fact that they were British agents. Certainly, many ceased to pass as French and informed their interrogators of their affiliation to a British organisation. For example, following her arrest in April 1943, Odette Sansom did not try to conceal her SOE identity from her interrogators. Instead, she pretended that she was married to Peter Churchill, her organiser, and alleged that he was the British Prime Minister's nephew. Thus, Sansom courted danger for the greater protection that it might offer in the belief that the Germans would execute neither Churchill nor herself but rather use them as diplomatic prisoners who could later be exchanged for high-ranking Germans who had been caught by the British. This would appear to have been a successful assumption, confirmed by a remark to Churchill made by the Abwehr agent who had arrested them: 'What would you say to the idea of being exchanged for Rudolf Hess? … The closer your relationship with Winston Churchill, the further your distance from the firing squad.'[3] Moreover, although Sansom was deported to Ravensbrück concentration camp, she was held in solitary confinement and, immediately prior to its liberation on 30 April 1945, the camp commandant Fritz Suhren still believing Sansom to be related to Winston Churchill, drove her to the American lines and tried to plea-bargain with American officials.

While Sansom and many others did not dissimulate their paramilitary identities, it becomes apparent from the limited material available that several agents continued to pass after their arrest because they recognised that their best chance of survival would be to hide their SOE identity and take on alternative personae. If it became known that they were British agents working for the SOE, they would almost certainly have been executed as the Geneva Conventions concerning prisoners of war did not protect them. Hence, incarceration required a different form of passing. For example, Yvonne Baseden, who was arrested in June 1944 following operation CADILLAC, the first daylight drop of arms, kept to her story that she was a local shorthand typist who had become involved with members of the regional Resistance group. Because Baseden was caught having a meal with her fellow Resistance comrades following the operation, rather than being captured at her wireless set, she was able to pass as a local Frenchwoman. The Gestapo were unaware that she was a wireless operator for some time: 'I implied that I was just another French Resistance worker with a group of people and I was helping them ... There was nothing very much pinned to me, so to speak, except being with a group of French resistants.'[4] She was then taken to be interrogated: 'In all fairness I wasn't put to any form of distress, if you like, till someone who had been arrested said I was a radio operator and probably come from England.'[5] Following that information, the Gestapo began to implement harsher interrogations to coerce Baseden to send a transmission to England. Despite the efforts of her interrogators to try and catch her out by speaking English to her and by observing her reactions while showing her a book illustrated with pictures of HQ staff of various British organisations to see whether there were any she recognised, she continued to affirm that she was French. Consequently, the Gestapo were unable to prove that she was a British agent and she was deported to Ravensbrück as 'Marie Bernier', a French political prisoner. Thus, despite being arrested, Baseden managed to continue to successfully pass as a French national.

Some agents who persisted in passing following capture chose identities that were gender-specific. Male agents and members of the French Resistance who were arrested while undertaking non-Resistance acts could hope to conceal their clandestine identities by pretending to be black-marketeers in the hope that they would shortly be released with a reprimand. Guido Zembsch-Schreve attended a rendezvous in March 1944 because his courier was unable to attend. He was warned by a prostitute that the meeting was a trap and upon meeting his contact, Zembsch-Schreve immediately pretended to be a black-marketeer as this was a lesser crime than resisting: 'I said to the [Abwehr] agent that I was a black-marketeer who off and on did a job for one or the other if they wanted me to deliver a parcel ... That I was a black-marketeer first, that I hated people who were active from the Resistance.'[6] By passing as a black-marketeer, Zembsch-Schreve thought that the Abwehr would not realise that they had captured the head of a successful Resistance network. To build on this, he also pretended to dislike Bolsheviks as he was aware that most Nazis were virulently anti-communist. By concealing his paramilitary identity, he improved his chances of survival. Although this strategy was successful for some time, Zembsch-Schreve was eventually handed over to the Gestapo, who were more rigorous than the Abwehr. Zembsch-Schreve, who concealed the fact that he could speak German, overheard his captors make several remarks including 'This isn't the man we're after', 'he's of minor interest' and he's 'only a little fish',[7] which suggested that they believed his cover story. Nevertheless, because he was suspected of knowing something about Resistance activities, Zembsch-Schreve was accused of being a terrorist, brutally tortured and threatened with execution. Following an interrogation in which he was beaten and endured the 'baignoire' or bath, in which his head was repeatedly immersed in cold water until he almost drowned, he overheard the interrogating officer state: 'I reckon he's telling the truth.'[8] In spite of this declaration of belief in Zembsch-Schreve's story, further interrogations ensued. He kept to his cover story and his paramilitary identity was never exposed.

Like Zembsch-Schreve, Bob Sheppard and fellow SOE agent Edward Zeff also instantaneously resolved to conceal their clandestine identities when they were arrested in March 1943 while crossing the Pyrenees, having been betrayed by their guide. Sheppard recalled how they opted to pass as British airmen:

> We acted. We pretended at once to be pilots of the Royal Air Force. Could only speak English. We didn't know anything. And it went on rather well with the German Army who arrested us. They treated us as two pilots and then we were sent up to Paris to the prison at Fresnes ... Two or three interrogations with the German police and Gestapo. It went on well ... Then I was called back to the Gestapo with a car ... and they took me to the cellar first and opened the door and I saw Ted Zeff, face broken, poor state, and he told me in English, 'They know all about it.' And then I turned round and I said, 'Qu'est ce qu'on peut dire d'autre?' in French. 'What can I say then?' and they started my interrogation.[9]

The Germans were aware of the existence of escape lines which had been established throughout France by resisters to enable Allied airmen to return to Britain and rejoin their squadrons. Thus, Sheppard's and Zeff's ploy of passing as RAF pilots had a chance of being successful and, initially, their ruse worked. When the Gestapo agents extracted a confession from Zeff, passing ceased to be an option for Sheppard as his identity had been exposed.

In contrast to the relative leniency shown to those regarded as wartime criminals by the Nazis such as black-marketeers or to Allied airmen, individuals who were identified as British agents were kept in solitary confinement in French prisons, taken on a daily basis for interrogations which often included physical torture, given the label 'Nacht und Nebel', meaning 'Night and Fog', which constituted a death sentence, and deported to concentration camps, where they were overworked, starved and mistreated, and from which they were not expected to return. The deliberate maltreatment of SOE agents was enshrined in a document written by Heinrich Himmler, the head of the SS, which noted: 'The agents should die, certainly, but not before torture, indignity and interrogation had drained from them that last shred and scintilla of evidence which should lead to the arrest of others. Then, and only then, should the blessed release of death be granted to them.'[10] These agents who believed that it was advantageous to attempt to conceal the fact that they were British agents were proved retrospectively to have followed the right course.

Occupations like airmen and black-marketeers were either exclusively or predominantly undertaken by men so they were not appropriate cover for female agents. Acting out a vacuous femininity was one of the few options available. The numerous examples of women undertaking performances of naivety and innocence suggest that women themselves felt they had no other recourse. We have already seen that performances of types of femininity could benefit female agents in dangerous situations. Their strategies following arrest were often a continuation of this. Female agents' endeavours not to reveal themselves as SOE combatants while in captivity were often accomplished through feigning ignorance and naivety as noted in a report: 'A woman agent "admitted" to having been engaged in subversive activity, but said she had gone into it with her eyes closed and, at first, had no idea of what she was doing. Later, when she did realise, she was afraid to give it up. In this way, she was able to represent herself as having been locally recruited, when in fact she was a parachuted agent.'[11] This anonymous female agent was able to play upon stereotypically feminine traits, such as foolishness, innocence, lack of common sense, anxiousness and timidity, in order to fool her captors into believing she was a local Frenchwoman who had become mixed up in something she did not understand.

This woman was not the only female SOE agent to choose this strategy. When direction-finding vans picked up a signal indicating where Brian Stonehouse was operating his set in October 1942, twenty-four-year-old Stonehouse (who was homosexual) and forty-two-year-old courier Blanche Charlet quickly made the decision to pretend to be lovers. Stonehouse recollected that he was clad in his dressing gown and 'so we sat down and started kissing like mad, pretending we were having a thing.'[12] Stonehouse undertook a performance of heterosexuality to facilitate both his and Charlet's passing as law-abiding civilians. However, the WT set was soon located and both Charlet and Stonehouse were arrested. Upon her return to Britain following her successful escape from prison, she was debriefed. This report indicates that her tactics for concealing her British identity were all clearly gendered: she concocted elaborate stories about lovers, feigned ignorance of the political consequences of her resistance and pretended to faint. Initially, she denied having connections to the Resistance but eventually the Gestapo discovered her codename: 'Informant was asked if she was really Christiane. She pretended to faint and, when she recovered, pretended to play the part of a stupid woman who had wanted to play her glorious part in the Resistance but knew nothing about it.'[13] Confronted with her codename, Charlet admitted to being involved in the Resistance but created the impression that she had little knowledge of what the work entailed. Feigning faintness and pretending to be ignorant proved successful as it tapped into long-standing (Nazi) assumptions that women were too emotional to be involved in political activities.

Eileen Nearne, who was caught at her wireless set in July 1944, also created the impression that she was imprudent and unaware of the political implications of her involvement. James Gleeson, a journalist who interviewed her in the 1950s, maintained that she fooled her interrogators by claiming that she was 'a bit of a scatterbrain and tomboy' 'who was helping the Resistance for fun and excitement.'[14] M. R. D. Foot noted that Nearne 'put on her act of being a sweet little thing who knew nothing she ought not'[15] and that, consequently, she 'brought off a dexterous bluff, and persuaded the Gestapo she was only a foolish little shopgirl who had taken up Resistance work because it was exciting; they never discovered she was half-English.'[16] This was a gendered strategy that was open only to women. Nearne had been informed by her training instructors that she was a good liar and found that during interrogations she could improvise plausible explanations and remain calm: 'All sorts of things I pulled from my head. And the more I was lying, the more I wanted to and the more it was easy coming to me.'[17] It was her conscious strategy 'to act confusion and misunderstanding'.[18] This was a ploy of which she had much experience. Maisie McLintock, a FANY coder who had been close friends with Nearne throughout their FANY training, recalled several episodes when Nearne had deliberately disobeyed rules, such as having baths after hours. McLintock recollected that when confronted by her FANY superiors, Nearne would always 'play the daft lassie' by pretending not to understand and she asserted that Nearne had employed this strategy once arrested:

> She was very clever, I think. It explained a lot when she survived the Germans and that concentration camp using the same method as she had done when she was a FANY. Wide-eyed innocence ... One of the first things she said when she was telling me about her experience, she was taken to the Avenue Foch in Paris, that was where she got her preliminary going over, and she said, 'You see, Mac, I did what you said, I played the daft lassie with them' ... She was still getting through life somehow, looking innocent and not quite sure why she was there.[19]

Nearne tried to alleviate the seriousness of the situation by performing a particular type of femininity. Feigning innocence and naivety was a way of removing suspicion: Gestapo agents were unlikely to believe that a foolish, childlike and unsophisticated young woman was a British agent. Moreover, by pretending to crave excitement and fun, Nearne depoliticised her Resistance involvement which further distanced her from her British paramilitary identity. Interestingly, Nearne decided to plead her innocence, claiming she was unaware of the Resistance, despite being caught at her wireless set and found to possess a weapon. The decision to perform in such a stereotypically feminine manner was not then always dependent upon the limited extent of the captor's knowledge of their involvement in the Resistance.

This practice suggests that several female agents followed gendered conventions by pretending to be vulnerable and naive. This appeared to them to be the strategy most likely to succeed, partly perhaps because of the success that they had had while operational. Thus, despite undermining conventional gender norms by undertaking a paramilitary role, captured female agents often tried to manipulate their interrogators by resorting to gender stereotypes and exploiting their perceived femininity. Although agents' passing undoubtedly saved some from being identified as SOE agents and executed as 'foreign spies', their performances in themselves neither precipitated their release nor protected them from torture.

Gendered torture

Before being despatched to France, agents were aware of the dangers they would face. Vera Atkins, F Section's Intelligence Officer, asserted: 'They knew if they were arrested they were likely to receive very rough treatment.'[20] In their testimonies, those who were mistreated recounted being beaten with implements, kicked, toenails being extracted, toes being trampled upon by boots, chained to furniture, deprived of sleep and made to remain awake during lengthy interrogation sessions, denied light, food and medical treatment, threatened with mock executions, fingers being crushed, immersed in water to the point of drowning, burned with hot pokers, hearing others being tortured or shot, subjected to electric currents surging through their bodies and being kept in solitary confinement. Agents sustained numerous injuries, such as broken ribs, fractured fingers, teeth being knocked out, bruises and cuts as the Gestapo were eager to extract information about colleagues, arms dumps and wireless codes by any means possible.

Given that some women enjoyed success with their performances of vulnerability, it might be presumed that women were treated differently than men by the Gestapo. Certainly, some female agents, such as Blanche Charlet and Violette Szabo, were not tortured. However, this is not to say that while all their male colleagues were tortured, female agents were spared. Evidence from veterans' testimonies suggests that once captured, women were not automatically shielded from torture because of their sex and, similarly, not all male agents experienced abuse. Women were just as likely to endure physical mistreatment as their male colleagues. Certainly, the three female SOE agents who were repatriated from concentration camps all experienced physical torture, as well as several other forms of mistreatment. All were beaten. In addition, Odette Sansom had her toenails extracted and a poker laid on her spine, Eileen Nearne experienced the 'baignoire' and Yvonne Baseden endured her bare toes being trampled upon by guards in army boots and a mock execution was staged. Indeed, the violence inflicted upon women's bodies by male interrogators was often gender-based. Personal testimonies indicate that female political prisoners experienced punishment with distinct sexist and sexual overtones. The torture meted out by Gestapo interrogators was often directed against body parts associated with female sexuality which might suggest that women were seemingly being punished by the Gestapo for transgressing their allotted gender role by participating in the masculine task of combat. Testimonies of locally-recruited French Resistance workers note that some women had electric currents run through their nipples, electrodes inserted into their vaginas, their nails extracted, their breasts severed and some were raped by guards.

The rape of civilian women has been used as a weapon of war in many conflicts and is commonly perceived as 'accepted' soldierly behaviour: about two million women in eastern Germany were raped by Soviet soldiers in 1945, which in part led to the 1949 Geneva Conventions which explicitly forbade rape. Despite this legal prohibition, sexual violence perpetrated by soldiers continues to occur: the rape of Vietnamese women by American GIs was, according to one soldier, 'an everyday affair; you can nail just about everybody on that – at least once'.[21] The rape of Bengali women by Pakistani soldiers in 1971 during the Bangladesh war of independence, the ethnic cleansing campaign embarked upon by Serbian and Croatian soldiers in ex-Yugoslavia which involved the rape of female Bosnian Muslims and the rape of Kuwaiti women by Iraqi troops in 1990 confirm Cynthia Enloe's assertion that sexual violence during war is symptomatic of its gendered nature.[22]

There was widespread sexual mistreatment of women by German soldiers during the Second World War. SOE agent Edgar Hargreaves, who served in Yugoslavia until his capture in 1943, recalled that in his interrogation sessions in Belgrade he was forced to observe the sexual mistreatment of female prisoners: 'I saw a number of occasions, girls particularly were brought in and they were always stripped and raped and I saw one girl having her nipples cut off. That was much, much worse than anything that ever happened to oneself.'[23] He considered that he was treated better than partisan women who were both physically mutilated and sexually abused. Evidence from women who befriended female SOE agents during captivity indicates that some of the women who were executed experienced sexual intimidation. A documentary about Violette Szabo featured a woman who had shared a cell with her in Limoges immediately following her capture. Resistance worker Hugette Desore recalled that Szabo had told her that an SS man had put his pistol into her neck, said he could kill her tomorrow if he so desired and then raped her.[24] This abuse of power by male guards was clearly not an exception. There is some evidence to suggest that Noor Inayat Khan was raped the night that she was shot[25] and two of the three women who survived deportation recollected intimidating moments. Yvonne Baseden recounted one occasion when she thought that she was going to be raped: 'I felt a threat once … I was in solitary confinement at the time and somehow or other I had a feeling that there was something afoot to possibly try to get me down into the cellars by two or three of the guards. But this is something I vaguely understood through their shouting and things like that. Certainly nothing like that happened. I wasn't raped.'[26]

The sexual intimidation experienced by Odette Sansom is alluded to in the film *Odette* in which a scene shows Neagle, with her open blouse revealing an undergarment, being scrutinised by three male interrogators

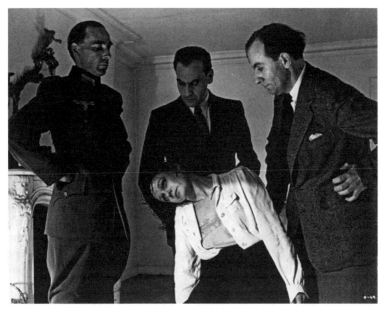

5 Captured female agents were sexually vulnerable as depicted by Anna Neagle in an interrogation scene from the film *Odette*, 1950.

(see Figure 5). The film is based on the biography by Jerrard Tickell who had access to various official documents and interviewed members of the SS and Sansom herself. In the biography, Tickell claims that the interrogator's assistant 'began leisurely to unbutton her blouse. She said, "I resent your hands on me or on my clothes. If you tell me what to do and release one hand, I will do it." "As you wish, unbutton your blouse."' Having been burnt by a poker on her spine, she was then told to remove her stockings and her toenails were extracted. 'To be tortured by this clean, soap-smelling, scented Nordic was one thing. To be touched by his hands was another.' Before her fingernails were removed, a higher-ranking officer stopped the interrogation, but she was warned, 'If you speak about what has happened to a living soul, you will be brought here again and worse things will happen to you.' Tickell concludes his description of this interrogation by writing: 'Though she had kept silent, she was filled with sickness and fear for she had heard of some of the other things that the Gestapo could do to women's bodies.'[27] Sansom appears to have accepted torture as an inevitable and 'appropriate' consequence of her capture but, paradoxically, she also feels vulnerable owing to her femininity. This description of Sansom's interrogation as narrated by Tickell indicates the additional concerns of female captives – or they may, of course, reveal more about his construction of femininity under threat than Sansom's actual experiences.

While rape has been used by soldiers as a weapon of war to reward themselves, to humiliate and emasculate the enemy who cannot protect 'their' women or for purposes of ethnic cleansing, the use of rape by guards had very different motivations. The gender-based violence inflicted upon women arrested for their Resistance activities may have been a way for male guards and interrogators, who perhaps felt emasculated by female prisoners' participation in actions traditionally perceived as masculine, to express their disapproval and to displace their impotence. Women arrested for their Resistance activities were strong, independent women who destabilised conventional notions of what it means to be a woman: weak, dependent, inferior and submissive. Nazi views of ideal femininity, underpinned by the glorification of domesticity in which women's activities were to be limited to *'Kinder, Kirche und Küche'*, were challenged by these women who were active in the public domain. Because of the pervasiveness of an ideology which placed women firmly in the home, it was not surprising that Nazi interrogators perceived that their female captives had transgressed conventional gender boundaries in such an explicit way. Being sexually aggressive was a way to reclaim their masculinity and to refeminise their prisoners.

Sexual violence or the threat of it was used against female political prisoners as a supplementary punishment which suggests that, because women were sexually vulnerable, their experiences of captivity were always tinged with this ominous threat, however vague. In contrast, no male veterans have mentioned this concern in their accounts. Although French interrogators sometimes used sex to humiliate Arab nationalists during the Algerian war in the 1950s, attaching wires to their genitalia and forcing men to masturbate and rape other prisoners, there is scant evidence to indicate that this took place during the Second World War. One possible explanation for the lack of evidence for the sexual abuse of male prisoners is that it is harder for men to discuss such overt challenges to their masculinity. A 1996 ChildLine study focusing upon boys' reticence in talking about abuse noted that while girls had support networks available to them, boys were much more inhibited in confiding in someone because they often felt ashamed that they could not defend themselves, perceived a failure of their masculinity and wondered whether they had unwittingly attracted male sexual attention because they were gay.[28] Moreover, despite hating the abuse after it had occurred, many of the subjects in the study recollected feeling sexual pleasure while it was occurring. There was, then, confusion over arousal and consent which inhibited many in talking about their experiences. These various explanations may account for the absence of rape within the testimonies of male political prisoners – or it simply may not have occurred.

More common were accounts of physical abuse which focused upon signifiers of masculinity, such as the penis and testicles. Edward Yeo-Thomas, who was arrested for his SOE activities and survived incarceration, wrote down his memories of captivity which two biographers used to reconstruct his experiences.[29] He recollected an interrogation session in which two men restrained him, while three others rained blows down on his testicles: 'They concentrated on the most vulnerable part of my anatomy. I could not restrain a scream, the agony was intense and they continued to slam away.'[30] Edgar Hargreaves also recollected an incident during his captivity in which his genitals were the focus of abuse: 'One of the sort of petty but unpleasant things that happened during one of my interrogations, all my clothes had been removed ... [and] one of the Germans was smoking a large cigar and he thought it would be a very amusing thing to come across and stub it out on my penis ... [Later that day, a doctor] put the tip of the syringe into my penis and injected corrosive acid into my bladder.'[31]

In addition to the physical mistreatment of male genitalia, another gendered aspect of interrogation sessions was the use of laughing women to 'unman' male prisoners, to strip them of their dignity and to fracture their morale. Yeo-Thomas was repeatedly immersed in water to the point of drowning while uniformed female clerks looked on: 'I could hear voices, laughs, feminine laughter. What was so funny? Me, of course. I must look a fool, wilting like a doll that has lost its stuffing.'[32] The explicitly gendered experiences of captivity for male and female political prisoners continued within concentration camps.

Passing in concentration camps

Once agents had been interrogated, and either refused to talk or divulged information and had ceased to be of any use to the Germans, they were sent to concentration camps across Nazi-occupied Europe, where it was expected that they would disappear without trace. Seven women, all of whom were known to be British agents, were executed immediately upon arrival: Andrée Borrel, Vera Leigh, Diana Rowden, Noor Inayat Khan, Yolande Beekman, Madeleine Damerment and Eliane Plewman. The other captured agents endured months of camp life, many being executed in the last few months of the war. Most did not pass during their incarceration in concentration camps as it was either unnecessary or impossible. For example, when Bob Sheppard arrived at Saarbrucken, he was handed his camp uniform and a red triangle bearing the initial 'E' for Englander which he had to sew on to his shirt. During the morning roll call, a guard shouted to him, 'Agh. You are the British officer?' which Sheppard confirmed.[33] Attempting to pass would have been futile as Sheppard's badge marked him out as British.

Some agents however, who had successfully passed during their interrogations and who were deported as French nationals, continued to pass throughout their incarceration. This was motivated by the necessity of not being identified as British or by the desire to escape. Yvonne Baseden continued to conceal her British identity and recollected that when she was deported to Germany in September 1944: 'I was just part of a group of French women, which probably saved me in the end.'[34] As a French political prisoner, she was given a red triangle adorned with a black 'F' and the words 'Politischer Franzose' in black. If she had been identified as a British paramilitary, she would probably have shared the fate of Violette Szabo, Denise Bloch and Lilian Rolfe who had also been deported to Ravensbrück and were shot in 1945. Although Baseden met up with them at Saarbrucken on the way to Ravensbrück, she was not with them inside the camp: she neither belonged to the same barrack nor was she on the same work transport. She recollected: 'They were all going off on a transport ... in another part of Germany and I thought I must try and get in with them, which was crazy of course and thank goodness I didn't achieve that. They were not particularly keen. They could see both sides of me going with them.'[35] The inducements for Baseden joining the group were presumably that she would no longer be on her own and would have the support, companionship and protection of fellow SOE comrades. The disincentives were undoubtedly the exposure of her British clandestine identity which she had endeavoured to conceal throughout her interrogations. If Baseden had succeeded in joining her fellow SOE comrades on the transport, it was highly likely that her British identity would have become known. Having decided not to draw attention to herself by asking to be placed on the same work transport as her SOE colleagues, Baseden, according to M. R. D. Foot, 'worked there [in Ravensbrück] as inconspicuously as she could, as a farm labourer under armed guard.'[36] She later worked in the camp hospital where she was equally unassuming. Baseden's survival was a direct result of her passing as a locally-recruited French resister during her interrogation sessions in Dijon and her decision to continue concealing the fact that she was a British agent while imprisoned in Ravensbrück.

Eileen Nearne also met Violette Szabo in Ravensbrück. The following statement by Liane Jones is based on her interview with Nearne:

> Didi warned Violette that she was passing herself off as French. Violette asked her what the Gestapo had done to her and, when Didi told her about the 'baignoire' in the Rue des Saussaies, she was horrified. She told Didi that neither she nor Lilian nor Denise had been tortured, and she advised Didi to change her story and admit her British nationality. 'She said, "You should have said you were English. English girls are better treated than the French", but I said, "No, I'm sticking to my story"' ... She was wary of being seen with the British women; her alias of Jacqueline du Tertre was important to her as a way of protecting her SOE knowledge, and it was as Jacqueline that her fellow prisoners knew her.[37]

Because Szabo and her colleagues had not been mistreated during their interrogations, they believed that they would be protected by their British nationality in the camp. But following discussions with the three SOE women, both Nearne and Baseden opted to retain their cover as French resisters and not identify themselves as agents, which, with hindsight, was prudent.

Were men's ways of passing different to women's? Another motivation for continuing to pass during incarceration in concentration camps was to assist escape. Zembsch-Schreve was deported as a French national which meant that like Baseden, he was given a red triangle with a black F. Throughout his imprisonment, he looked for ways of escaping. He managed to acquire a patch of green cloth, which signified that the wearer was a German criminal prisoner. Most 'Greens' had been incarcerated when the camps first opened and as such they had acquired the trust of the guards and gained positions of responsibility as 'Kapos' (the block leaders who distributed food and allocated work placements): 'My escape plan envisaged passing myself off as a "Green", and I had already procured the requisite clothing and the triangular green patch ... Transforming myself into one of the German "Greens", a plan devised and perfected during long nights of cogitation at Dora would not be difficult because I spoke their language ... [I] metamorphosed myself into a "Green"'.[38] Zembsch-Schreve, who had been allocated the number 77249 at Buchenwald, the first concentration camp to which he was sent, erased the first digit in order to pass as a prisoner of long standing. With twelve comrades, Zembsch-Schreve later managed to escape from Ravensbrück.

Two other SOE agents incarcerated at Buchenwald were able to escape: Harry Peulevé, who was captured at his set in March 1944 having been denounced to the Germans by a neighbour who, noticing the number of people entering and leaving the house, suspected him of black-market activity, and RF Section organiser Edward Yeo-Thomas. After thirty-one F Section agents had been executed at the camp, moves were made to try to save some of the remaining SOE prisoners. The Allies' advance in March 1945 offered an opportunity. The SS doctor, Ding-Schuler, was persuaded to allow three inmates (Yeo-Thomas, Peulevé and Hessel, an agent of the Gaullist-run Deuxième Bureau) to exchange their identities with three Frenchmen who were dying of typhus. This would entail substituting their camp uniforms which bore the number of each inmate. In return, they would testify at a post-war trial on behalf of Ding-Schuler. When the three SOE agents were summoned for execution, the Frenchmen, who had since died, were cremated in their place. Following the successful substitution, the three agents were able to use their new identities to pass as French political prisoners and they soon managed to leave the main camp on work transports, from which they succeeded in escaping.

Other agents were not as fortunate as Peulevé in evading their summons and many went to their deaths still using cover names. Denise Bloch, for example, was executed as 'Danielle Williams' and a Frenchwoman called 'Madame Jacqueline Gautier' who died at Belsen concentration camp after its liberation was later identified as Yvonne Rudellat. Throughout their captivity, many agents maintained their cover stories and retained their cover names in desperate attempts to conceal the fact that they were British agents.

Gendered perceptions in concentration camps

Did gender, like passing, continue to be of significance during agents' incarceration in the camps? It would appear to have been noteworthy in other contexts, such as in the Gulag. In a chapter specifically on women, Alexander Solzhenitsyn asserts that between the first years of the Revolution and the end of the Second World War when camps were mixed-sex, life was 'easier for women' as they could prostitute themselves. Women's position in the camps changed, however, in 1946 when men and women were separated and women could no longer capitalise on finding a 'taker.'[39] Gender was clearly a structuring force in the Gulag. Was it so significant in the concentration camps, such as Ravensbrück, the women's camp near Berlin to which female political prisoners were sent, where there was less opportunity for sexual bargaining? And how have male veterans' remembered their camp experiences? Certainly, from 1942, women from Ravensbrück could volunteer to staff the brothels in men's camps in Mauthausen, Buchenwald and Sachsenhausen. Male prisoners received a nominal pay for their work which they could spend in the camp on sex, tobacco, food or clothing.[40] Although male political prisoners were unlikely to have access to the brothel, its existence and the fact that it was staffed by female prisoners who were promised improved living conditions, clothing and diet and their release following six months' service – unsurprisingly, these guarantees were not honoured – indicates that gender was of significance within the concentration camp system.

Moreover, the experiences of prisoners suggest that incarceration was gender-specific. Lillian Kremer, in her research on Jewish survivors of the Holocaust, argued that, although male and female prisoners endured similar hardships during their captivity within camps, their highly gendered socialisation produced very different responses.[41] Camp initiation was one of the most traumatic experiences, not only because this was their first encounter of camp life during which they were confronted with skeletal inmates, the vast overcrowding of the camp and the crematorium chimneys belching acrid smoke but also due to its generally dehumanising routines. Prisoners were ordered into shower rooms where they were told to undress, were disinfected, had their hair shorn, were given camp uniform and were allocated a number in order to strip them of their individuality. Kremer noted that male survivors have described their loss of personal dignity and autonomy during this initial phase of camp life. Like the Jewish male writers whose accounts Kremer analysed, male SOE agents experienced the camp initiation as eroding their self-respect. Bob Sheppard recollected an episode following his arrival at Neubremme, near Saarbrucken, when he was compelled to undress before he emptied the latrines. He asserted: 'Now after a few weeks or months in camp, getting undressed was nothing at all. We lived like that. But just imagine for us coming out of normal life. Getting undressed suddenly in the afternoon and I was absolutely naked.'[42] Sheppard was singled out and had to undress in front of other (clothed) inmates who observed this degrading spectacle, which undoubtedly added to his humiliation. Sheppard regarded his initiation into camp life as the beginning of a new phase. On four separate occasions during the interview, he commented upon this: 'After an experience, it was normal life. It was another world, a normal life'; 'we were entering a new life, a new world. It was fantastic, the change. Really a new world'; 'This was the beginning of a new life in concentration camp'; and 'That was the start of a new life'.[43] Brian Stonehouse also commented upon the indignity of the camp initiation when he arrived at Mauthausen and like Sheppard reflected upon it as a different world to that in which he had been living: 'Stripped of everything, all your clothing, and your hair is shaved off. You're nothing but a hunk of meat, a slave. It was difficult to connect that with the world I knew. This complete, this complete savagery … We had been robbed of everything. Not just our lives, but our dignity.'[44] It would seem that male agents, like the Jewish writers that Kremer analysed, experienced the camp initiation as diminishing their self-esteem.

In contrast to male Jewish survivors who have borne witness to their experiences of camp initiation, Kremer argued that women, socialised by both religious teaching and by gendered values to be modest, were likely to experience this humiliating process as a form of sexual assault. Kremer asserted that women were 'shamed and terrified by SS men who made lewd remarks and obscene suggestions and poked, pinched and mauled them in the course of delousing procedures and searches for hidden valuables in oral, rectal and vaginal cavities.'[45] Kremer also noted that female survivors emphasise in their testimonies the humiliation associated with having shorn hair and the replacement of their personal items of clothing with deliberately ill-fitting and mismatched garments. Cessation of menstruation, fear of sterilisation and frequent sexual harassment were further identified by Kremer as being significant in the writings of Jewish women who survived the camps.

Certainly, female SOE agents were likely to have felt embarrassed by having to strip naked given the sense of modesty that prevailed at this time. Women were unlikely to have been seen naked by members of their own family and thus the shock and humiliation of being observed by others is likely to have been extreme. Inmates who had lice had their hair shaved: this could also include the removal of pubic hair. Scissors and razors were likely to have been blunted by the processing of hundreds of new inmates and thus shaving often left cuts and scratches which could become infected. Those who received anti-typhus inoculations were sometimes injected in the breast rather than the arm by large veterinary syringes. Female prisoners had to stand naked, often for hours, waiting to be scrutinised by male SS doctors. Added to the humiliation of being frequently made to parade naked were the sexual comments made by male doctors. Older women made desperate attempts to look younger, in order to boost their chances of survival, smearing dirt into their scalps to conceal grey hairs and trying to hold themselves upright. This became even more urgent following the arrival of Hungarian Jews in Ravensbrück in spring 1944 when the camp was severely overcrowded and selections were made. Every few days, older women were forced to strip to the waist and run past male doctors who would select the oldest and weakest. Yvonne Rudellat, a forty-eight year old SOE courier, tried to colour her grey hair with a boiled onion skin that she had found but her thick hair, which had become brittle from persistent dying, would not change colour. Instead, she resorted to wearing a piece of cloth like a turban to mask her grey hair.

Sometimes these cursory checks indicated signs of illness. Cecily Lefort, a forty-three-year-old SOE courier, was forced to undergo further tests and was found to have cancer of the stomach. Even within the camps, medical experiments were undertaken, most famously by Josef Mengele on twins in Auschwitz. Treiter, an SS doctor at Ravensbrück, was eager to operate on her as he was interested in post-operational treatment. He put her on a diet of porridge and thick vegetable soup, but despite successful treatment, she was not saved from being sent to the gas chamber.

Another source of humiliation upon arrival was the camp clothing that the women were obliged to wear. Deliberately mismatching and ill-fitting clothes were distributed: short women were often given baggy garments which enveloped their bodies, while tall women were provided with insufficient clothing. Yvonne Baseden, for example, recollected that upon arrival at Ravensbrück, she was allocated a pleated red skirt and a sailor boy's shirt, 'dished out just enough to cover yourself with.'[46] Prisoners were forbidden to exchange their outfits.

A further psychological hardship for female inmates may have been the complete dearth of make-up, especially in view of the investment in glamour to signify respectability which had been a crucial strategy of many while operational. Kremer noted: 'Women socialised to invest in their physical appearance – to use make-up, to dress well, to style their hair – were radically defeminised.'[47] Although make-up, fashionable clothing and hairstyles cannot be compared with the privations of lack of food and water, overcrowded sleeping quarters, disease, overwork and poor sanitary conditions, it may have further undermined an already desperately low morale. The importance of appearance to female agents during their imprisonment is illustrated in the film *Carve Her Name with Pride*. In one scene set in Ravensbrück concentration camp, the camera pans on to the actress playing Denise Bloch who is powdering her face:

Second inmate: Face powder. Where did you get it?
Denise Bloch: Whitewash from the wall in the kitchen.
Second inmate: Why, what's the use?
Denise Bloch: I don't know, just makes me feel better.[48]

This scene was perhaps suggested by Odette Sansom, one of the technical advisers on the film, who used margarine from her food allowance as face cream.[49] She also turned her skirt an inch every day so that it would not look worn in the same place and put rags from her stockings in her hair every night to act as rollers. She recollected: 'I used to put them on every evening religiously in case they would fetch me the next morning to put me to death. I wasn't going to be seen going to my death without my curls.'[50] Hair, an important signifier of femininity and individuality, was clearly important to female prisoners who fought to reclaim some dignity.

Testimonies indicate that having one's head shaved upon arrival in the camps was experienced as highly defeminising and disempowering. Erika Buchmann, a German political prisoner, noted that a frequent response among her fellow prisoners was to commit suicide immediately following this procedure.[51] This affront to femininity can be seen in other contexts in which women's heads were shaved as a gendered form of punishment. An early reference to the indignity of shaved hair is made by Paul in his epistle to the Corinthians: 'It was a disgrace for a woman to have her hair cut or shaved off'.[52] This symbolic act of purification was forced upon Frenchwomen who slept with Germans in 1918, on German women who consorted with French soldiers in the 1920s during the occupation of the Rhineland, on German women caught with foreign workers in the early 1940s and was also witnessed on a wider scale in some French towns following the liberation. Upon arrival at the camps, many women underwent this procedure which represented the reduction of the individual to a uniform mass, but it was also used as a form of punishment to undermine morale and to reinforce social control. During her incarceration at Ravensbrück, Eileen Nearne refused to work in a factory assisting the German war effort, whereupon guards shaved her head and threatened her with execution.

Women also had to cope with diarrhoea, cystitis, the humiliation of communal toilets and the lack of sanitary products until they ceased menstruating. Without rags, menstruating women had no choice but to let the blood run down their legs. There was a widespread belief that the SS had put chemicals, such as bromide, in their soup to stop the menstrual cycle, which increased fears about future fertility. It was, however, likely that severe malnutrition, coupled with excessive exercise (required by manual labour) caused oestrogen levels to drop, which prevented ovulation. For some women, this had already occurred following lengthy imprisonment in France.

Female agents therefore experienced both the humiliation and loss of personal dignity that their male counterparts endured, as well as suffered more gendered hardships, such as sexual harassment, loss of menstruation and low morale from the lack of feminine accoutrements.

Kremer also noted that many male Holocaust survivors have commented upon the lack of support from other inmates. She cited Primo Levi who asserted: 'Here the struggle to survive is without respite because everyone is desperately and ferociously alone.'[53] Testimonies of male SOE agents, however, suggest that there was group affiliation among political prisoners and that this was crucial in coping with camp life. Bob Sheppard recalled: 'Pat [O'Leary], Tom [Groom], Brian [Stonehouse], I: they were the four. It was really the team together. It was the creation of a real strong family. It was a great help in getting together.'[54] This was not an exception. The biography of the Newton brothers emphasised the friendships between Alfred and Henry Newton, Christopher Burney, Maurice Southgate and Maurice Pertschuk (known as Martin Perkins to his SOE colleagues). Pertschuk was suddenly, without forewarning, instructed to report to the gate: 'Only Burney was with him. He walked with his friend to the *appel* [roll call] square. Then Martin went on, alone, towards the gate. Watching the slim, boyish figure striding away, head erect and shoulders squared, Burney's cold, realistic mind failed him. His throat choked and the tears ran down his cheeks unashamedly.'[56] It is necessary to be cautious about easy assessments of solidarity.

One explanation for the apparent lack of cohesion experienced by Jewish prisoners might be that Jews had little power and status in the camps in contrast to other prisoners and, consequently, Communists and national groups gained little by forming alliances with Jews. This does not explain, however, why there was little solidarity *among* Jewish prisoners. Although the individual hero involves one version of masculinity, there were other modes of masculinity, especially in the context of war, which emphasise male camaraderie. Kremer's argument that Jewish male prisoners did not experience solidarity and mutual support does not appear to relate to the experiences of male SOE agents.

In contrast to Jewish men, Kremer noted that Jewish women have testified to the solidarity and mutual cooperation which existed between female camp inmates and many attribute their survival to friends who found extra food and nursed them through sickness. Despite this being a prevalent idea in survivors' testimonies[56] and with historians,[57] this emphasis on sisterhood has, however, been challenged. There was much mistrust between different groups, in particular between Communists and Catholics and between political prisoners and 'asocials'. This can be evidenced in personal accounts in which there is a marked stigmatisation, especially against prostitutes, gypsies and lesbians. There is also evidence to suggest that there was little cohesion within categories. Jewish inmate Rosi Muskopf, who arrived at Ravensbrück in late 1944, aged sixteen, recollected: 'I experienced neither friendship not solidarity with fellow prisoners.'[58] Such testimonies suggest that Kremer's argument that there was widespread female solidarity is perhaps not the whole picture.

What do the accounts of female agents indicate? Yvonne Baseden recollected that on one occasion she was nearly killed by a guard.[59] A feather from a pillow that she was unloading from a truck landed on his uniform. He immediately raised his truncheon to strike her but a fellow inmate pushed her out of the way and instead of hitting her head the weapon landed on Baseden's thigh. Her life was saved by someone she did not know, who risked turning the guard's anger upon herself. As a result of her intervention, this unknown woman was severely beaten by the guard. Baseden, who was later diagnosed as having tuberculosis, was also saved from being transferred to Belsen concentration camp by another woman who managed to take her name from the list and get her admitted to the hospital block. It is likely that in Belsen, where conditions were worse as a result of rampant typhus, Baseden would have died, as did Yvonne Rudellat, who left Ravensbrück in relatively good health. These episodes illustrate Kremer's contention that female prisoners looked out for one another. The development of a close bond with other inmates was important in providing information, advice and protection and could also be crucial in reinforcing one's sense of worth.

One woman who did not experience companionship was Odette Sansom who was kept in solitary confinement for two years in the camp prison as a direct result of her alleging that she was married to Churchill's nephew. While in solitary confinement, Sansom occupied her mind by visualising the domestic chores that wives and mothers routinely undertake, including making clothes for her daughters and decorating rooms: 'I imagined what I wanted them to wear, then I would get the pattern, then the material, lay it out, cut it out and stitch it. Every single stitch I'd sew until it was all finished. Then I would refurnish all the houses of people I'd known, starting with walls, carpets, curtains.'[60] While incarcerated in Paris before her deportation, Sansom, a mother of three girls, had succeeded in making two dolls out of scraps of material that she found, which are now on display at the Imperial War Museum. Her homemaking skills, either real or imagined, were therefore crucial to her endurance of imprisonment. She was not unique in being creative: female inmates crafted purses, small bags, handkerchiefs, doilies and scarves with scraps of material, and sang and told stories. Nor was Sansom exceptional in reflecting upon routine domestic tasks: survivors' testimonies indicate that female prisoners often dreamed about food, swapped recipes during roll calls and planned menus for imaginary banquets. These peculiarly gendered coping strategies enabled women to connect with their lives prior to incarceration. Psychiatrist Judith Herman noted: 'Prisoners tenaciously seek to maintain communication with a world outside the one in which they are confined. They deliberately practise evoking mental images of the people they love in order to preserve their sense of connection.'[61] The example of Sansom suggests that there was often a gendered element to this particular coping strategy.

Conclusion

This examination of the testimonies of political prisoners of the Nazis has revealed that, despite being captured, many continued to pass. Whatever identities they adopted, agents were motivated by the belief that their chosen personae would increase the likelihood of them surviving the war. Although it did not necessarily prevent them from being tortured and deported, passing could save them from being executed. Analysis of agents' accounts has also uncovered the gender dynamics that were in operation during interrogations and in concentration camps. Female captives could not escape the fact that they were guarded and interrogated by men who belonged to a regime which held distinctly sexist attitudes. The intention here has not been to suggest that women suffered more during captivity than men, but that the violence inflicted upon women's bodies by male interrogators was gender-based and that there were gendered differences in their experiences of suffering in camps. Indeed, as a Harley Street dentist said to Odette Sansom when she visited him shortly after her release from Ravensbrück, 'I understand you were a prisoner of war in Germany ... how very tiresome for a woman.'[62]

Notes

1 Buckmaster, *They Fought Alone*, p. 74.
2 B. Harris, 'Lt. Arthur Staggs, Wireless Operator: Hero of the French Resistance', available online at: http://users.tpg.com.au/berniezz/page3%20Arthur.htm [Accessed 2006].
3 Churchill, *The Spirit in the Cage*, p. 38.
4 Baseden, *Secret Agent* (BBC2).
5 Personal interview with Yvonne Baseden.
6 Zembsch-Schreve, *Secret Agent* (BBC2).
7 Zembsch-Schreve, *Pierre Lalande*, p. 119 and p. 124.
8 Zembsch-Schreve, *Pierre Lalande*, p. 125.
9 Personal interview with Bob Sheppard.
10 Cited in J. Wheeler-Bennett, *Nemesis of Power* (London: Macmillan, 1954), p. 662.
11 National Archives, HS 7/66.
12 IWM SA, 9852 Stonehouse.
13 National Archives, HS 6/568.
14 Gleeson, *They Feared No Evil*, p. 80.
15 Foot, *SOE in France*, p. 430.
16 Foot, *SOE in France*, p. 409.
17 Jones, *A Quiet Courage*, p. 278.
18 Jones, *A Quiet Courage*, p. 282.
19 Personal interview with Maisie McLintock.
20 Personal interview with Vera Atkins.
21 Member of Charlie Company cited in D. Russell, 'Rape and the Masculine Mystique', in E. Whitelegg et al. (eds), *The Changing Experience of Women* (Oxford: Martin Robertson, 1982), p. 331.
22 C. Enloe, *The Morning After: Sexual Politics at the End of the Cold War* (London: University of California Press, 1993.)
23 IWM SA, 5378, Hargreaves.
24 *Homeground: Secret Agent: The True Story of Violette Szabo* (Channel 4)
25 Basu, *Spy Princess*, pp. 179.
26 Personal interview with Yvonne Baseden.
27 Tickell, *Odette*, pp. 222–6.
28 A ChildLine Study, *We Know it's Tough to Talk: Boys in Need of Help* (London: ChildLine, 1996.)
29 B. Marshall, *The White Rabbit: The Secret Agent the Gestapo Could not Crack* (London: Cassell, 2000); M. Seaman, *Bravest of the Brave: The True Story of Wing Commander 'Tommy' Yeo-Thomas – SOE Secret Agent – Codename 'The White Rabbit'* (London: Michael O'Mara, 1999).
30 Seaman, *Bravest of the Brave*, p. 147.
31 IWM SA, 5378 Hargreaves.
32 Seaman, *Bravest of the Brave*, p. 141.

33 Personal interview with Bob Sheppard.
34 Personal interiew with Yvonne Baseden.
35 Personal interview with Yvonne Baseden.
36 Foot, *SOE in France*, p. 430.
37 Jones, *A Quiet Courage*, pp. 313–14.
38 Zembsch-Schreve, *Pierre Lalande*, pp. 167–8.
39 A. Solzhenitsyn, *The Gulag Archipelago, Volume 2: An Experiment in Literary Investigation, Pts. III–IV* (London: Collins, 1976), p. 217.
40 Thomas, *No Banners*, p. 309.
41 L. Kremer, *Women's Holocaust Writing: Memory and Imagination* (Lincoln: University of Nebraska Press, 1999), p. 10.
42 IWM SA, 10445 Sheppard.
43 Personal interview with Bob Sheppard.
44 IWM SA 9852 Stonehouse.
45 Kremer, *Women's Holocaust Writing*, p. 10.
46 Personal interview with Yvonne Baseden.
47 Kremer, *Women's Holocaust Writing*, p. 10.
48 BFI film script S13981.
49 Churchill, *Spirit in the Cage*, p. 233.
50 Sansom in Jones, *A Quiet Courage*, p. 303.
51 J. Morrison, *Ravensbrück: Everyday Life in a Women's Concentration Camp, 1939–45* (Princeton: Markus Wiener Publishers, 2000), p. 33.
52 1 Corinthians 11 v. 6
53 Levi cited in Kremer, *Women's Holocaust Writing*, p. 18.
54 Personal interview with Bob Sheppard.
55 Thomas, *No Banners*, pp. 326–7.
56 See for example, C. Delbo, *None of Us Will Return* (Boston: Beacon Press, 1968).
57 J. Ringelheim, 'Women and the Holocaust: A Reconsideration of Research', *Signs*, 10 (1985).
58 Cited in Morrison, *Ravensbrück*, p. 73.
59 Personal interview with Yvonne Baseden.
60 M. Nicholson, *What Did You Do in the War, Mummy?* (London: Pimlico, 1995), p. 242.
61 J. Lewis Herman, *Trauma and Recovery: From Domestic Abuse to Political Terror* (London: Pandora, 1998), p. 81.
62 Jones, *A Quiet Courage*, p. 341.

8

'So many happy memories': demobilisation and the return to civvy street

This concluding chapter serves as an epilogue by recording the experiences of agents following demobilisation from the organisation. It examines how the SOE men and women, trained in unarmed combat and silent killing techniques, who had operated behind enemy lines under penalty of death and who may also have experienced captivity, fitted back into civilian life. It also considers how they look back on the war, noting that for some their experiences have been incorporated into the rest of their lives, while for others the war years have had a lingering significance.

Liberations

Following the liberation of French towns in 1944, the work of the SOE agents was completed and those who had not been arrested began to return to Britain. Some volunteered for new roles: Claire Everett and her organiser assisted the American Army in gathering intelligence about German troop movements and at one point their car was fired upon. Upon entering a nearby town, her organiser and several others were temporarily taken hostage and Everett, as previously mentioned, was attacked by two German soldiers. She returned to Britain on 4 November 1944, while her organiser, like many of the men including Roger Landes, Gaston Cohen, Sydney Hudson and Bob Maloubier, volunteered to continue serving with the SOE by joining Force 136 to fight the Japanese. Others, such as Yvonne Cormeau, returned to France with Maurice Buckmaster on his 'Judex' mission to meet the people who had assisted the SOE operatives ensuring they got adequate financial reparations, creating lists of people worthy of decoration and pensions and collecting equipment that might be useful in the ongoing war with Japan.

For those agents who were incarcerated in concentration camps, the liberation was of less immediate significance. The war continued for many more months, as did their captivity. American and Soviet soldiers finally advanced across Germany in April 1945.[1] Bob Sheppard recalled an encounter with an American officer who was one of the first into Dachau on 29 April:

> On the day of the liberation, an American officer said, 'Can you take me into the camp so that I can see immediately how it was?' So we took him into the camp and along the barracks there. We toured around and showed him the barracks and suddenly we saw him stopping and being sick from the piles of corpses and at the end we didn't even take notice of that and we had the proof of that on the day of the liberation. To show you how we were used to that, Brian [Stonehouse] turned round and said, 'What happened to him? He's sick'.[2]

Sheppard and Stonehouse had become immune to the sight of dead bodies. The American soldiers, however, had not and were so appalled at what they saw, that they ordered the camp guards down from their watch-towers and shot them. Sheppard and Stonehouse intervened to protect one from being killed as they were determined that someone should stand trial.[3] Temporary accommodation in an SS house was arranged for them while Intelligence Officers verified their identities and, three days after its liberation, they finally left Dachau. In his Imperial War Museum interview, Stonehouse recalled that despite 'great joy at having survived', the return was somewhat anti-climatic as no one met him at the airport.[4] The delayed reunion with his parents was an awkward one and, fifty years after the war, he still perceived that there had been an unbreachable divide between them as a result of his captivity: 'I never spoke to my family, my parents about the war and they never asked, which I resented for many years … they didn't seem to want to know. They pretended that I was still the same person and that nothing had happened in between. That I found very irritating'.[5] Stonehouse's recovery was hampered by this silencing of his experiences and he recalled that he felt more like a Holocaust victim than a POW, despite the fact that 'I don't have the feeling of guilt that I'm told a lot of Jewish people had who survived'.[6]

While Stonehouse's family struggled to cope, Sheppard's parents were able to empathise with their son as they had been interned in 1940 as enemy aliens (his French mother became a British national upon marriage to his English father) and had spent the years of occupation in the prison in Vittel before being exchanged in 1944 for German prisoners held in Britain. Sheppard remembered the reunion with his parents: 'Immediately after landing, Buck[master] and Vera [Atkins] dropped me in front of the house of my father and mother in Oakley Square in London … My mother looked at me after five years of war and everything I went through and she looked at me and said, "You look tired, my boy." [laughs] So sweet. "Oh you look tired!" "Yes, a little."'[7]

Both men had lost a considerable amount of weight. Before his capture, Sheppard had weighed roughly 75 kg; upon his return from the camps, he was a mere 48 kg.[8] They were sent to an SOE school in London to recover from their ordeal. Stonehouse's obituary records an incident while he was in London which illustrates the difficulty he had in overcoming his traumatic experiences: 'When Stonehouse returned to London, an emaciated shadow of his former self, two of his former FANY friends hardly recognised him. And when, in their horrified compassion, they invited him to the flat they shared and cooked him a lunch of chops – their entire week's meat ration – he rushed out into the street as the frying pan sizzled, crying, "I can't bear the smell of burning flesh."'[9] Sheppard also, understandably, found the first few days overwhelming, recalling in particular the celebrations on VE Day: 'We went on the 8 May in front of Buckingham Palace and the crowd and the people were shouting and I couldn't support it. I go home. I can't. Too much, too much.'[10]

When I asked Sheppard whether he had ever experienced nightmares, he replied: 'No. Not at all. No, it's strange, but no, I never dreamt of the past or things like that.'[11] Other survivors, however, were plagued by reminders of their incarceration. Although Harry Peulevé had escaped from Buchenwald, M. R. D. Foot noted: 'He never recovered from it: it haunted his dreams for the rest of his life … When he had had a few drinks, he developed a tendency to become quarrelsome with other men, total strangers he accused of being SS in disguise, come to persecute him.'[12] Similarly, Guido Zembsch-Schreve was troubled by ill-health in the immediate post-war period, both physically, suffering from perforated stomach ulcers and oedema, and mentally: 'My mind had been affected even more than my body. Utterly disoriented, I suffered from mood swings and fits of irritability … [and was] haunted by harrowing nightmares of life in captivity'[13] and in the epilogue to his autobiography, he wrote: 'My dreams have been haunted by nightmare visions from the past. Half a century has done nothing to dull their intensity.'[14] Dorothy Temple, an SOE-FANY who years after the war went on holiday to the south of France with Yeo-Thomas, who had escaped with Peulevé from Buchenwald, and his wife recollected: 'Barbara would tell us that they'd beaten him about the head so much that he'd had these appalling headaches and he was almost insane when he had them. He'd get violent, you know, and rather beastly to her, that sort of thing. And you couldn't reconcile it with Tommy.'[15] Edgar Hargreaves, who had been operational in Yugoslavia before being captured, also experienced long-term physical and psychological problems as a result of his imprisonment, which impacted upon his ability to lead a normal life. In an interview with the Imperial War Museum, he asserted:

> I still suffer … this is something of course that has affected me for the rest of my life … It took a tremendous amount of readjustment … A lot of very, very unpleasant memories. I found I was intolerant, very bad-tempered, very, very hard to live with. I was married in 1945 but it was not a happy marriage and I think the fault was mostly mine. I couldn't make the necessary adjustments and it was very, very difficult. You become unreasonable. You know you're being unreasonable and you know you're being impossible but there just seems to be, you can't control it. It's very, very difficult indeed.[16]

These reactions to their war experiences were by no means exceptional. Research undertaken by practicing psychiatrists and psychologists on the effects of captivity on Second World War Resistance fighters of French,[17] Dutch,[18] Danish[19] and Norwegian[20] nationality indicate that many repatriated prisoners responded in this way. These studies reveal the prevalence of psychosomatic problems such as neurological syndromes, as well as reduced concentration levels, heightened irritability, emotional instability and increased fatigue. Ex-POWs experienced flashbacks and nightmares reliving traumatic events and had difficulty establishing and maintaining personal relationships. Since 1980, sufferers of these symptoms have been recognised as having Post-Traumatic Stress Disorder. In retrospect, it would appear that Peulevé, Zembsch-Schreve, Yeo-Thomas and Hargreaves were all suffering from PTSD and that it destroyed Hargreaves' marriage (and, as we shall see, Peulevé's also.)

For the three female agents who survived incarceration at Ravensbrück, the return to Britain was equally challenging. Odette Sansom, who had been driven to the American lines by the Camp Commandant who believed she was related by marriage to Winston Churchill, was reunited with her three daughters. She was plagued by ill-health, suffering from TB, articular rheumatism, a weakened heart and anaemia. Because of her swollen feet, a result of having had her toe nails extracted and walking on her heels for two years, she could only wear men's shoes when she first returned.[21] Her personal file includes several letters from doctors testifying to her poor physical and mental health. Six months after her release from Ravensbrück, the doctor was concerned at the 'very poor state of her health' and it was reported that Sansom 'stills feels very tired and exhausted and is still very worried at the condition of her hair.'[22] Maintaining her femininity had been a crucial survival strategy for Sansom while incarcerated as we saw in the last chapter and regaining her appearance was clearly a concern in the immediate aftermath. A request was put to the finance officer for the cost of Sansom's treatment to be borne by the organisation. It was also noted that there were 'some trouble-some symptoms which, I feel, are in the most part psychological and are undoubtedly a direct result of her two years in solitary confinement.'[23] In a letter dated 12 December 1945, a doctor wrote of the state of health of both Sansom and fellow survivor Eileen Nearne:

> The above-named ex-agents have been under my care for some months. They have both been seen by specialists and no evidence of serious organic disease has been detected. They are, however, in my opinion, both suffering from psychological symptoms which undoubtedly have been brought on by their service in the field. These symptoms interfere to a considerable extent with their efficiency for future employment and it is likely they may continue to do so for some time to come. This being so, it is hoped that this Organisation will see its way to giving these two gallant women the appropriate compensation ... At the present I would assess Mrs Sansom's disability at 70% and Miss Nearne's at 50%.[24]

Sansom remained in a fragile state of health for several years. Recalling that she first heard about receiving the George Cross from a journalist who knocked on her door, she noted: 'I was trying to get my bearings, recover completely with the children in a little cottage at Petersfield'[25] and, in an article on the unveiling of the FANY memorial in May 1948, it is noted that Sansom was 'frailest of all, and with the suffering still on her pretty young face.'[26]

While Sansom was thrust into the limelight as a result of the unexpected awarding of the George Cross, Didi Nearne, upon her escape from Ravensbrück, withdrew from society, cutting herself off even from her SOE colleagues. Yvonne Baseden, who was also incarcerated, noted that Nearne 'was affected in a different way by Ravensbrück ... I knew Didi quite well but I haven't seen her since the war, only because she's never wanted to. Vera [Atkins] told me this, she said, "Don't worry, don't try to contact her. She's better left as she wants to be left."'[27] Similarly, Maisie McLintock, who had known Didi during their FANY training, remarked:

'Didi suffered terribly, was very stoic about it, but she eventually broke down completely … she finally cracked … Odette [Sansom] told me she was in a mental home in France and she was very, very bad. However, she recovered and she came back to London and I believe trained as a nurse.'[28] Because of her breakdown, Nearne did not attend the unveiling of the plaque to remember the women who died and was nursed for some time by her older sister, Jacqueline, who had starred in *School for Danger*. She did, however, agree to be interviewed by journalist Liane Jones in the 1980s, telling her, 'These things live with you'[29] and appeared in a television programme entitled *Timewatch: Secret Memories*[30] in 1997, identified only by the pseudonym 'Rose'. It is believed that Nearne is still alive; she did not respond to my letter requesting an interview.

The third survivor of Ravensbrück, Yvonne Baseden, left the camp on the last convoy of three coaches run by the Swedish Red Cross a fortnight before the camp was liberated. She was driven into Denmark and then caught a boat to Sweden. From Malmo, officials were able to contact Vera Atkins who verified her identity and informed her father that she was alive. She was then put on a plane to Leuchars and made her way to London for an emotional reunion with her father. In the final instalment of three articles she wrote for the *Sunday Express* in 1952, she noted: 'I came home to England on a Saturday afternoon. Before me lay nine months in hospital, a lung operation, pain, and nights tormented by fearful dreams.'[31] Baseden, who married two months after attending the unveiling of the FANY memorial[32] and subsequently moved to Rhodesia (present-day Zimbabwe), withdrew from the public eye. She declined to be interviewed by Liane Jones in the 1980s and her acceptance of my request for a meeting was unexpected. Although willing to talk about her experiences, she clearly found it upsetting. The first of my two interviews with Baseden was ended when she began to sob while talking about fellow comrades who did not return from the camp. Before I met her a second time, she was interviewed in preparation for the *Secret Agent* documentary. The transcript stated that on twenty separate occasions she became distressed and the interviewer often had to pause while she composed herself as, according to the transcriber, she was 'too upset to continue'.[33] Although Baseden had lived a full life since the war, her harrowing wartime experiences still had the capacity to unsettle her.

Post-war adjustment

Clearly, incarceration had a devastating effect on agents' physical and mental health. Yet, even agents who were not deported experienced problems in adjusting to civilian life. Tony Brooks noted: 'It was very difficult to adapt … it was very difficult to settle down'[34] and Sydney Hudson recalled: 'I did not fit back very well', slowly accentuating each word.[35] Societal expectations of female dependency (on fathers or husbands) and male wage-earning meant that it was perhaps harder for male agents to find a new role to fulfil. After the excitement, danger and adventure of life behind enemy lines, peacetime must have felt somewhat flat and drab. After the war, Hudson moved to Israel to work for Shell: 'It's very exciting to negotiate with the Algerian trade unions and the Israeli trade unions, but somehow it's a bit less exciting than the other stuff.'[36] The transition to peacetime was a slow process and many missed the companionship and camaraderie of the Resistance. When I asked Roger Landes why he volunteered to carry on with the special forces by joining Force 136, noting that he 'could have stopped', he remarked: 'Oh yes, I could have done, but I couldn't stop … I couldn't take a regular life. You know, it took me seven years to adjust myself after the war, mentally. Difficult to let go.'[37] Others took even longer. Jos Mulder-Gemmeke, an agent who was operational in Holland, remarked in her Imperial War Museum interview that she had never really overcome the strain: 'You are affected because you are never relaxed. I still am not relaxed … After the war, I was always and I still am very tense and when I am sleeping, I have my fists clenched … I think that's from all the years you have to be tense. Always being on your alert … Years after the war when a car stopped at night, I jumped out of my bed and I was packing something because I thought it was the SS.'[38] That agents who had not been deported experienced difficulties in adjusting mentally to civilian life suggests that their service with the SOE irrevocably changed them. The months of living with anxiety, the constant pressure and ever-present threat of arrest took its toll and many found the return to a normal existence fraught with difficulties.

Seemingly, one of the responses to their wartime experiences was to marry quickly. Edgar Hargreaves married in 1945 and Bob Sheppard, who returned to Britain in May 1945, married in September the woman that he had been engaged to since 1940. They had five children and had been married almost 57 years when I interviewed him. Roger Landes married the daughter of one of his Resistance colleagues in July 1947 and they had one son. Similarly, the majority of female agents, it would seem, eagerly embraced marriage and motherhood. Of the twenty-six who returned, just four remained single; three returned to their husbands, three had been widowed (two of whom later remarried) and the others married within five years of the war ending. In a radio script from 1950, Vera Atkins, F Section's Intelligence Officer, asserted: 'Today the greater number are happy wives and mothers, and the others have settled into different everyday jobs.'[39] This prevalence for marriage in the immediate post-war period mirrored the general trend. The Registrar General's report of 1961 stated that while the pre-war average number of weddings was 325,813 per year, rising to 370,997 during the war, the figure for 1947 increased to 401,210.[40]

In addition to increased marriage rates, the birth rate soared. Whereas the pre-war average number of babies born annually was 580,413, 881,025 babies were born in 1947.[41] The Registrar General's Statistical Review of Britain also indicated a steep rise in both birth rates and general fertility after the war:

Table 2 Birth rates, 1936–50, England and Wales, Scotland and N. Ireland

Date	Births in England and Wales per 1000 population	Births in Scotland per 1000 population	Births in N. Ireland per 1000 population
1936–40	14.7	17.6	19.8
1941–45	15.9	17.8	19.8
1946–50	18.0	20.0	22.0

Source: Compiled from D. A. Coleman, 'Population', Table 2.1(a) 'Birth – and death – rates and natural increase, 1901–1985, England and Wales, and Scotland (per 1000 population)' and Table 2.1(b) 'Birth – and death – rates and natural increase, 1901–1985, N. Ireland (per 1000 population)' in A. H. Halsey, *British Social Trends Since 1900: A Guide to the Changing Social Structure of Britain* (Basingstoke: Macmillan Press 1988), p. 40.

Young men and women, who had put their lives on hold while they fought the Nazis, were eager to get married and have children. It seems rather surprising that women, especially, who had been employed as combative agents, trained in offensive manoeuvres such as how to kill silently, infiltrated behind enemy lines and who had actively participated in clandestine warfare, were content to withdraw from the adventure and danger in order to settle down. These women had broken down established Western divisions of male and female tasks in war by partici-

Table 3 General fertility rates, 1936–50, England and Wales, Scotland and N. Ireland

Date	Live births in England and Wales per 1000 women aged 15–44	Live births in Scotland per 1000 women aged 15–44	Live births in N. Ireland per 1000 women aged 15–44
1936–40	60.9	73.3	84.5
1941–45	67.2	75.9	93.2
1946–50	80.6	87.6	95.1

Source: Taken from D. A. Coleman, 'Population', Table 2.2 'General fertility rate: live births per 1000 women aged 15–44, 1901–85, England and Wales, Scotland and N. Ireland' in A. H. Halsey, *British Social Trends Since 1900*, p. 42.

pating actively at the 'front line'. Their involvement in such a masculine organisation suggests that societal norms underwent a considerable reconstruction and yet, because heterosexual conventions were fairly systematically reinforced following demobilisation with female agents generally assuming more traditional roles by returning to the home as wives and mothers, it becomes apparent that the blurring of gender roles was only temporary. Indeed, several newspaper articles revelled in the irony of women trained as killers who slipped into quiet domesticity. In an article about Marguerita Knight's wartime escapades, James Gleeson wrote: 'A strange story. It seemed all the more incredible as Mrs Peggy Smith told it the other day, leaning over a sink and washing her baby's clothes in her little Wanstead home.'[42] A report on her being awarded the United States Medal of Freedom with Bronze Palm noted that she said: 'I can't stay long. I have got to get home and put the two children to bed.'[43] Similarly, a headline, 'Mrs Smith: Train-wrecker, spy and Nazi-killer', and the caption under a photograph of her playing with her two children, 'Croix de Guerre ... M.B.E... . mother', as well as the article itself, indicate this fascination with her antithetical wartime and post-war roles:

> In her handbag Mrs Smith has her shopping list – a little different from the past. For six months she carried code messages and radio sets in her suitcase through the German lines ... As she wheels her pram to the shops she is using her keen brown eyes to spy out some apples for Peter ... About two and a half years ago the same keen eyes spied out German strongpoints ... The most exciting thing in her life now is to watch her children grow up. In May 1944, the most exciting thing was to be parachuted at night into German-occupied Bergundy.[44]

Presented in this way, any possible concerns that the public may have had about the use of women to fight the Nazis behind enemy lines were alleviated. These women may have been secret agents, but the public were reassured in the tabloid press that they were not masculine in appearance and they had returned to conventional womanly roles after their wartime adventures. Smith, herself, asserted: 'I honestly think my present job as a housewife is more exacting.'[45]

It might be presumed that because of their wartime role, the SOE women had a greater transition to make in order to adjust to a life of domesticity. Yet perhaps it was their experiences during their employment with the SOE that prompted them to lead quiet, private lives. Despite their extraordinary experiences, these were ordinary women and their decision to become paramilitaries was purely a temporary measure in order to rid France of its Nazi occupiers. If they eluded the Gestapo and survived, these women expected to return to their pre-war lives once their mission had been successfully completed. Most left the labour force entirely, choosing conventional roles as wives and mothers, as women in wider society did also. Even Nancy Wake at first seemed to settle into a provincial and rather uneventful post-war life, making a radio programme called 'Nancy Wake, the Housewives' Friend', in which she talked about the price of meat, and helped organise the Miss New South Wales beauty contest.[46]

It must also be remembered that while F Section's apparently progressive approach to women's involvement in the war effort suggests a destabilisation of conventional gender norms, analysis of their experiences reveals that there was little conflict concerning women overstepping traditional gender delineations. Any disruption which women's inclusion in the organisation might have caused was limited by the extremely small numbers of women recruited and trained as agents, their allocation to female-appropriate roles and their recourse to conventional gender acts in order to undertake their clandestine work, which was, moreover, explicitly recognised as 'for the duration'. Thus, the potential to destabilise gender relations was never fully realised and established Western traditional divisions of male and female tasks in war and stereotypical notions of femininity remained largely intact, unscathed by women's militarisation in the SOE. In this light, the transition to a life of domesticity is not perhaps so astonishing. While more recent conflicts such as the first Gulf War have witnessed much greater instabilities with women undertaking traditionally masculine tasks, including being in charge of men within the combat zone, in the Second World War military women were concentrated in particularly female-appropriate positions. The enthusiasm with which women greeted the post-war roles of wife and mother, which in themselves are the most gender-apposite that women in peacetime can embody, is perhaps, then, less surprising than might first appear.

Although the post-war marriage and birth rates increased exponentially, the number of couples wanting to separate also soared, indicating that individuals were less inclined to tolerate unsatisfactory marriages. In 1938, 9,970 petitions for divorce were filed in England and Wales; this increased to 34,443 in 1949.[47] Yet divorce was not the only option. Magistrates Courts granted Maintenance Orders, acknowledging marital separation, and the numbers in receipt of an Order also dramatically increased: 10,538 Orders were made in 1938–39 and 25,400 in 1945–46.[48] The high rate of marital breakdown in the mid to late forties was undoubtedly a result of hasty marriages contracted during wartime, lengthy separation, women's new roles during the conflict, which led to tension in the home in the post-war period, the armed forces' assistance in dissolving marriages as well as the simplifications to the divorce procedure as a result of the passing of the Matrimonial Causes Act in 1937. These factors would also have affected the marriages contracted by SOE personnel and, while some were happy, lasting a lifetime, others ended in divorce. Instead of returning to his wife and daughter, Sydney Hudson first volunteered for Force 136 and then went to help process Japanese POWs. When he did finally return to Switzerland where he had lived before the war with his wife, it was clear that his marriage was over: 'We ended up by being divorced. I was living in a different world.'[49]

For some couples, it was the war that both brought them together and led to their separation. Mary Herbert, who had given birth to her organiser's child in November 1943, married him after the liberation of France. Lise de Baissac, Claude's sister, told me that if Herbert had not become pregnant, 'he wouldn't have married her … A child had been produced. It was right to give it a proper father so they got married but they never lived together.'[50] When de Baissac met someone else while he was working in Africa, he asked Herbert, who had remained in Britain, for a divorce. Working for the SOE also brought together Odette Sansom, who was already married, and Peter Churchill, but they found they had little else in common and it was Churchill's inability to put the war behind him, according to Sansom, that led to the collapse of their marriage after nine years:

> It was the war that broke up Peter Churchill and me. I loved him very much and he loved me but we were so very different in the way that we thought

about it. He wanted to go on with it, writing about it and lecturing about it.[51] He did not want to leave it behind. The war had been for him the best years of his life … Every time we sat in front of food, he would say, 'How marvellous it is to have this food.' And I would say, 'No, it's not marvellous, it's normal.'[52]

Sansom, in contrast, wanted to move on, despite the media interest in her war story. An article reporting on her award of the George Cross quoted her as saying: 'It was a secret mission of which I do not care to talk. I am trying here in this quiet spot to forget it all … all I want is rest. I am going to stay at home and do some knitting.'[53]

Sansom and Churchill were not the only repatriated prisoners whose post-war marriages failed. We have already seen that Edgar Hargreaves' marriage ended in divorce. Harry Peulevé, who survived Buchenwald, married in 1952 and had two children, but his need for independence put additional pressure on the relationship and his wife filed for divorce on the grounds of desertion.[54]

The prevalence of divorce among SOE agents (as well as reading Angus Calder's seminal text *The People's War*[55]) allegedly inspired David Hare to write *Plenty* (1978)[56] in order to examine the effects of the Second World War on personal relationships. The play depicts the post-war disillusionment of Susan Traherne who, we learn through flashbacks, served with the French Resistance during the Second World War. Her manic depression, madness, promiscuity, drug-taking, incessant smoking and drinking, passionate arguments with her husband and a hinted-at lesbian relationship testify to the war's impact on one individual. One character, Mick, says, 'She is actually mad', while Brock, her husband, threatens to have her committed to an institution. In her book on Hare's plays, Carol Homden notes that Traherne, 'a schizophrenic icon',[57] is 'a woman who serves as a reflection of a disjuncture in the society of which she is part.'[58]

Hare recognised that the war could have a profound effect on veterans' lives and for some, like the fictitious character Susan Traherne, it could be highly destructive leading to poor mental health and marital breakdown. For others, the war is fondly looked back upon as the best of times, a testing period in which they rose to the challenge and proved themselves. Others have incorporated the war years into the rest of their lives, while some moved on completely, looking ahead to the future and leaving the war firmly in the past.

Looking back or moving on

As we have seen, Odette Sansom asserted that Peter Churchill could not leave the war behind him: he sought to recapture that period by writing and lecturing about it and by moving to the South of France where he had been operational. The rest of his life was led in the shadow of the war. Some veterans I interviewed provided 'Golden Age' accounts of their involvement with the SOE: Roger Landes asserted that it constituted 'the best years of my life ... made me a man.'[59] That he named his house 'Aristide', after his codename, suggests that he is still absorbed in the war. Nancy Wake also provided a very positive account of her war years: 'I got so many happy memories from those days, happy memories.'[60] When I asked her whether or not her work with the SOE was the focal part of her life, she replied: 'Well, let's face it, my dear, of course it was.'[61] The war clearly has had a lingering significance in the rest of her life. Wake has been involved in several projects, has been the subject of a mini-series and has assisted two biographers, as well as written her own life story. She has made arrangements that when she dies, her ashes are to be flown over to Mont Mouchet in the Auvergne 'where I was with the men.'[62] For Wake, the war was the pivotal part of her life and, despite attempts to be the 'Housewives' Friend', she found it difficult to readjust to mundane civilian life. In *The Australian*, she is quoted as saying: 'It was dreadful because you've been so busy and then it all fizzles out.'[63] Under the headline 'Bored Heroine' on *The Star*'s 'diary' page on 22 April 1948, the 'Star Man' reported:

> Over the phone from Paris today a musically girlish voice asked me: 'Can you get me an exciting job? I'm so bored.' Owner of the voice was Mrs Nancy Fiocca, wartime heroine who has just been presented with the George Medal for exploits in France in 1944 ... Mrs Fiocca assured me today she is ready for more. ('I'll do anything and go anywhere – to the North Pole, if possible.') At the moment grey-eyed, dark-haired Mrs Fiocca works in the visa section of the British Embassy. She has a furnished flat, gives dinner parties and goes to occasional cinemas and theatres. But all the time she hankers after life with the partisans.[64]

Even agents who were deported have tended to stress the positive aspects of their captivity, such as comradeship, survival techniques, independence, development of skills and humour. In an interview held in 1996, Brian Stonehouse noted: 'I now feel that I was lucky, if you can put it that way, to have gone through this because now I know who I am and I'm not afraid anymore ... It gives you a different sense of values ... what is important changes ... I should have died 51 years ago.'[65] Similarly, Bob Sheppard asserted:

> It's a wonderful part of my life, even including the concentration camps. I look back with sadness for all the friends I left everywhere but, for myself, I think it was a tremendous experience. I very often wonder would I be what I am (if I am something) without these experiences? It's an enormous experience and probably more the concentration camps too, for human contact, respect of the other and all that which was very important. The concentration camp in its horror and awfulness was also a lesson of the human being ... Respect yourself and respect others. That's what camp brought me.[66]

The construction of positive memories by those who endured highly traumatic experiences was possibly, as Alistair Thomson maintained, 'an unconscious way of dealing with deeply repressed experiences and feelings.'[67] Or it might simply be that they had come to terms with their experiences and had successfully integrated them into the rest of their lives. During the interview, I wanted to make sure that Sheppard was comfortable talking about his experiences of captivity. He replied: 'It is a part of my life'[68] and indeed it remained so until he died. When I interviewed him in July 2002, aged eighty, he was the honorary International President of Mauthausen (having been previously elected International President), still remembered his different camp numbers like many survivors and still retained the physical signs of his mistreatment having chosen not to have them operated upon.[69] When I asked him what it was like the first time he returned to the camps, he asserted: 'It was coming back into a part of my life. [pause] Natzweiler, Mauthausen, it's rather amazing. Coming back is feeling at home. Do you see what I mean? Feeling relieved there, the others did not, hard to explain but we were there.'[70]

While many agents, including Churchill, Landes, Wake, Stonehouse and Sheppard, look back on their involvement with the SOE as the defining part of their lives and shaped who they became, others had clearly put their experiences behind them. Lise de Baissac, for example, emphasised, unprompted, that the war was only one aspect of her varied life: 'I've lived a full and happy life. SOE is just one part of it ... But that's all. I mean I never talk about it. A lot of people don't know anything about my past lives ... I've turned the page a long time ago. It's such a long time ago. I don't look back on my life. I never think about anything like that. I always look forward despite being 97.'[71] For her, the war was over and it had no real lasting meaning: 'I don't think it has changed me.'[72] Claire Everett said that neither she nor her husband, another SOE agent, talked about their wartime work: 'The war's gone. That was then and this is now, let's get on with life. I'm looking ahead and I'm not looking back ... It just didn't seem to fit in with our lives. It was part of our life then, that was the war, the war was then over and you just get on with life.'[73] Although they may have succeeded in putting the war behind them and getting on with their lives, their memories of the war were bound to return at some point. Judith Lewis Herman, writing about trauma and recovery, noted that when survivors reach new milestones in their lives, such as marriage, divorce, illness, death of a relative or retirement, memories re-emerge and this is when subjects return to the 'unfinished work of integrating the traumatic experience.'[74] Herman's understanding of the re-emergence of traumatic memories can be extended and applied to recollections about war more generally. Everett's decision to be interviewed about her wartime experiences appear to be linked to the death of her husband in 1999.

Sydney Hudson also felt that it was necessary to move on, especially given the difficulties he had in readjusting to civilian life. When I asked him whether he had kept in contact with wartime friends, he replied: 'No. For the best part of fifty years I felt that I was just not in the right; it's very easy, I know, to get yourself saturated in the past and I've met people who've done that. So I thought I wouldn't do that. I had a lot of other things to do. I'm not at all sorry that I separated myself totally from it, 1950s onwards.'[75] While Hudson was reluctant to maintain friendships with wartime colleagues, perhaps fearful of getting stuck in the past, most agents kept in close contact with some of the French people with whom they worked and this was certainly a common theme in veterans' testimonies. For example, Francis Cammaerts noted: 'The friendship was something that you couldn't find under other circumstances. The important thing was that the friendship was lifelong and very profound'[76] and Yvonne Cormeau remarked: 'I'm still friendly with them ... I went back every year ... It forged a kind of friendship which will always last, I think, because we shared difficulties and we shared the risks ... we haven't forgotten each other.'[77]

For many, both those who survived imprisonment and also those who were fortunate not to have been arrested, the war left an indelible mark – some continued to be haunted by their experiences, while others, to varying extents, have lived their lives in the shadow of that period with its concomitant adventure, personal development and great friendships. When I asked Vera Atkins, F Section's Intelligence Officer, who remained in touch with the agents after the war, about the transition from agent to civilian, she replied: 'Very difficult. In fact, I don't know anyone who doesn't remember every day of their life what they've been through. It colours them. They were the highlight of their lives. They live it all the time. You don't shake it off.'[78]

Post-war lives

Involvement with the SOE impacted upon agents' lives in other ways, opening up opportunities and enabling them to find interesting employment. Sydney Hudson acknowledged this: 'I have to admit that, on the whole, it probably made my life pleasanter. Ever since, I had rather nice jobs. Maybe that wasn't the reason why they gave me the rather nice jobs. I think it certainly counted in my favour.'[79] Equally, Lise de Baissac recognised that having her war record on her CV certainly helped.[80] A memo dated 7 March 1945 illustrates that the SOE also tried to assist some of its agents to find jobs: 'Col. Buckmaster has tried to obtain employment for Lt. Col. Cammaerts (Jockey). It was considered that he would do well with the Foreign Office, but was turned down because his father is Belgian.'[81] Interestingly, Yvonne Cormeau felt that there might have been a gendered element to this, with only some male agents receiving assistance: 'I can see a lot of women not getting their fair due', but again the interviewer did not press her further.[82] Francis Cammaerts thought that only some who were well liked by Vera Atkins, like himself, had assistance in finding positions after the war: 'Vera is one of the responsible people. She gave high priority to the people she regarded as "her boys", and Auguste Florias [Cammaerts' wireless operator] and Christine Granville [his courier] didn't belong to "her boys", so they didn't get her leg-up.'[83] For Granville, this had particularly tragic consequences. Struggling to find her niche in life, she undertook a variety of low-paid and low-status jobs and eventually became a steward on a shipping line. In 1952, a colleague began stalking her when she rejected his advances and, despite attempts to distance herself from him by changing her shifts, he fatally stabbed her. Francis Cammaerts, however, was one of Vera's 'boys', as he himself recognised. He worked for the British Military Control Commission, responsible for food and agriculture in the British sector of Berlin. He resumed his teaching career and became a Professor of Education at Nairobi University in Kenya and was one of the first presidents of the university and college lecturers' union, NATFHE. He and his wife, who had three children, returned to live in the South of France. Cammaerts, who was well decorated after the war having been awarded a D.S.O.[84] from the British, the *Légion d'honneur*[85] from the French and the Medal of Freedom[86] from the Americans, died in July 2006.

Bob Sheppard was also one of Vera's favourites. He recalled that the day after he and Stonehouse had returned from Dachau, she had said: 'Ah boys, I must think of getting a medal for you.'[87] He was given a Mention in Despatches[88] and was awarded the *Légion d'honneur*. After the war, he was sent to Germany as a Denazification Officer and was demobbed in early 1947. He later worked in Belgium and retired to the north of France where he wrote his autobiography which was published in French. Sheppard died in 2002, shortly after I interviewed him.

The other veterans I interviewed were all decorated and many had post-war employment which used some of the skills they had acquired with the SOE. Cyril Watney, who had a prominent position within the Canadian intelligence service between 1949 and 1951, was awarded an M.C.[89] and the *Croix de Guerre*.[90] Bob Maloubier enlisted with Force 136 and served in Ceylon and India. After the war, he worked in the French Secret Service ('the equivalent of the SOE'[91]) and received a D.S.O. and an M.C. He is currently living in France, and on the day of our meeting in Paris had just finished writing the last line of a biography of Violette Szabo who was a member of the same Resistance network. Sydney Hudson also joined Force 136, serving in Ceylon, India and Thailand and then moved to Germany to work, like Cammaerts, with the Control Commission dealing with industrial relations. After his divorce, he married a German woman whose Jewish mother was shot in spring 1945 just days before the end of the war. They moved to Israel where Hudson worked for Shell and then to Scotland. In 2001, Hudson was reunited with his courier Sonya Butt whom he had not seen since 1944. Hudson, who was awarded two D.S.O.s[92] and a Croix de Guerre, died in 2005. Roger Landes, who was ordered to leave France immediately by Charles de Gaulle who wanted to remove all British officers so that he could begin rebuilding France without any outside assistance, joined Force 136, serving in Malaya. He then worked in Intelligence until 1947, interpreting photographs taken by reconnaissance planes flying over Russia. He returned to France, married the daughter of a Resistance colleague and, rather than becoming an architect as he had planned, took up his father's profession as a jeweller. Landes' wife died in 1983 and, in 1990, he remarried. He was awarded the *Croix de Guerre*, the *Légion d'honneur* and an M.C. He lives in the South of England. Gaston Cohen, who was awarded an M.C., volunteered for active service in Force 136. He returned to live in Paris where he had been operational and is now Gaston Collins; he elected to keep the name that SOE had given him during his training, changing his name by deed poll after the war. His brother, George, who was deported to Germany as a Jew, did not return. At the time of interview in 2002, Cohen was trying to find out what had happened to him. Cohen died in 2007.

The female agents were also well decorated. Claire Everett was awarded an M.B.E.[93] and Yvonne Baseden was awarded an M.B.E. and the *Croix de Guerre*. She returned to the WAAF after recovering from her experiences of captivity and, like Roger Landes, interpreted aerial photographs. She was demobbed in 1948, when she married Desmond Bailey, moved to Rhodesia in 1949 and had a son in 1951. Vera Atkins, F Section's Intelligence Officer asked her to agree to be the subject of 'This is Your Life' and, despite not wanting to, she relented. When I went to interview her, she showed me the 'big red book', the pictorial record of the event, broadcast on 25 September 1955.[94] She later remarried and was widowed. Yvonne Burney currently lives in London. Nancy Wake, who was awarded the George Medal,[95] the *Légion d'honneur*, the *Croix de Guerre* and the Medal of Freedom, was the most highly decorated servicewoman of the Second World War. She returned to Marseille to find that her husband had been tortured and killed by the Nazis who, failing to locate her, arrested him in her place. In 1949, the 'Bored Heroine' found a new role to occupy herself: she returned to Australia and entered politics. Standing for the Liberal Party, Wake contested the federal seat of Barton, cutting the margin of the incumbent, Labour candidate and Deputy Prime Minister Dr Clive Evatt, from 11,112 to 2,644. She tried again in 1951, polling just 127 votes less than Evatt. Wake then moved to Britain, joined the Air Ministry and married John Forward in 1957, before returning to Australia to give politics one last try in 1961. Widowed in 1997, Wake moved back to Britain in 2001 and I attended her ninetieth birthday party in 2002. Lise de Baissac joined the BBC, something she had wanted to do prior to joining the SOE, working as a translator in the French section. She stayed with the BBC until 1950 before leaving, aged forty five, to marry a man who had first proposed to her in 1922. They lived together in Marseille and she was widowed in 1978. Lise Villameur died aged ninety-eight in 2004. She was awarded the *Légion d'honneur* and the *Croix de Guerre* and was recommended for the O.B.E., but a letter in her personal file dated 18 October 1945 stated that it was 'downgraded to M.B.E. – issue being fought'.[96] A memo entitled 'Some examples of discrepancies in civil/military awards', dated 22 October 1945, noted that de Baissac 'declined the M.B.E. (Civil)'[97] and her file at the National Archives contains a letter from Vera Atkins about this: 'I should therefore be very grateful if you would write me a note setting out your reasons for wishing to refuse the M.B.E. (Civil).'[98]

De Baissac was not the only woman to turn down the M.B.E. Pearl Witherington was nominated for an M.C. but, as women were ineligible for receiving this honour, she was awarded an M.B.E. instead, which was a civilian decoration. She returned it claiming that she was not a civilian and had not done anything 'civil'. In the same memo cited above, it is noted:

> Her exploits over a very long period compare favourably with those for which a D.S.O. or M.C. is normally given. She was awarded an M.B.E. (Civil) on the grounds that:
>
> i) The holder of an Honorary Commission is not eligible for a military award. [Witherington held an Honorary Commission in the WAAF as she had belonged to that service prior to her recruitment.]
>
> ii) Her low rank limits her to this grade of the British Empire Order.
>
> She has declined this honour on the grounds that her work was not appropriate to the M.B.E. (Civil), which incidentally she does not disparage. She prefers no award to an inappropriate one.[99]

The memo also noted that 'a number of these young women have given service in the field which, had they been male officers, would have earned between them gallantry awards or other recognition of every grade from D.S.O. and C.B.E. (Mil) downwards. They are, however, debarred from receiving most of such awards.' It then listed why women were excluded, stating that 'women are not eligible' for the D.S.O., the M.C. or the Distinguished Conduct Medal despite the fact that there is no debarring authority in the warrants, that both FANY personnel and Honorary Officers in the WAAF are 'deemed to be civilians' and that 'there is no award available to British Women Officers up to Lt. Col. rank for gallantry in the face of the enemy except the M.B.E. (Civil)'. However, they were eligible for the Victoria Cross, the George Cross, the George Medal, the Military Medal and Mentions in Despatches. This clearly angered Lise de Baissac and Pearl Witherington who refused their M.B.E.s, as well as fellow agent Sydney Hudson: 'I think it's disgraceful that our women were given civilian decorations, not military ones.'[100]

In October 1944, Pearl Witherington married her fiancé Henri Cornioley, whom she had worked alongside and they had a child. She embarked upon a two-month lecture tour in America in 1945 and then worked in banking. She is now widowed and is living in France. She replied to my letter but decided that, because her husband had only just died, she did not want to be interviewed. Of the other people mentioned in this book, little is known of their post-war lives as the focus in the official records and interviews has been on their wartime experiences. However, it is known that Anne-Marie Walters, who was awarded the M.B.E (Civil), married M. Comert, a Frenchman, and lived in France and Spain. Jacqueline Nearne starred in the documentary *School for Danger*, looked after her sister Didi upon her release from Ravensbrück and then moved to New York to work with the United Nations. In an article in the *Evening Standard*, entitled 'He and She, 'chutists, start new jobs', she is quoted as saying: 'I have to do no parachuting now, not even as a Sunday hobby. Just to stand on the top floor of this 1,250 foot building makes me giddy these days.'[101] Nearne remained single and died in 1982. Both Jacqueline and her younger sister Eileen, known as Didi, were awarded the M.B.E. and a *Croix de Guerre*. Yvonne Cormeau worked for the Control Commission in the Ruhr and then for the Embassy in Brussels. In her Imperial War Museum interview, she asserted: 'I settled perfectly all right.'[102] Like Yvonne Baseden, she was also the subject of 'This is Your Life' (broadcast on 8 November 1989.) She was awarded an M.B.E., the *Légion d'honneur* and the *Croix de Guerre*. Cormeau remarried in 1989, becoming Mrs Farrow, and died on Christmas Day 1997. Sonya Butt M.B.E. went to live in Canada with her husband Guy d'Artois. They had six children. Paddy O'Sullivan married an SOE trainer and had two children. Françine Agazarian, who got a Mention in Despatches, returned to Britain, but her husband Jack, a fellow agent, did not: he was executed at Flossenberg in March 1945. In a letter to the journalist Liane Jones, she wrote of her visit to Flossenberg to see his cell and to walk to the yard where he was shot: 'I have not been able to free myself entirely from grief.'[103] Odette Wilen married, becoming Mrs de Strugo, and is currently living in South America. Odette Sansom, as has been noted, became something of a celebrity, bolstered by the fairy tale romance with her organiser, Peter Churchill. Sansom gave evidence in 1946 at the War Crimes trial of Ravensbrück staff dressed in her FANY uniform. In 1956, Sansom got married a third time to a man who had also been in the Special Forces. Odette Hallowes G.C. died in 1995. After his divorce, Peter Churchill moved to France and remarried. He died in the 1960s. Brian Stonehouse, who was awarded a military M.B.E., joined the Allied Control Commission in Germany. While assisting with the prosecution of war criminals, he came across someone who had interrogated him and refused the gun given to him to exact revenge. In late 1946, he moved to the United States to work as a fashion artist for *Vogue* and *Harper's Bazaar*. He returned to Britain in 1979 to paint portraits: the Queen Mother was one of his subjects. He died in December 1998, aged eighty. Jacques Poirier, who was awarded a D.S.O., worked for a large oil company in Africa, Venezuela, Argentina, the Netherlands, France and

Britain and, following his retirement, wrote his autobiography which was published in both French and English. Guido Zembsch-Schreve, who had Dutch parents, was sent to the Netherlands to investigate the capture of agents and to interrogate war criminals. He married, worked in the oil and gas industries and wrote his autobiography during his retirement. Zembsch-Schreve died in 2003. Ted Zeff, Bob Sheppard's colleague who was arrested with him, survived both Mauthausen and later cancer. After the war, he returned to his shirt-making business in Paris. Robert Boiteux, Sheppard's organiser, who was awarded the M.B.E. and the M.C., volunteered for service in Force 136, assisted the evacuation of Allied POWs and worked with displaced persons in Germany. He married, had two children and moved to Australia where he changed his name to Burdett. Harry Peulevé joined Shell but he struggled to overcome his experiences as a concentration camp prisoner (which had precipitated the end of his marriage) and he resigned. He died in 1963, aged just forty-seven.

While the experiences of serving with SOE lived on with many veterans, the organisation itself did not. The new Prime Minister, Clement Atlee, with Ernest Bevin, Sir Alan Brooke (Chief of the Imperial General Staff) and Sir Stewart Menzies (Head of MI6, the Secret Intelligence Service), made the decision to dissolve the SOE in January 1946. A month later, a fire broke out on the top floor of a Baker Street building which housed the SOE files. Whether this was a deliberate ploy to destroy sensitive material or was purely accidental is open to conjecture. Up to 85 per cent of the files were estimated to have been lost in that fire.

In order to ensure that those who had served with the organisation should not lose touch, several surviving members of the SOE had decided that a Special Forces Club should be formed. In August 1946, the Club bought the lease for a property just around the corner from Harrods in Knightsbridge. It has just celebrated its sixtieth anniversary and some of the surviving F Section veterans attended the celebration. Running the length of its many staircases are the photographs of its agents, many of which have blacks frames – a poignant reminder of SOE's heavy loses.

Conclusion

Having begun by examining the recruits to the organisation, noting their upbringing and various occupations they undertook before joining, the book has come full circle, recording what the survivors went on to do after the war. The ordinariness of their pre- and post-war roles is striking and reminds us that these were just normal people who were given an opportunity to participate in an extraordinary organisation which demanded great sacrifice. Odette Sansom, the most well-known of the SOE agents, asserted: 'I am a very ordinary woman to whom a chance was given to see human beings at their best and at their worst.'[104] The personal testimonies analysed for this book are replete with comments which downplay their contributions and it is evident that few of their neighbours and friends knew about their war records. These individuals, who successfully passed during the war, have, to varying degrees, continued to conceal this aspect of their fascinating history.

Notes

1 11 April 1945 – Buchenwald; 15 April – Bergen-Belsen; 22 April – Sachsen-hausen; 23 April – Flossenberg; 29 April – Dachau; 30 April – Ravensbrück; 7 May – Mauthausen.

2 Personal interview with Bob Sheppard. For some American soldiers, the experience of liberating the camps was to have a troubling effect in their post-war lives. In an interview published in the *Guardian*'s weekend magazine, one of the soldiers who had liberated Buchenwald asserted: 'I have post-traumatic stress syndrome, and still have horrific dreams ... I go to a group therapy session every week. For the fiftieth anniversary of the liberation of Buchenwald, they asked me to return, but I didn't want to bring back those memories.' *Guardian* (16 September 2006).

3 IWM SA, 10445, Sheppard.

4 IWM SA, 18156 Stonehouse.

5 IWM SA, 18156 Stonehouse.

6 IWM SA, 18156 Stonehouse.

7 Personal interview with Bob Sheppard.

8 Personal interview with Bob Sheppard.

9 Obituary, *The Times* (10 December 1998).

10 Personal interview with Bob Sheppard.

11 Personal interview with Bob Sheppard.

12 M. R. D. Foot, *Six Faces of Courage* (London: Eyre Methuen, 1978), pp. 73–4.

13 Zembsch-Schreve, *Pierre Lalande*, p. 194; p. 188.

14 Zembsch-Schreve, *Pierre Lalande*, p. 195.

15 Personal interview with Dorothy Temple.

16 IWM SA, 5378 Hargreaves.

17 X. Vic-Dupont, L. F. Fichez and S. Weinstein cited in L. Eitinger and A. Strøm, *Mortality and Morbidity After Excessive Stress: A Follow-Up Investigation of Norwegian Concentration Camp Survivors* (New York: Humanities Press, 1973).

18 E. Cohen, *Human Behaviour in the Concentration Camp* (London: Jonathon Cape Ltd, 1954).

19 P. Helweg-Larsen et al., 'Famine Disease in German Concentration Camps: Complications and Sequels', *Acta Psychiatrica Scandinavica, Supplementum, 83* (1952).

20 L. Eitinger, 'Pathology of the Concentration Camp Syndrome', *Archives of General Psychiatry*, 5 (1961), p. 86.

21 IWM SA, 9478 Hallowes.

22 National Archives, HS 9/648/4, letter from RWL/F, dated 8 November 1945.

23 National Archives, HS 9/648/4, letter from AQ/MED to D/FIN, dated 14 November 1945.

24 National Archives, HS 9/648/4.

25 IWM SA, 9478 Sansom.

26 O. Franklin, 'Britain pays tribute to her war heroines: women secret agents at unveiling of memorial', *Daily Graphic* (8 May 1948).

27 Personal interview with Yvonne Baseden.

28 Personal interview with Maisie McLintock.

29 Jones, *A Quiet Courage*, p. 334.

30 *Timewatch: Secret Memories* (BBC2).

31 Y. Baseden, 'An English Secretary in the torture cells of the Gestapo', *Sunday Express* (23 March 1952).

32 Her picture, along with one of the Corps Commander placing a wreath under the new plaque, appeared in the *Daily Graphic* (8 May 1948). The same picture is used, along with photographs of Vera Atkins, Odette Sansom holding five-year-old Tania Szabo and Princess Alice, Countess of Athlone, unveiling the memorial, in *London Illustrated News* in an article entitled 'Heroines of the Second World War'.

33 Baseden, *Secret Agent* (BBC2).

34 IWM SA, 16568 Brooks.

35 Personal interview with Sydney Hudson.

36 Personal interview with Sydney Hudson.

37 Personal interview with Roger Landes.

38 IWM SA, 12297 Mulder-Gemmeke.

39 *Now it can be told*, broadcast 4 April 1950.

40 Cited in R. Adam, *A Woman's Place, 1910–1975* (London: Chatto and Windus, 1975), p. 159.

41 Adam, *A Woman's Place*, p. 167.
42 Gleeson, 'Commando Girls: Beginning today'.
43 Article untitled and undated. Held at FANY HQ. [1947 or 1948]
44 S. Rodin, 'Mrs Smith: Train-wrecker, spy and Nazi-killer', date and newspaper unknown, clipping held at FANY HQ.
45 Rodin, 'Mrs Smith'.
46 Grice, 'Return of the White Mouse'.
47 B.Turner and T. Rennell, *When Daddy Came Home: How Family Life Changed Forever in 1945* (London: Pimlico, 1995), p. 142.
48 Turner and Rennell, *When Daddy Came Home*, p. 144.
49 Personal interview with Sydney Hudson.
50 Personal interview with Lise de Baissac.
51 For example, in March 1947, he and two other non-SOE men who had each endured solitary confinement took part in a discussion chaired by fellow agent Harry Rée. *The Radio Times* records that this programme focused on 'how their experiences have affected their outlook on life'. *Radio Times*, (21 March 1947). Peter Churchill also told his story in a two-part series in *John Bull*, on 10 and 17 October 1953, in addition to publishing three volumes of his autobiography.
52 Jones, *A Quiet Courage*, p. 343.
53 W. O'Brien, 'G.C. woman withstood red-hot iron torture', *Daily Graphic* (undated) [August 1946]. Clipping held at FANY HQ.
54 Foot, *Six Faces of Courage*, p. 74.
55 A. Calder, *The People's War* (London: Cape, 1969).
56 *Plenty* was Hare's first original play for the National Theatre shown in 1978. It was later turned into a film, for which Hare wrote the screenplay, starring Meryl Streep (1985). In 1999, Cate Blanchett took the part of Traherne at the Albery Theatre.
57 C. Homden, *The Plays of David Hare* (Cambridge: Cambridge University Press, 1995), p. 82.
58 Homden, *The Plays of David Hare*, p. 65.
59 Personal interview with Roger Landes.
60 Personal interview with Nancy Wake.
61 Personal interview with Nancy Wake.
62 Personal interview with Nancy Wake.
63 *The Australian*, 25 April 1983. Quoted in Fitzsimons, *Nancy Wake*, p. 281.
64 'Bored Heroine', *The Star* (22 April, 1948).
65 IWM SA, 18156 Stonehouse.
66 Personal interview with Bob Sheppard.
67 Thomson, *Anzac Memories*, p. 26.
68 Personal interview with Bob Sheppard.
69 As well as losing a tooth from being punched during an interrogation, a toenail had been extracted: 'I still keep it. I didn't want to be operated. I still have it the old way. It's like a little bone. It doesn't look like a nail.' Personal

interview with Bob Sheppard.

70 Personal interview with Bob Sheppard.
71 Personal interview with Lise de Baissac.
72 Personal interview with Lise de Baissac.
73 Personal interview with Claire Everett (pseudonym).
74 Herman, *Trauma and Recovery*, p. 174.
75 Personal interview with Sydney Hudson.
76 Personal interview with Francis Cammaerts.
77 IWM SA, 8885 Cormeau.
78 Personal interview with Vera Atkins.
79 Personal interview with Sydney Hudson.
80 Personal interview with Lise de Baissac.
81 National Archives, HS 9/258/5.
82 IWM SA, 8885 Cormeau.
83 Personal interview with Francis Cammaerts.
84 The Distinguished Service Order is a British military decoration established in 1886 and is awarded to officers of the armed forces during wartime for commendable service.
85 The *Légion d'honneur*, which was instituted in 1802 by Napoleon Bonaparte, honours soldiers for exceptional acts of valour.
86 The Presidential Medal of Freedom is America's highest civilian award and was established by Truman in 1945 to recognise distinguished service in the war.
87 Personal interview with Bob Sheppard.
88 If a combatant's gallant actions are referred to in their commanding officer's report from the field, they have been 'Mentioned in Despatches'. The despatches were often printed in the *London Gazette* and they were later issued with a small bronze oak leaf.
89 The Military Cross was established in 1915 and is awarded to commissioned officers for gallant and distinguished services in battle.
90 The *Croix de Guerre* was instituted in 1915 to recognise acts of bravery in the face of the enemy.
91 Personal interview with Bob Maloubier.
92 A bar is added to the D.S.O. for a second award.
93 An M.B.E. is awarded for services and/or gallantry in the war by civilians at home and servicemen in support positions.
94 The programme was broadcast live and no copies were made of the programme.
95 The George Medal, which was instituted in 1940 along with the George Cross, is the second highest award for civilian bravery.
96 National Archives, HS 9/77/1.
97 'Some examples of discrepancies in civil/military awards', 22 October 1945, held in box labelled 'SOE' at FANY HQ.
98 National Archives, HS 9/77/1.

 99 'Some examples of discrepancies in civil/military awards'.
100 Hudson, *Behind Enemy Lines* (Channel 4).
101 'He and She, 'chutists, start new jobs', *Evening Standard* (undated), held at BFI.
102 8855 Cormeau, IWM SA.
103 Jones, *A Quiet Courage*, p. 330.
104 BFI, *Odette* film programme, 1950.

Appendix:
biographies of the twenty interviewees
whose testimonies have been referred to

Vera Atkins

Interviewed Vera Atkins, 2 July 1999, Sussex. (Unwilling to talk about herself.)

Born 15 June 1908 in Romania; Jewish father; two brothers, Ralph and Guy.

Had links with British intelligence whilst living in Romania in the 1930s; moved to Britain in 1937; joined Chelsea ARP (Air Raid Precaution) in 1940.

Name put forward for SOE by Leslie Humphreys who worked for Section D; interviewed February 1941; appointed as an Intelligence Officer for F Section; remained a civilian (known as Miss Atkins); particular responsibility for the female agents.

Became Squadron Leader in the WAAF in order to go to Germany to trace missing agents; interviewed prison and concentration camp staff; worked at the Central Bureau for Educational Visits and Exchanges; worked as a consultant for both *Odette* and *Carve Her Name with Pride*.

Awarded *Croix de Guerre, Légion d'honneur* and a CBE; died in 2000.

Lise de Baissac

Interviewed Lise Villameur, 17 April 2002, Provence.

Born 11 May 1905 in Mauritius; French parents, two older brothers, Jean and Claude; educated in Paris; at outbreak of war, journeyed to England, via Spain and Portugal; worked in office in London.

Was one of the first women to be recruited to the SOE; was on second training course (women only); was the second woman to be parachuted into France (preceded by Andrée Borrel seconds earlier) on 24 September 1942; codenamed 'Odile'; set up ARTIST, a base in Poitiers; assisted new agents upon their arrival in France; called back to England as group penetrated; collected by Lysander.

Became a conducting officer while in England; broke leg during a practice parachute jump; remained in England for five months; landed by Lysander on 9 April 1944.

Second mission as liaison agent to PIMENTO; did not get on well with PIMENTO, a socialist group; asked permission to join her brother Claude's SCIENTIST network in Normandy; worked as a courier for SCIENTIST; codenamed 'Marguerite'.

Awarded *Légion d'honneur, Croix de Guerre* and made a Member of the British Empire; worked for five years at the BBC as a translator in the French section; married a French architect in 1950 whom she had known before the war; she died in 2004, aged 98.

Yvonne Baseden

Interviewed Yvonne Burney, 28 August 1999 and 11 April 2000, London.

Born 20 January 1922 in France; English father, engineer; French mother, a singer, had driven an ambulance in the First World War, worked for the French Red Cross, put in charge of a canteen on the Maginot Line in 1939–40; older brother, Rex.

Lived for eight years in France, before travelling with her parents to Belgium, Holland, Poland, Italy and Spain; left Spain at the beginning of the Spanish Civil War; returned to Arcachon in France; joined a women's ice hockey team and enjoyed clay-pigeon shooting; studied in France and England; completed secretarial courses in English (Pitman) and French (Prevost-Delaunay).

Tried to join de Gaulle's Free French Section but rejected because of English father; joined the WAAF as a Craft GD (Aircraft Woman General Duties); met F Section agent Pearl Witherington who recommended her; recruited for the SOE by Selwyn Jepson; trained as a wireless operator.

Parachuted into Auch for SCHOLAR circuit on 18 March 1944; codenamed 'Odette'; based in Dôle, near Dijon; took part on 26 June in operation CADILLAC, the first daylight drop of supplies; betrayed and arrested on 26 June 1944; taken to Dijon prison; deported to Ravensbrück concentration camp near Berlin, given number 62,947; left on the last convoy run by Swedish Red Cross in April 1945, a fortnight before camp was liberated; spent nine months in King Edward VII's Sanatorium in Midhurst recovering from TB.

Awarded an M.B.E. and *Croix de Guerre* with Palm; married Desmond Bailey; one son, Simon; lived in Rhodesia; remarried to a descendant of Fanny Burney, the first women correspondent in South Africa; has never returned to Ravensbrück; lives in London.

Derrick Duesbury (pseudonym)

Interviewed Derrick Duesbury, 27 August 1999, Oxfordshire.

Born 25 February 1913; educated at Cambridge University; was a pacifist; joined the Security Section.

Appendix

Claire Everett (pseudonym)

Interviewed Claire Everett, 19 June 2002, London.

Born 14 May 1924 in Kent; parents separated for many years, finally divorced in 1939.

Lived in France with mother from age three; educated in France and a convent in Italy; returned to England after war broke out; joined WAAF.

Recruited by Selwyn Jepson; trained as a courier; parachuted in May 1944; after liberation worked for Americans, collecting intelligence by crossing the lines back and forth; on one occasion the car her organiser and her were travelling in was ambushed; was raped by two German soldiers.

Awarded M.B.E.; married fellow SOE agent; now widowed.

Francis Cammaerts

Interviewed Francis Cammaerts, 28 July 1999, Languedoc-Roussillon.

Born 1916 in England; English mother, a Shakespearean actress; Belgian father, teacher, journalist, and poet, wrote *A Child of Divorce*, a 'peaceful anarchist' who never shaved during his whole lifetime and made his own clothes; one brother.

Brought up in England; educated by father; met future SOE agent Harry Rée at Cambridge University; teacher; registered as a conscientious objector; resigned from teaching and became a farm labourer on a pacifist community in Lincolnshire where he met Nan; married; daughter born; RAF brother killed; retracted his objection to the war.

Recruited by Jepson; underwent training as an organiser; parachuted 1 March 1943 to establish JOCKEY; codenamed 'Roger'; based in south-east France; second daughter born while in France; arrested in August 1944 – travelling with SOE colleagues Xan Fielding and Major Sorenson in a car driven by Claude Renoir, the son of the Impressionist painter, stopped at a German roadblock, pretended to be strangers hitching a lift but some of the bank notes which they were carrying were from the same series; courier Christine Granville blackmailed Gestapo chief to release them; liberated and returned to Britain.

Awarded D.S.O., *Légion d'honneur* and Medal of Freedom with Silver Palm; resumed job as a teacher; died in 2006.

Gaston Cohen

Interviewed Gaston Collins, 31 July 2002, Paris.

Born 10 October 1918; English father, educated in France; Jewish French mother; one brother, George, who was deported to Germany and did not survive incarceration, and one sister.

Brought up in the West End of London; attended a French Protestant School in London; joined Hampshire Yeomanry regiment of the British Army (artillery);

staffed anti-aircraft batteries in Southampton during the Battle of Britain.
Interviewed by Selwyn Jepson in 1942; trained as a wireless operator; parachuted
into Versailles May 1943; code named 'Justin'; based in Paris; worked for the
PELICAN circuit, a sub-section of PROSPER.
Crossed Pyrenees following penetration of PROSPER in September 1943; arrested
by Spanish guards; imprisoned at Saragossa.
Second mission to France; parachuted on 6 March 1944; based in Marseille with
GARDINER circuit.
Trained a French commando unit in England; joined Force 136; stationed in
Poona; changed name by deed poll to Collins.
Awarded Military Cross, *Légion d'honneur* and the *Croix de Guerre*; has never
married; died in 2007.

Gervase Cowell

Interviewed Gervase Cowell, 3 June 1999, London.
Born 4 August 1926 in Cheshire; educated by Jesuits at St Bede's College,
Manchester; volunteered in 1944 for the RAF; learnt Japanese and Russian;
worked for GCHQ until 1948; studied Russian and French at St Catherine's
College, Cambridge.
Joined MI6 (Secret Intelligence Service) in 1951, posted to Germany to work in the
Control Commission until it disbanded in 1952; worked for MI6 in London,
Amman, Moscow, Bonn, Paris and Tel Aviv; ran Soviet agent Oleg Penkovsky
during the Cuban missile crisis of 1962; retired in 1981.
In 1985, undertook research in MI6's archive; in 1988, became the Foreign Office's
adviser on the wartime work of the SOE; retired from this post in 1996; became
Chairman of the historical sub-committee of the Special Forces Club.
Awarded an M.B.E.; designed two plaques commemorating the SOE agents, one
at Westminster Abbey and one at Ravensbrück concentration camp; died in
2000.

M. R. D. Foot

Interviewed M. R. D. Foot, 1 April, 1999, Hertfordshire.
Born 1919 in London; educated at Winchester and New College, Oxford.
Junior Intelligence Officer at Command Operations Headquarters in 1942; became
Intelligence Officer in the SAS in 1944, serving for six months; awarded *Croix
de Guerre*.
Lecturer at St. Catherine's College, Oxford; asked to write the official history of
F Section in 1959; spent two years researching and writing; took four years to
pass the sensors; *SOE in France* published in 1966; libelled by Odette Sansom
and Peter Churchill; second edition appeared with omitted sections about
Sansom and Churchill; Professor of Modern History at Manchester for six

years; published many books including *Resistance* (London: Eyre Methuen, 1976), *Six Faces of Courage* (London: Eyre Methuen, 1978) and *SOE: An Outline History of the Special Operations Executive 1940–46* (London: BBC, 1984); lives in Hertfordshire.

Sydney Hudson

Interviewed Sydney Hudson, 8 June 2002, East Lothian.

Born 1 August 1910 in England; father half-German, half-British, consul in Switzerland; English mother.

Lived in Switzerland; privately educated; sold chemicals; married Joan; returned to England after outbreak of war; joined Royal Fusiliers, then Auxiliary Units; recruited by Lewis Gielgud; trained as organiser; daughter Jennifer born day before parachuted.

Parachuted into France on 24 September 1942 to lead HEADMASTER circuit; codenamed 'Marc'; based in the Puy de Dôme; arrested on 8 October 1942 when people with whom he was staying were betrayed; was under Vichy control as arrested before southern France was occupied; sentenced to five years' hard labour; escaped with fifty prisoners on 3 January 1944; crossed Pyrenees.

Returned April 1944; codenamed 'Albin'; based in the Sarthe; joined by courier Sonya Butt with whom he had a relationship.

Served in Force 136 in Far East; processed prisoners of Japanese POW Camp; demobilised; divorced wife; worked in Germany with Controlled Commission; married Ruth Risse, a German Jew, in 1954.

Awarded two D.S.O.s and a *Croix de Guerre* with *Palme*; died in 2005.

Roger Landes

Interviewed Roger Landes, 25 August 1999, Hampshire.

Born 16 December 1916 in Paris; British father (spoke little English as he lived in France), jeweller; Russian-born French mother; two brothers, Marcel and Claude.

Left school aged thirteen, started work with a building firm; went to evening classes to become a chartered surveyor; father bankrupted, left France for England in 1933 with wife and Claude; Roger remained in France until 1938; worked in rescue service in Islington during the Blitz; called up to the Royal Corps of Signals in March 1941; trained as a wireless operator.

Interviewed by Lewis Gielgud; parachuted into France as a wireless operator for the SCIENTIST network on 31 October 1942; codenamed 'Stanislas'; based in Normandy; realised group penetrated by an informer, Grandclement; Grandclement was shot following a tribunal supervised by Landes; Landes shot Grandclement's wife as none of his group would kill a woman; crossed Pyrenees; captured by Spanish guards and imprisoned in Miranda de Ebro.

Lectured at Beaulieu; infiltrated a second time as an organiser for ACTOR network; based in Bordeaux; codenamed 'Aristide'; his group undertook much sabotage around D-Day; met de Gaulle who ordered him out of France.

Joined Force 136; underwent jungle training in Sri Lanka; dropped into Malaya.

Awarded the Military Cross with bar and *Légion d'honneur*; married Ginette Corbin, the daughter of a fellow resister on 29 July 1947; became a jeweller; was widowed and remarried; lives in Hampshire.

Bob Maloubier

Interviewed Robert Maloubier, 31 July 2002, Paris.

Born 2 February 1923 in Paris; French parents; teachers in Brooklyn, New York.

Studied at lycée in Paris; after invasion, cycled down to Bordeaux ahead of German army, strafed by Stukas; enlisted with French Air Force in Neuilly; posted to Bizerta (Tunisia) at the time of Operation TORCH, the Allied landing; escaped shortly after the Germans landed in Bizerta; joined Special Detachments in Algiers; met F Section staff member Jacques de Guelis in Algiers; travelled to England; joined SOE; trained as a saboteur.

Dropped into Normandy in August 1943; codenamed 'Paco'; operational in Rouen in SALESMAN circuit; caught by the local Feldgendarmerie on 20 December 1943, shot in lung and liver; returned to England on 6 February 1944; Violette Szabo joined network as courier; involved in the liberation of Limoges.

Enlisted with Force 136 in October 1944; based in Ceylon, then India.

Awarded the D.S.O.; married twice; three children; lives in Paris.

Maisie McLintock

Interviewed Maisie McLintock (née Sim) 24 October 1999, Morayshire.

Born 30 November 1916 in Edinburgh; worked for the Civil Service; because of the marriage bar, left the Civil Service when she married in February 1941; brought back due to labour shortage; worked in Ministry of Labour, responsible for recruiting female labour in Scotland; received file about FANY and joined.

Undertook FANY training with Eileen Nearne; also saw Yvonne Baseden on courses; became a coder.

Bob Sheppard

Interviewed Robert Sheppard, 30 July 2002, Normandy.

Born 1 March 1922 in Paris; British father, fought in the First World War, worked in a plywood factory in Nantes; French mother, worked for the Metro; both arrested by the Germans and sent to a prison in Vittel – were exchanged with German civilian prisoners who were imprisoned in England in 1944.

Studied at the lyéee up to the baccalaureate in Nantes; helped British servicemen to escape from France; decided to get to England and join the British Army; crossed the Pyrenees, was arrested by Spanish guards and imprisoned at Arida, Saragossa and Miranda de Ebro; released after a couple of months, moved to Gibraltar, boarded a ship to Liverpool.

Was recruited by Lewis Gielgud; underwent the training and allotted role of saboteur; parachuted on 1 June 1942 and arrested immediately upon landing – he landed on the roof of the gendarmerie; escaped within days with the assistance of friendly gendarmes; codenamed 'Patrice'; based in Lyon; began work as a saboteur.

Was recalled to London with fellow SOE agent Edward Zeff; arrested while crossing the Pyrenees on 1 March 1943, betrayed by their guide; tortured (beaten up and toenails extracted) and deported to Germany; imprisoned in Neubremme near Saarbrucken, Mauthausen, Natzweiler and Dachau; liberated on 29 April 1945.

Following his recuperation, sent to Germany as a Denazification Officer; demobilised with the rank of Major in February 1947; awarded *Légion d'honneur* and a Mention in Despatches; elected International President for Mauthausen concentration camp; married pre-war fiancé Lisette, in September 1945; five children; died in 2002.

Eric Sheppard

Interviewed Eric Sheppard, 22 September 1999, Cheshire.

Born 28 June 1920 in Cheshire; three brothers and one sister; left school aged fourteen to work in parents' knitwear business; joined Fairey Aviation and worked alongside Arthur Lowe (Captain Mainwaring in *Dad's Army*).

Joined the Territorial Army in the Royal Corps of Signals attached to the Fifth Kings Own Regiment; brought out of Dunkirk on 3 June 1940 on H.M.S. Windsor; caught meningitis which affected his hearing and prevented him serving overseas; called to interview to become an SOE instructor in communications.

Demobilised; returned to Fairey Aviation; worked at the British Embassy but resigned before being posted to Iran; returned to family business; worked at Kelloggs until retirement. Married twice; died in 2003.

May Shrewsbury

Interviewed May Shrubb, 23 July 1999, Buckinghamshire.

Born 11 December 1919 in London; six brothers and four sisters; left school aged fourteen to become a dressmaker; trained and qualified as a dressmaker; worked for Berketex.

Joined ATS in 1943; six weeks' training in Pontefract; posted to the Thatched

Barn where she worked as a dressmaker; married and very quickly widowed; demobilised August 1945; remarried.

Dorothy Temple

Interviewed Dorothy Wakely, 20 June 2002, Somerset.

Born 4 July 1915 in Essex; brought up in India; worked as a journalist in Fleet Street, 1941–2.

Joined the FANYs in 1943; seconded to SOE as a Signals Planner; posted to Algiers and then Bari in Italy; joined the British Embassy in Paris after VE Day.

Nancy Wake

Interviewed Nancy Wake-Forward, 18 August 1999, London.

Born 30 August 1912 in Wellington, New Zealand; English father, a journalist; half-Maori, half-French mother; lived in New Zealand and Australia; parents separated; five older siblings (three sisters and two brothers).

Came to London and Paris in 1930s; worked as a journalist; saw Hitler when in Berlin on assignment; married Henri Fiocca; after outbreak of war worked on Garrow escape line (later PAT line) helping downed airmen return to Britain; called 'The White Mouse'; crossed Pyrenees when too dangerous; husband killed by Germans.

Recruited by Selwyn Jepson; trained as a courier; parachuted 29 April 1944; codenamed 'Helene'; based in the Auvergne; lived on hillside with thousands of maquisards; undertook sabotage actions.

Awarded George Medal; worked at British Passport Control Office; ran for seat against Deputy Prime Minister Dr Clive Evatt, narrowly losing; worked at Air Ministry in Whitehall; married John Forward in 1957; widowed in 1997; living in London at the Royal Star and Garter Home for ex-Servicemen and -women.

Cyril Watney

Interviewed Cyril Watney, 11 August 2000, Essex.

Born 29 September 1922 in Calais; British father, born in France, educated in England; English mother.

Lived in France; returned to England in 1940; learned radio and Morse at Oxford University; joined British Army.

Interviewed by Selwyn Jepson; trained as a wireless operator; went to shooting galleries with Violette Szabo during his training; parachuted on 7 January 1944; based in the Lot at Saint-Céré; codenamed 'Eustache'; worked for FOOTMAN circuit; undertook much sabotage around D-Day.

Awarded Military Cross and the *Croix de Guerre*; became head of Canadian Intelligence 1949–1951; lives in Essex.

Pru Willoughby

Interviewed Prudence Hannay, 20 June 2002, London.
Born 22 April 1918 in Hertfordshire; four sisters; educated at St Hilda's, Oxford.
Worked for MI5 until August 1942; transferred to SOE's Security Section at Baker
Street working in counter-espionage; went to Italy in February 1944.

Bibliography

1 Archival sources

1.1 Files held at the National Archives, formerly the Public Record Office,
Kew, London

CAB 66/7 – 'British Strategy in a Certain Eventuality.' Report by the Chiefs of Staff, 25 May 1940.

CAB 121/305 – 'Organisation and Control of the Special Operations Executive (SOE).'

CO 537/1210 – 'Revision of British Nationality and Status of Aliens Act: Married Women', 1946.

HS 6/568 – France: Circuit and mission reports and interrogations: Cammaerts to Cruzel, 1944–1945.

HS 6/569 – France: Circuit and mission reports and interrogations: Dennery to Duquesne, 1944–1945.

HS 6/573 – France: Circuit and mission reports and interrogations: Istria to Knight, 1944–1945.

HS 6/576 – France: Circuit and mission reports and interrogations: Nearne to Noyer, 1944–1945.

HS 7/55 – Histories and War Diaries: Lecture folder STS 103; Part 1, 1943–1944.

HS 7/66 – Histories and War Diaries: SOE Group B training manual regional supplement: France, Netherlands and Norway [c.1940–1945].

HS 7/135 – Histories and War Diaries: Evaluation of SOE activities in France 1941–1944 [c.1941–1944].

HS 8/371 – Ministry of Economic Warfare, Special Operations Executive and Successors: Headquarters: Records: Recruitment and training: Lectures and statistics, 1942 Jan 01 – 1942 Dec 31.

HS 8/858 – Ministry of Economic Warfare, Special Operations Executive and

Bibliography

Successors: Headquarters: Security: Publications, 1942 Jan 01 – 1948 Dec 31.

HS 9/10/2 – Personal File, Françoise Agazarian [also know as Françine Agazarian].

HS 9/11/1 – Personal File, Jack Agazarian.

HS 9/77/1 – Personal File, Lise de Baissac.

HS 9/114/2 – Personal File, Yolande Beekman

HS 9/165/8 – Personal File, Denise Bloch.

HS 9/183 – Personnel File, Andrée Borrel.

HS 9/250/2 – Personal File, Muriel Byck.

HS 9/258/5 – Personal File, Francis Cammaerts.

HS 9/298/6 – Personal File, Blanche Charlet.

HS 9/314 – Personnel File, Peter Churchill.

HS 9/339/2 – Personal File, Anne-Marie Walters.

HS 9/457/6 – Personal File, Yvonne Fontaine.

HS 9/612 – Personal File, Christine Granville.

HS 9/648/4 – Personal File, Odette Sansom.

HS 9/747/4 – Personal File, Christopher Sydney Hudson.

HS 9/836/5 – Personal File, Noor Inayat Khan.

HS 9/910/3 – Personal File, Vera Leigh.

HS 9/1240/3 – Personal File, Harry Rée.

HS 9/1419/8 – Personal File, Brian Stonehouse.

HS 9/1435 – Personal File, Violette Szabo.

LO 3/604 – British Nationality and Status of Aliens Act, 1914.

1.2 SOE box held at FANY HQ

Memo – 'Some examples of discrepancies in civil/military awards', 22 October 1945.

2 Oral History

2.1 Conducted by author

Date of interview	Interviewee	Wartime occupation
01/04/99	M. R. D. Foot	Author of official history of SOE
03/06/99	Gervase Cowell	Ex-SOE Adviser, Foreign Office
02/07/99	Vera Atkins	Intelligence Officer, F Section
23/07/99	May Shrubb (née Shrewsbury)	ATS Tailoress
28/07/99	Francis Cammaerts	SOE agent, F Section.
18/08/99	Nancy Wake-Forward (née Wake)	SOE agent, F Section
25/08/99	Roger Landes	SOE agent, F Section
27/08/99	Derrick Duesbury	Security Section
28/08/99	Yvonne Burney (née Baseden) (1)	SOE agent, F Section
22/09/99	Eric Sheppard	Instructor
24/10/99	Maisie McLintock (née Sim)	SOE-FANY Coder

21/11/99	Dorothy Wakely (née Temple)	SOE-FANY Signal Planner
11/04/00	Yvonne Burney (née Baseden) (2)	SOE agent, F Section
11/08/00	Cyril Watney	SOE agent, F Section
17/04/02	Lise Villameur (née de Baissac)	SOE agent, F Section
08/06/02	Sydney Hudson	SOE agent, F Section
20/06/02	Pru Hannay (née Willoughby)	Security Section
19/06/02	Claire Everett (pseudonym)	SOE agent, F Section
30/07/02	Bob Sheppard	SOE agent, F Section
31/07/02	Gaston Collins (né Cohen)	SOE agent, F Section
31/07/02	Bob Maloubier	SOE agent, F Section

2.2 Transcripts of media interviews

Name of interviewee	Programme	Channel	Year
Sonya Butt	Behind Enemy Lines: The Real Charlotte Grays	Channel 4	2002
Ralph Beauclerk	Churchill's Secret Army	Channel 4	2000
Yvonne Burney (Baseden)	Secret Agent	BBC2	2000
Francis Cammaerts	Churchill's Secret Army	Channel 4	2000
Francis Cammaerts	Secret Agent	BBC2	2000
Francis Cammaerts	Behind Enemy Lines: The Real Charlotte Grays	Channel 4	2002
Henri Diacono	Secret Agent	BBC2	2000
Peter Lake	Churchill's Secret Army	Channel 4	2000
Roger Landes	Secret Agent	BBC2	2000
Jacques Poirier	Churchill's Secret Army	Channel 4	2000
Claudia Pulver	Secret Agent	BBC2	2000
Lise Villameur (de Baissac)	Behind Enemy Lines: The Real Charlotte Grays	Channel 4	2002
André Watt	Churchill's Secret Army	Channel 4	2000
Guido Zembsch-Schreve	Secret Agent	BBC2	2000

2.3 Taped interviews with ex-SOE members held at the IWM SA

Name of interviewee	IWM tape number	Source	Date of interview
Robert Boiteux-Burdett	9851	IWM SA	1988
Tony Brooks	16568	'Reminiscences of a British Agent' (lecture at IWM)	1995
Maurice Buckmaster	8680	BBC Radio 4, Set Europe Ablaze	1983
Maurice Buckmaster	9452	IWM SA	1986
Yvonne Cormeau	7369	IWM SA	1984
Yvonne Cormeau	8885	BBC Radio 4, Set Europe Ablaze	1983
Pearl Cornioley (Witherington)	8689	BBC Radio 4, Set Europe Ablaze	1983

Name of interviewee	IWM tape number	Source	Date of interview
Pearl Cornioley (Witherington)	10447	IWM SA	1988
Harry Despaigne	9925	IWM SA	1987
Edgar Hargreaves	5378	IWM SA	1981
Selwyn Jepson	9331	IWM SA	1986
Peter Lee	7473	IWM SA	1984
Kenneth Mackenzie	18154	IWM SA	1996
Jos Mulder-Gemmeke	12297	BBC Radio 4, *Set Europe Ablaze*	1983
Harry Rée	8688	BBC Radio 4, *Set Europe Ablaze*	1983
Harry Rée	8720	IWM SA	1995
Odette Hallowes (Sansom)	9478	IWM SA	1986
Bob Sheppard	10445	IWM SA	1988
Brian Stonehouse	9852	IWM SA	1987
Brian Stonehouse	18156	IWM SA	1996

3 Correspondence

3.1 Written correspondence

Pearl Cornioley (Witherington) – 8 July 1999.
Sydney Hudson – 14 March 2002.
Duncan Stuart – 25 February 1999.
André Watt – 17 January 2003.
Anonymous combatant in Greece – 28 March 2000.
Anonymous combatant in Greece – 14 October 1999.
Anonymous combatant in the Middle East – 3 November 1999.

3.2 Email

Shrabani Basu, biographer, 12 October 2006.

3.3 Telephone conversations

Yvonne Burney (Baseden) – 6 November 2000.

4 Newspapers

Simpson, W., 'WAAF girls parachuted into France', *Sunday Times* (11 March 1945).
'Girl who was dropped over France missing', *News of the World* (17 March 1946).
'Story of the woman who knew how to die: Nazi firing squad was moved', *News Chronicle* (30 March 1946).

Bibliography

'The story behind a tragic picture: women agents' death mystery solved: last hours in concentration camp after parachute leap', newspaper unknown (31 March 1946).

'British women burned alive: German camp staff charged', *Daily Telegraph and Morning Post* (30 May 1946).

Lane, M., 'The story of four British Secret Service women: parachutists did not return'. Newspaper unknown and undated. Clipping held at FANY HQ.

O'Brien, W., 'G.C. woman withstood red-hot iron torture', *Daily Graphic* (undated). [August 1946].

'First British Woman GC: Fought gun battle alone with the Gestapo', *Daily Graphic* (and *Daily Sketch*) (18 December 1946).

'Girl who was dropped over France missing', *News of the World* (1946).

'Odette G.C. wed today' (newspaper unknown and undated) [1947].

'Couple who fooled Gestapo marry' (newspaper unknown and undated) [1947].

Review of *School for Danger*, P. Kirwan, *Evening Standard* (6 February 1947).

Review of *School for Danger*, *To-day's Cinema*, Vol. 68, No. 5457 (7 February 1947).

Review of *School for Danger*, *The Times* (7 February 1947).

Review of *School for Danger*, 'A seat in the stalls', *Sunday Express* (7 February 1947).

Review of *School for Danger*, C. C. Lejeune, *Observer* (9 February 1947).

Review of *School for Danger*, 'Reviews for Showmen', *Kinematograph Weekly*, No. 2078 (13 February 1947).

Review of *School for Danger*, R. Mortimer, *The New Statesman and Nation* (15 February 1947).

Review of *School for Danger*, *Showmen's Trade Review* (22 February 1947).

Review of *School for Danger*, 'At the Pictures – round up', *Punch or the London Charivari* (5 March 1947).

Review of *School for Danger*, F. Majdalany, *Daily Mail* (undated). Clipping held at the British Film Institute, Item 31.

Review of *School for Danger*, R. Winnington, *News Chronicle* (undated). Clipping held at the British Film Institute, Item 31.

Review of *School for Danger*, *Daily Graphic* (undated). Clipping held at the British Film Institute.

'He and She, 'chutists, start new jobs', *Evening Standard* (undated). (Item 31: *School for Danger/Now It Can Be Told* file, held at British Film Institute.

Title unknown, *Radio Times* (21 March 1947).

'Bored Heroine', *The Star* (22 April 1948).

Franklin, O., 'Britain pays tribute to her war heroines: women secret agents at unveiling of memorial', *Daily Graphic* (8 May 1948).

'Heroines of the Second World War', *London Illustrated News* (undated) [May 1948].

Rodin, S., 'Mrs Smith: Train-wrecker, spy and Nazi-killer', date and newspaper unknown [1948]. Clipping held at FANY HQ.

'British Films Take Honours: Five among six winners at Great Britain's box offices during year', *Motion Picture Herald* (6 January 1950).

Gleeson, J., 'Commando Girls: Beginning today: a story that will thrill you and make you proud', *Daily Herald* (24 April 1950).

Gleeson, J., 'Commando Girls: Part II: Peggy blows up a German convoy', *Daily Herald* (25 April 1950).

Gleeson, J., 'Caught by the Gestapo: today's instalment of Commando Girls', *Daily Herald* (26 April 1950).

Gleeson, J., 'Torture – despair then rescue', *Daily Herald* (27 April 1950).

Gleeson, J., 'Commando Girls: Her bluff saved three men from death', *Daily Herald* (1 May 1950).

Gleeson, J., 'Commando Girls: the radio "widow"', *Daily Herald* (2 May 1950).

Gleeson, J., 'Commando Girls: the mother who died and the sisters', *Daily Herald* (3 May 1950).

Gleeson, J., title unknown, *Daily Herald* (5 May 1950).

Gleeson, J., 'Commando Girls: she led 3,500 guerillas', *Daily Herald* (6 May 1950).

Review of *Odette*, *Daily Express* (7 June 1950).

Baseden, Y., 'The tremendous things that happened to a quiet little English secretary: Secret Mission', *Sunday Express* (9 March 1952).

Baseden, Y., 'The tremendous things that happened to Yvonne Baseden: an English secretary meets the Gestapo', *Sunday Express* (16 March 1952).

Baseden, Y., 'An English Secretary in the torture cells of the Gestapo', *Sunday Express* (23 March 1952).

Gleeson, J., 'The secret heroines', *Sunday Graphic* (22 June 1952).

Churchill, P., title unknown, *John Bull* (10 October 1953).

Churchill, P., title unknown, *John Bull* (17 October 1953).

Billings, J., *Kinematograph Weekly*, n.26367 Vol. 25, No. 291 (1 April 1958).

'Painful Memories', *Time* (15 December 1958).

Author and title unknown, *The Australian* (25 April 1983).

Grice, E., 'Return of the White Mouse', *Daily Telegraph* (7 June 1994).

Obituary of Brian Stonehouse, *The Times* (10 December 1998).

'Weekend' magazine, *The Guardian* (16 September 2006).

5 Posters, adverts, newsreels and films

5.1 Posters and adverts

'Serve in the WAAF with the men who fly' (1941), artist Jonathon Foss.

'Just a good afternoon's work' (c.1942), artist unknown.

'On a man's job and equal to it', Weetabix, *Picture Post*, 6 June 1942.

5.2 Newsreels

All in a fighter's day's work (7 October 1940), Gaumont British.

Jane Brown changes her job (1942), Ministry of Information, Dir. H. Cooper.

Nightshift (1942), Dir. P. Roth.

Bibliography

5.3 Films

The Gentle Sex (1943), Dir. L. Howard, starring J. Howard, R. John and J. Greenwood.

Millions Like Us (1943), Dirs. S. Gilliat and F. Launder, starring P. Roc and A. Crawford (Gainsborough Pictures).

School for Danger/Now It Can be Told (1944), Dir. T. Baird, starring H. Rée and J. Nearne (RAF Film Unit/Ministry of Information).

Odette (1950), Dir. H. Wilcox, starring A. Neagle, T. Howard and P. Ustinov.

Carve Her Name with Pride (1958), Dir. L. Gilbert, Prod. D. Angel, starring V. McKenna.

Gallipoli (1981), Dir. P. Weir, starring M. Gibson and M. Lee.

Plenty (1985), Dir. F. Schepisi, Prods. E. Pressman and J. Papp, starring M. Streep.

Charlotte Gray (2002), Dir. G. Armstrong, Prods. S. Curtis and D. Rae, starring C. Blanchett.

5.4 Film scripts held at the British Film Institute

School for Danger (also known as *Now It Can Be Told*), Box 10 Item 5, Thurold Dickinson Collection.

Odette – S8909 – 'Release script'. Also S3070 – 'Storyline' donated by Anna Neagle; S6244 – 'Screenplay', dated 26 June 1950, donated by Anna Neagle; S6245 – 'Screenplay', dated 5 December 1949, donated by Anna Neagle.

Carve Her Name with Pride, S13981 – Domestic version, post-production script.

6 Radio and television

6.1 Radio

Now It Can Be Told, broadcast 4 April 1950.

6.2 Television series

'Allo 'Allo!, BBC1, 1982–1992.

Dad's Army, BBC1, 1968–1977.

Secret Army, BBC2, 1977–9.

Wish Me Luck, ITV, 1987.

6.3 Television documentaries

The History of the Female Spy, The History Channel, 1984.

For Valour: Pearl Witherington, BBC1, 1995.

The Story of Nancy Wake, Codename The White Mouse, 1997, White Mouse Productions.

Timewatch: Secret Memories, BBC2, 1997.

Churchill's Secret Army, Channel 4, 2000.

Conflict, The History Channel, 2000.

Secret Agent, BBC2, 2000.

Bibliography

Behind Enemy Lines: The Real Charlotte Grays, Channel 4, 2002.
Gladiators of World War Two, Channel 5, 2002.
Homeground: Secret Agent: The True Story of Violette Szabo, Channel 4, 2002.

7 Internet Sources

Forbes, A., 'The Princess who would be Spy', available online at: www.the-south-asian.com/Sept2001/Noor%20Inayat%20Khan1.htm [Accessed 2002].
Harris, B., Lt Arthur Staggs, Wireless Operator: Hero of the French Resistance', available online at: http://users.tpg.com.au/berniezz/page3%20Arthur.htm [Accessed 2006].

8 Official Publications

Foot, M. R. D., *SOE in France: An Account of the Work of the British Special Operations Executive in France 1940–1944* (London: HMSO, 1966).
Hooks, J., *British Policies and Methods of Employing Women in Wartime* (Washington: US Government, 1944).

9 Autobiographies

Altbeker Cyprys, R., *A Jump for Life: A Survivor's Journey from Nazi-Occupied Poland*, ed. E. Potter (London: Constable, 1997).
Bleicher, H., *Colonel Henri's Story* (London: William Kimber, 1954).
Buckmaster, M., *Specially Employed* (London: Batchworth Press, 1952).
Buckmaster, M., *They Fought Alone: The Story of British Agents in France* (London: The Popular Book Club, 1959).
Burney, C., *The Dungeon Democracy* (London: William Heinemann Ltd, 1945).
Burney, C., *Solitary Confinement* (London: Clerke and Cockeran, 1952).
Churchill, P., *Of Their Own Choice* (London: Hodder and Stoughton, 1952).
Churchill, P., *Duel of Wits* (London: Hodder and Stoughton, 1953).
Churchill, P., *The Spirit in the Cage* (London: Hodder and Stoughton, 1954).
Cowburn, B., *No Cloak, No Dagger* (London: Jarrolds, 1960).
Delbo, C., *None of Us Will Return* (Boston: Beacon Press, 1968.)
Hahn Beer, E. and S. Dworkin, *The Nazi Officer's Wife: How One Jewish Woman Survived the Holocaust* (New York: Little, Brown and Company, 2000).
Heslop, R., *Xavier: The Famous British Agent's Dramatic Account of His Work in the French Resistance* (London: Rupert Hart-Davis, 1970).
Hudson, S., *Undercover Operator: An SOE Agent's Experiences in France and the Far East* (Barnsley: Leo Cooper, 2003).
Langelaan, G., *Knights of Floating Silk* (London: Hutchinson, 1959).
Millar, G., *Maquis* (London: William Heinemann Ltd, 1945).
Millar, G., *Horned Pigeon* (London: William Heinemann Ltd, 1946).

Bibliography

Moszkiewiez, H., *Inside the Gestapo: A Young Woman's Secret War* (London: Warner Books, 1998).

Neagle, A., *Anna Neagle Says: 'There's Always Tomorrow': An Autobiography* (London: W.H. Allen, 1974)

Poirier, J., *The Giraffe Has a Long Neck* (London: Leo Cooper, 1995).

Rake, D., *Rake's Progress* (London: Leslie Frewin, 1968).

Rochester, D., *Full Moon to France* (London: Robert Hale Limited, 1978).

Sheppard, R., *Missions Sécrètes et Déportation* (Paris: Heinandal, 1999).

De Vomécourt, P., *Who Lived to See the Day* (London: Hutchinson, 1961).

Wake, N., *The Autobiography of the Woman the Gestapo Called The White Mouse* (Melbourne: Macmillan, 1985).

Walters, A-M., *Moondrop to Gascony* (London: Macmillan, 1947).

Zembsch-Schreve, G., *Pierre Lalande: Special Agent. The Wartime Memoirs of Guido Zembsch-Schreve* (London: Leo Cooper, 1996).

10 Biographies

Basu, S., *Spy Princess: The Life of Noor Inayat Khan* (Stroud: Sutton, 2006).

Braddon, R., *Nancy Wake: The Story of a Very Brave Woman* (London: The Book Club, 1956).

Cookridge, E., *They Came From the Sky: The Stories of Lieutenant-Colonel Francis Cammaerts, DSO, Légion of Honour, Major Roger Landes, MC and Bar, Légion of Honour and Captain Harry Rée, DSO, OBE* (London: Heinemann, 1965) (London: Corgi, 1976).

Fitzsimons, P. *Nancy Wake: The Inspiring Story of One of the War's Greatest Heroines* (London: Harper Collins, 2002).

King, S., *Jacqueline: Pioneer Heroine of the Resistance* (London: Arms and Armour Press, 1989). (On Yvonne Rudellat.)

Le Chêne, E., *Watch for Me by Moonlight: A British Agent with the French Resistance* (London: Eyre Methuen, 1973). (On Robert Boiteux-Burdett.)

Marshall, B., *The White Rabbit: The Secret Agent the Gestapo Could Not Crack* (London: Cassell and Co, 2000). (On Edward Yeo-Thomas.)

Masson, M., *Christine: A Search for Christine Granville* (London: Hamish Hamilton, 1975).

Minney, R., *Carve Her Name with Pride: The Story of Violette Szabo* (London: George Newnes, 1956).

Nicolson, D., *Aristide: Warlord of the Resistance* (London: Leo Cooper, 1994). (On Roger Landes.)

Ottoway, S., *Violette Szabo: The Life That I Have: The Heroic Tale of a Female Spy in Nazi-Occupied France* (Barnsley: Leo Cooper, 2002).

Overton Fuller, J., *Madeleine: The Story of Noor Inayat Khan, George Cross, MBE, Croix de Guerre with Gold Star* (London: Gollancz, 1951).

Overton Fuller, J., *Born for Sacrifice: The Story of Noor Inayat Khan* (London: Pan, 1957).

Overton Fuller, J., *Dericourt: The Chequered Spy* (Wilton: Michael Russell, 1989).

Seaman, M., *Bravest of the Brave: The True Story of Wing Commander 'Tommy' Yeo-Thomas – SOE Secret Agent – Codename 'The White Rabbit'* (London: Michael O'Mara, 1999). (On Edward Yeo-Thomas.)

Thomas, J., *No Banners: The Story of Alfred and Henry Newton* (London: WH Allen, 1955).

Tickell, J., *Odette: The Story of a British Agent* (London: Chapman and Hall, 1949). (On Odette Sansom.)

11 Unpublished Theses

Josephine Dolan, 'National Heroines: Representing Femininity and the Past in Popular Film and Literature, 1930–1955' (Ph.D. thesis, Lancaster University, 1997).

Julia Rosenzweig, 'The Construction of Policy for Women in the British Armed Forces: 1938–1948' (M.Litt. dissertation, University of Oxford, 1993).

12 General bibliography

Adam, R., *A Woman's Place, 1910–1975* (London: Chatto and Windus, 1975).

Anderson, B., *Imagined Communities: Reflections on the Origin and Spread of Nationalism* (London: Verso, 1983).

Baker, R., *Drag: A History of Female Impersonation in the Performing Arts* (London: Cassell, 1994).

Bakhtin, M., *Problems of Dostoevsky's Poetics* (Manchester: Manchester University Press, 1984).

Beecher Stowe, H., *Uncle Tom's Cabin or Negro Life in the Slave States of America* (London: C.H. Clarke, 1852).

Bell, L., *Sabotage: The Story Of Lieutenant-Colonel J. Elder Wills* (London: T. Werner Laurie Limited, 1957).

Berger, J., *Ways of Seeing* (London: BBC, 1975).

Binney, M., *The Women Who Lived For Danger: The Women Agents of SOE in the Second World War* (London: Hodder and Stoughton, 2002).

Binney, M., *Secret War Heroes: Men of the Special Operations Executive* (London: Hodder and Stoughton, 2005).

Bourdieu, P., 'The School as a Conservative Force: Scholastic and Cultural Inequalities', in Dale, R., Esland, G. and MacDonald, M., *Schooling and Capitalism: A Sociological Reader* (London: Routledge & Kegan Paul, 1976).

Bourdieu, P., *Outline of a Theory of Practice* (Cambridge: Cambridge University Press, 1977).

Bourdieu, P., *Sociology in Question* (London: Sage, 1992).

Bourke, J., *An Intimate History of Killing: Face-to-Face Killing in Twentieth-Century Warfare* (London: Granta Publications, 1999).

Bibliography

Braybon, G., *Women Workers in the First World War: The British Experience* (London: Croom Helm, 1981).

Braybon, G., and P. Summerfield, *Out of the Cage: Women's Experiences in Two World Wars* (London: Pandora, 1987).

Brownmiller, S., *Femininity* (London: Hamish Hamilton Ltd, 1984).

Butler, J., *Bodies That Matter: On The Discursive Limits of Sex* (London: Routledge, 1993).

Butler, J., *Gender Trouble: Feminism and the Subversion of Identity* (New York: Routledge, 1999).

Calder, A., *The People's War* (London: Cape, 1969).

A ChildLine Study, *We Know it's Tough to Talk: Boys in Need of Help* (London: ChildLine, 1996.)

Cohen, E., *Human Behaviour in the Concentration Camp* (London: Jonathon Cape Ltd, 1954).

Coleman, D., 'Population', in Halsey, A. (ed.) *British Social Trends Since 1900: A Guide to the Changing Social Structure of Britain* (Basingstoke: Macmillan Press, 1988).

Connell, B., *Masculinities* (Cambridge: Polity Press, 1995).

Connell, B., *The Men and the Boys* (Cambridge: Polity, 2000).

Craft, W., *Running a Thousand Miles for Freedom: The Escape of William and Ellen Craft from Slavery* (London: William Tweedie, 1860).

Dawson, G., *Soldier Heroes: British Adventure, Empire and the Imagining of Masculinities* (London: Routledge, 1994).

DeGroot, G., "Whose Finger on the Trigger?': Mixed Anti-Aircraft Batteries and the Female Combat Taboo', *War in History*, 4:4 (1997).

Deutsch, K., *Nationalism and Social Communication: An Inquiry into the Foundations of Nationality* (Cambridge, MA: The M.I.T Press, 1966).

Dudink, S., K. Hagermann and J. Tosh (eds), *Masculinities in Politics and War: Gendering Modern History* (Manchester: Manchester University Press, 2004).

Eitinger, L., 'Pathology of the Concentration Camp Syndrome', *Archives of General Psychiatry*, Vol. 5, October (1961).

Enloe, C., *The Morning After: Sexual Politics at the End of the Cold War* (London: University of California Press, 1993.)

Escott, B., *Mission Improbable, A Salute to the RAF Women of SOE in Wartime France* (Sparkford: Patrick Stephens Limited, 1991).

Foot, M. R. D., *Resistance* (London: Eyre Methuen, 1976).

Foot, M. R. D., *Six Faces of Courage* (London: Eyre Methuen, 1978).

Foot, M. R. D., *SOE: An Outline History of the Special Operations Executive 1940–46* (London: BBC, 1984).

Fussell, P., *The Great War and Modern Memory* (Oxford: Oxford University Press, 1975).

Gilman, S., *Seeing the Insane: A Cultural History of Madness and Art in the Western World* (Wiley: New York, 1982).

Bibliography

Ginsberg, E. (ed.), *Passing and the Fictions of Identity* (Durham: Duke University Press, 1996).

Gleeson, J., *They Feared No Evil: The Stories of the Gallant and Courageous Women Agents of Britain's Secret Armies, 1939–45* (London: Hale, 1976).

Grinker R. and J. Spiegel, *Men Under Stress* (Philadelphia: Blakiston, 1945).

Grinker, R., 'The Psychosomatic Aspects of Anxiety', in Simon, A., Herbert, C. and Straus, R. (eds), *The Physiology of Emotions* (Illinois: Springfield, 1961).

Hall, G., *Adolescence*, 1:4 (1904).

Harrison, B., 'Oral History and Recent Political History', *Oral History*, 1: 3 (1972).

Heidegger, M., *Being and Time* (Oxford: Basil Blackwell, 1962).

Helweg-Larsen, P. et al., 'Famine Disease in German Concentration Camps: Complications and Sequels', *Acta Psychiatrica Scandinavica, Supplementum*, 83 (1952).

Higate, P., *Military Masculinities: Identity and the State* (London: Praeger, 2003).

Homden, C., *The Plays of David Hare* (Cambridge: Cambridge University Press, 1995).

Hunt, F., *Gender and Policy in English Education: Schooling for Girls, 1902–44* (Hemel Hempstead: Harvester Wheatsheaf, 1991).

Jones, L., *A Quiet Courage: Women Agents in the French Resistance* (London: Corgi Books, 1990).

Kedward, R., *In Search of the Maquis: Rural Resistance in Southern France, 1942–1944* (Oxford: Clarendon Press, 1993).

Kessler, R. et al., 'Lifetime and 12–month Prevalence of DSM-III-R Psychiatric Disorders in the United States: Results from the National Comorbidity Survey', *Archives of General Psychiatry*, 51 (1994).

Kramer, R., *Flames in the Field: The Story of Four SOE Agents in Occupied France* (London: Penguin Books, 1995).

Kremer, L., *Women's Holocaust Writing: Memory and Imagination* (Lincoln: University of Nebraska Press, 1999).

Lewis Herman, J., *Trauma and Recovery: From Domestic Abuse to Political Terror* (London: Pandora, 1998).

Light, A., *Forever England: Femininity, Literature and Conservatism Between the Wars* (London: Routledge, 1991).

Maclaren, R., *Canadians Behind Enemy Lines, 1939–1945* (Vancouver: University of British Colombia Press, 1981).

Marwick, A., *The Deluge: British Society and the First World War* (London: Macmillan, 1965).

Marwick, A., *Britain in the Century of Total War: War, Peace and Social Change, 1900–67* (Fakenham: Cox and Wyman Ltd, 1968).

Morrison, J., *Ravensbrück: Everyday Life in a Women's Concentration Camp, 1939–45* (Princeton: Markus Wiener Publishers, 2000).

Mosse, G., *The Image Of Man: The Creation of Modern Masculinity* (Oxford: Oxford University Press, 1996).

Myrdal, A., and V. Klein, *Women's Two Roles: Home and Work* (London: Routledge, 1956).

Newton, E., *Mother Camp: Female Impersonators in America* (Chicago: Chicago University Press, 1979).

Nicholas, E., *Death Be Not Proud* (London: Cresset Press, 1958).

Nicolson, M., *What Did You Do In The War, Mummy?* (London: Pimlico, 1996).

Overton Fuller, J., *Double Agent? Light on the Secret Agents' War in France* (London: Pan Books, 1961).

Page Baldwin, M., 'Subject to Empire: Married Women and the British Nationality and Status of Aliens Act', *Journal of British Studies*, 40: 4 (2001).

Paris, M., *Over the Top: The Great War and Juvenile Literature in Britain* (Westport: Praeger, 2004).

Pattinson, J., '"The Best Disguise": Performing Femininities for Clandestine Purposes During the Second World War', in Smith, A. (ed.) *Gender and Warfare in the Twentieth Century: Textual Representations* (Manchester University Press: Manchester, 2004).

Rich, A., 'Compulsory Heterosexuality and the Lesbian Continuum', *Signs*, 5:4 (1980), pp. 631–60.

Riley, D., *Am I That Name?: Feminism and the Category of 'Women' in History* (London: Macmillan, 1988).

Ringelheim, J., 'Women and the Holocaust: A Reconsideration of Research', *Signs*, 10 (1985).

Robins, L., and D. Regier, *Psychiatric Disorders in America: The Epidemiologic Catchment Area Study* (New York: Free Press, 1991).

Rose, S., *Which People's War? National Identity and Citizenship in Britain, 1939–1945* (Oxford: Oxford University Press, 2003).

Russell, D., 'Rape and the Masculine Mystique', in Whitelegg, E. et al. (eds) *The Changing Experience of Women* (Oxford: Martin Robertson, 1982).

Sainsbury, J., *The F Section Memorial* (London: Hart Books, 1992).

Schwartz, P., 'Partisanes and Gender Politics in Vichy France', *French Historical Studies*, 16: 1 (1989), pp. 126–51.

Skeggs, B., *Formations of Class and Gender: Becoming Respectable* (London: Sage, 1997).

Slater, E., and J. Shields, 'Genetic Aspects of Anxiety', in Lader, M.(ed.), *Studies of Anxiety* (Ashford: Headley Brothers, 1967).

Smith, H., *War and Social Change: British Society in the Second World War* (Manchester: Manchester University Press, 1986).

Solzhenitsyn, A., *The Gulag Archipelago, Volume 2: An Experiment in Literary Investigation, Pts. III–IV* (London: Collins, 1976).

Stone, T., 'Creating a (Gendered?) Military Identity: The Women's Auxiliary Air Force in Great Britain in the Second World War', *Women's History Review*, 8:4 (1999).

Strongman, K., *The Psychology of Emotion* (Chichester: John Wiley and Sons, 1987).

Bibliography

Summerfield, P., *Women Workers in the Second World War: Production and Patriarchy in Conflict* (London: Croom Helm, 1984).

Summerfield, P., *Reconstructing Women's Wartime Lives: Discourses and Subjectivity in Oral Histories of the Second World War* (Manchester: Manchester University Press, 1998).

Summerfield, P. and C. Peniston-Bird, 'The Home Guard in Britain in the Second World War: Uncertain Masculinities?', in Higate, P. (ed.), *Military Masculinities: Identity and the State* (London: Praeger Publishers, 2003).

Thomson, A., *Anzac Memories: Living with the Legend* (Oxford: Oxford University Press. 1994).

Turner, B., and T. Rennell, *When Daddy Came Home: How Family Life Changed Forever in 1945* (London: Pimlico, 1995).

Vic-Dupont, X., L. Fichez and S. Weinstein cited in Eitinger, L. and A. Strøm, *Mortality and Morbidity After Excessive Stress: A Follow-Up Investigation of Norwegian Concentration Camp Survivors* (New York: Humanities Press, 1973).

Ward, I., *F.A.N.Y. Invicta* (London: Hutchinson, 1955).

Weitzman, L., 'Living on the Aryan Side in Poland: Gender, Passing and the Nature of Resistance', Ofer, D. and Weitzman, L. (eds) *Women in the Holocaust* (New Haven: Yale University Press, 1998).

Wheeler-Bennett, J., *Nemesis of Power* (London: Macmillan, 1954).

Index

Note: 'n.' after a page number indicates the number of a note on that page

Index

Index